Recipes & Remembering

Recipes & Remembering

Edith P. Middleton
1902 Tara Place
Dalton, GA 30720

First printing   -   May, 2005

ISBN # 0-9769597-0-4

WIMMER
COOKBOOKS

A CONSOLIDATED GRAPHICS COMPANY

800.548.2537   wimmerco.com

Table of Contents

# In Appreciation

This book has been a family project. The sketches and artwork were done by my daughter-in-law, Brenda Bennett. The photographs were done by my son-in-law, Chris Bock, my daughter, Kelly Bock and their children, Suzanne and Craig. My husband, Jay, has been supportive and has helped in too many ways to list. I have included recipes from my sisters and of some of my special friends.

◆　　◆　　◆

I have tried to put into this book my love for cooking and entertaining. I have always felt at home in the kitchen, wearing an apron, and preparing meals for people I love. I have delighted in sharing recipes with others and hope that my book will reach many people who love to cook. It truly is the way to a man's heart. I know that is old-fashioned but so am I.

I am fortunate to have grown up on a farm with wonderful parents and a large loving family. I was the seventh of eight children. The events in my 'Remembering" section of the book are exactly as I remember them.

◆　　◆　　◆

I want my children and grandchildren to know how life was growing up on a farm in North Florida in the thirties and forties without electricity or running water.

◆　　◆　　◆

I cannot give them the earthy smell of a field just plowed for planting; or the wonder of watching a butterfly emerge from its cocoon, flap its wings to dry, and flit among the summer flowers; or the sound of the autumn wind singing in the tops of the pine trees, but I can share with them my fascination with food. It began as I watched Mama prepare feather light biscuits in a wood-burning stove and has continued all my life.

◆　　◆　　◆

I have attended cooking classes in Atlanta, Savannah, Charleston and the Greenbriar Hotel taught by Ann Willan, founder of the Culinary Institute, La Varenne in Paris, but one of my favorite meals is still back bones and rice, collard greens and cornbread.

◆　　◆　　◆

My family and friends have encouraged me for years to compile a cookbook. I hope that everyone who shares this book enjoys the recipes as much as I have enjoyed preparing them for family and friends over the years.

Recipes

 *Hints*

I use:

- Hellmann's mayonnaise.
- White Lily self-rising flour for biscuits, cornbread and other quick breads.
- Martha White's self-rising cornmeal.
- Gold Medal all-purpose flour for yeast breads, rolls and pie crusts, and some cakes.
- Swans Down cake flour..
- Land-O-Lakes butter..
- Kraft's bar-b-que sauce with onion bits..
- Crisco shortening..
- Campbell's chicken and beef broths. (Unless I use home-made.)

◆   ◆   ◆

Note:

- When making yeast breads, make sure you do not kill your yeast using water or milk that is too hot.
- A pie crust always cooks more evenly and crisper if you freeze it a few minutes before baking.
- Do not over-mix quick breads. Biscuits and cornbread will be lighter and flakier with very little mixing and handling.
- Use a meat thermometer to roast or cook meats perfectly. My favorite is one I purchased from Williams-Sonoma that has a probe to be placed in the meat and a wire that comes out the oven door to a timer on the counter.
- I prefer to bake in a convection oven.

Appetizers & Beverages

Artichoke Spread

1	(14-ounce) can artichoke hearts, finely chopped
1	cup mayonnaise

8	ounces Parmesan cheese, freshly grated
	Tabasco sauce to taste

Mix together all ingredients and place in an ovenproof dish. Bake at 350 degrees for 30 minutes. Serve warm with plain crackers. Yield: 20 to 25 servings.

Bacon Wrapped Dates with Walnuts

Walnut halves
Pitted dates

Bacon slices

Place a walnut half into the opening of a pitted date. Cut bacon slices into thirds. Wrap each stuffed date with a piece of bacon and secure with a toothpick. Bake at 350 degrees for 10 minutes or until bacon is done. Drain and serve warm.

Baked Brie in Puff Pastry

4	frozen puff pastry patty shells, thawed
2	(4½-ounce) rounds Brie cheese
1	egg

1	tablespoon milk
3	ripe pears
3	crisp apples

Place 2 patty shells next to each other and roll together into a large circle. Place a cheese round in center. Bring edges of pastry together as if wrapping a package. Seal edges by pressing dough together. Repeat with remaining pastry and cheese. Beat together egg and milk. Brush each pastry round with egg mixture until well coated. Place rounds on a greased baking sheet. Bake at 425 degrees for 25 to 30 minutes or until puffed and brown. Serve with sliced fresh fruit. Yield: 8 servings.

Baked Crab, Brie and Artichoke Dip

1	medium leek, finely chopped, washed and drained	1	pound Brie, rind discarded, cut into ¼-inch pieces
1	medium Vidalia onion, finely chopped	3	tablespoons finely chopped fresh parsley leaves
2	tablespoons minced garlic		
2	tablespoons olive oil	2	tablespoons finely chopped fresh dill leaves
½	cup canned artichoke hearts, drained, rinsed and finely chopped	1	tablespoon finely chopped fresh tarragon leaves
½	cup frozen chopped spinach, thawed, squeezed dry and finely chopped	1	pound fresh jumbo lump crabmeat, picked over to remove shell
¼	cup Riesling or other medium-dry white wine	2	tablespoons Dijon mustard
⅔	cup heavy cream	1	teaspoon Tabasco sauce, or to taste
			Salt and pepper to taste

Cook leek, onion and garlic in olive oil in a large heavy skillet over medium heat, stirring until pale golden. Stir in artichoke hearts and spinach. Add wine and cook and stir 3 minutes. Add cream and simmer and stir for 1 minute. Add Brie and stir until cheese just starts to melt. Remove skillet from heat and stir parsley, dill and tarragon into mixture.

In a large bowl, stir together crab, mustard, Tabasco and salt and pepper. Stir in cheese mixture. Spread mixture evenly in a lightly greased 11-inch gratin or 6-cup shallow baking dish. Bake at 425 degrees in center of oven for 15 to 20 minutes or until golden. Serve hot with toasted baguette slices. Yield: 6 to 8 servings.

Boursin Cheese

1	(8-ounce) carton whipped butter	½	teaspoon dried chives
2	(8-ounce) packages cream cheese, softened	½	teaspoon dried marjoram
		½	teaspoon thyme
1	teaspoon dill seed	2	teaspoons lemon juice
½	teaspoon dried basil	2	cloves garlic, pressed

Cream butter and cream cheese together in a food processor or blender. Soften dill, basil, chives, marjoram and thyme in lemon juice for 5 minutes. Add garlic to herbs. Add herb mixture to creamed mixture and blend. Refrigerate or freeze Boursin in two 8-ounce cartons with tight lids. Yield: 2 cups.

Cheese Crisps

½	cup butter, softened		Dash of cayenne pepper or Tabasco
1	cup flour		sauce
1½	cups shredded sharp Cheddar cheese	1	egg, well beaten
1	cup Rice Krispies cereal		

Mix butter and flour until mixture resembles coarse meal. Add cheese, cereal and pepper. Stir well. Mix in egg. Roll out dough between 2 sheets of wax paper. Cut out shapes with cookie cutters. (For a wedding or Christmas party, you may make bells.) Bake at 350 degrees for 15 to 17 minutes.

Cheese Puffs

1	loaf white bread, unsliced	½	cup butter
1	(3-ounce) package cream cheese	2	egg whites, stiffly beaten
4	ounces sharp Cheddar cheese, shredded		

Trim crusts and cut bread into 1-inch cubes. Melt cheeses and butter in the top of a double boiler over hot water until smooth and thick. Remove from heat and fold in egg whites. Dip bread cubes into cheese mixture until well coated. Place on a baking sheet and refrigerate overnight.

When ready to serve, bake puffs at 400 degrees for 12 to 15 minutes or until puffy and golden brown.

Cheese Spread

1	pound Cheddar cheese	¼	teaspoon black pepper
1½	cups finely chopped pecans		Dash of cayenne pepper
2	tablespoons grated onion	¼	cup mayonnaise
2	tablespoons milk		Dash of garlic powder

Mix together all ingredients in a food processor. Serve with crackers.

Caviar Presentation

8	thin slices bread or unsalted water biscuits	½	cup chopped sweet onion
1	(2-ounce) jar caviar, well chilled	2	hard-cooked eggs, whites and yolks chopped separately
	Crushed ice	½	cup sour cream
1	lemon, cut into wedges		

Toast bread lightly, trim crusts and cut into triangles. Nestle opened jar of caviar in a large bowl of crushed ice. Set up an accompaniment platter with toast triangles, lemon wedges, onion, chopped egg white and yolk and sour cream. Guests can help themselves to caviar and add desired accompaniments. Saltier caviar benefit from the cooling contrast of sour cream, and many people enjoy a squeeze of lemon juice. Yield: 4 servings.

Do not serve caviar with a metal spoon. There are special spoons made for this purpose. You may use a china or ceramic spoon.

The caviars available on the market are labeled either fresh or pasteurized. The lightly salted fresh, however, has a refrigerator shelf life of 4 to 6 months. The more heavily salted pasteurized one is found on the grocer's shelf, and it does not require refrigeration until it has been opened. The caviars from the Caspian Sea or the Volga River have a mild, non-fishy flavor. These are the most popular:

Beluga: Large grain, pearly gray to black (most expensive).

Osetra: Medium grain, pearly gray to black with gold highlights.

Sevruga: Small grain, deep gray tones.

Pressed: Some intact grains, somewhat "jammy" consistency.

The other commonly imported caviar is lumpfish caviar from Icelandic waters. The caviar may be black or red (it is dyed these colors) or golden. The eggs, small and with a pronounced flavor, are good for dips and hors d'oeuvres.

Black and golden whitefish caviar come from sturgeon caught in the Great Lakes. The eggs are small with a firm texture and a delicate crunch. The black can be used like lumpfish; the natural golden is milder and is good for garnish, salads and pasta.

Salmon caviar comes from Pacific Northwest and has large, translucent grains. The red caviar comes from silver salmon while the natural, slightly paler caviar, comes from chum salmon. Flavorful and attractive, the caviar is good in omelets, canapés and toppings.

American caviar from rivers that empty into oceans, when processed properly, can be comparable to sevruga. It is mild, tangy and half the price.

Cheese Straws

1	pound sharp cheese, shredded	1	teaspoon baking powder
½	cup butter, melted and cooled	½	teaspoon paprika
2	cups unsifted flour	⅛	teaspoon cayenne pepper
1	teaspoon salt		

Mix cheese and butter. Sift together flour, salt, baking powder, paprika and cayenne pepper. Add dry ingredients to cheese mixture. Knead well. Working with one-fourth of dough at a time, roll out dough into a ⅓-inch thick rectangle. Cut into ½-inch wide by 4-inch long strips using a pastry wheel or sharp knife. Place strips on an ungreased baking sheet. Bake at 350 degrees for 10 to 12 minutes, but do not brown. Remove from oven, cool and store in an airtight container, placing wax paper between layers. Freezes well. Yield: About 6 dozen.

Cheese Wafers

1	cup butter, softened	1	teaspoon cayenne pepper
1	pound New York Cheddar cheese, shredded	1	teaspoon salt
			Pecan halves
3	cups sifted all-purpose flour		

Cream butter and cheese. Add flour, cayenne and salt and mix well. Use hands, if needed, to mix dough evenly. Divide dough into 3 equal parts. Shape each into a 1½-inch diameter log. Wrap each in wax paper and chill about 30 minutes, or freeze.

Slice chilled logs into ⅛-inch thick wafers. Place wafers on an ungreased baking sheet and press a pecan half into each. Bake at 350 degrees for 10 to 15 minutes. Yield: 3 dozen.

Classic Guacamole

4	avocados, seeded and peeled	¼	cup finely chopped onion
2	tablespoons lemon juice	¼	teaspoon ground cumin
1	clove garlic, crushed	3-4	drops Tabasco chipotle pepper sauce
1	tomato, finely chopped		Tortilla chips

Using a fork, coarsely mash avocado with lemon juice and garlic. Stir in tomato, onion, cumin and pepper sauce until blended. Garnish as desired and serve with tortilla chips. Yield: 8 to 10 servings.

Chicken Liver Pâté

1	pound chicken livers	¼	teaspoon ground cloves
1	small onion, chopped		Dash of hot pepper sauce
1	clove garlic, minced	1	cup chicken broth, divided
4	tablespoons butter	2	tablespoons brandy or wine
1	teaspoon salt	1	(¼-ounce) envelope unflavored gelatin
¼	teaspoon allspice		Olives for garnish
½	teaspoon ground ginger		

Sauté livers, onion and garlic in butter until livers are no longer pink inside. Add salt, allspice, ginger, cloves, hot sauce and ½ cup chicken broth. Cook, uncovered, for 5 minutes. Stir in brandy and cool. Process livers and pan juices in a food processor or blender. Dissolve gelatin in remaining ½ cup broth. Add dissolved gelatin to liver and process 30 seconds. Pour into a bowl or mold, cover and chill until set. Garnish with olives. Serve with crackers or Melba rounds. Yield: 2½ cups.

Crab Dip

1	(8-ounce) package cream cheese, softened	½	teaspoon seasoned salt
		1	tablespoon chopped fresh parsley
⅓	cup mayonnaise		Dash of garlic powder
1	teaspoon prepared mustard with horseradish	6	ounces crabmeat, picked over to remove shell
1½	tablespoons dried minced onion		Crackers

Blend together cream cheese, mayonnaise, mustard, onion and seasoned salt. Fold in parsley, garlic powder and crabmeat. Serve hot or cold with crackers. Yield: 1½ cups.

Gouda in Pastry

1	frozen puff pastry sheet, thawed	3	tablespoons Praline Mustard Glaze*
1	(4-ounce) Gouda cheese round		

Unfold thawed pastry and place cheese in center. Drizzle glaze over cheese. Pull pastry up over cheese and seal all edges where pastry comes together. Place on an ungreased baking sheet. Bake at 450 degrees for 15 minutes or until brown. Serve with crackers.

*Dr. Pete's of Savannah (available on the internet "Dr. Pete's Gourmet Foods")

For easier handling of pastry, dust hands and preparation surface with flour.

Fried Green Tomatoes
with Creamy Horseradish Sauce

Horseradish Sauce

1	(8-ounce) container sour cream (about 1 cup)	1	tablespoon Dijon mustard
2	tablespoons mayonnaise	1	tablespoon prepared horseradish
			Salt and freshly ground pepper to taste

Tomatoes

3-4	green tomatoes	½	cup self-rising cornmeal
	Salt	½	cup self-rising flour
1	egg white	½	cup butter
1	teaspoon black pepper		

Combine all sauce ingredients in a small bowl. Mix well, cover and refrigerate.

For tomatoes, cut green tomatoes into ⅜-inch thick slices. Sprinkle with salt and pepper. In a shallow dish, beat egg white with a fork. Combine cornmeal and flour in a separate shallow dish. In a large skillet over medium-high heat, melt 2 tablespoons butter. Dip tomato slices in egg white, then in cornmeal mixture to coat. Add coated tomato slices to skillet in a single layer. Cook over medium-high heat until golden brown; turn and cook until golden brown on other side. Drain on paper towels. Repeat with remaining tomato slices, adding butter to skillet as needed. Serve warm with horseradish sauce. Yield: 6 servings.

Marinated Mushrooms

⅔	cup tarragon vinegar		Freshly ground black pepper
½	cup salad oil	2	tablespoons water
2	medium cloves garlic, halved		Dash of Tabasco sauce
1	tablespoon sugar	1	medium onion, sliced into rings
1½	teaspoons salt	2	pints fresh mushrooms

Combine vinegar, salad oil, garlic, sugar, salt, pepper, water and Tabasco sauce, putting garlic on toothpicks for easy removal before serving. Add onions and mushrooms. Cover and refrigerate 8 hours, stirring several times.

Herbed Potato Garlic Spread

15 large cloves garlic, unpeeled
4 tablespoons olive oil, divided
  Salt and pepper to taste
1½ pounds russet potatoes, unpeeled and
  cut into 2-inch pieces
¼ cup chopped green onions

3 tablespoons chopped fresh basil
2 tablespoons chopped fresh parsley
1 tablespoon minced shallot
1 clove garlic, minced
½ cup sour cream

Place unpeeled garlic cloves in a small baking dish. Add 1 tablespoon olive oil and sprinkle with salt and pepper. Toss to coat. Cover dish tightly with foil. Bake at 350 degrees for 30 minutes or until garlic is golden brown and tender. Cool. Squeeze garlic between fingertips to release cloves from papery skin. Transfer cloves to a bowl and mash with a fork.

Cook potatoes in a large pot of boiling salted water for 25 minutes or until very tender. Drain and return potatoes to pot. Add mashed roasted garlic, remaining 3 tablespoons olive oil, green onions, basil, parsley, shallot and minced garlic and mash together. Mix in sour cream. Season with salt and pepper and serve on toast points. Yield: 4 servings.

Hot Spiced Pecans

4 tablespoons butter, melted
1 pound fresh pecans

1 tablespoon salt
1 tablespoon cayenne pepper

Pour melted butter over pecans. Add salt and cayenne and stir. Spread coated pecans on a baking sheet. Bake at 250 degrees for 30 minutes, stirring once or twice while baking.

You may leave out the cayenne pepper for good toasted pecans.

Hot Vidalia Onion Dip

1 cup finely chopped Vidalia onion
1 cup shredded Swiss cheese

1 cup mayonnaise

Mix together all ingredients and pour into a baking dish or pie plate. Bake at 350 degrees until bubbly. Serve with crackers.

Oysters Rockefeller

1½ tablespoons unsalted butter, divided	Salt and freshly ground white pepper to taste
1½ pounds raw spinach, washed, dried and stems removed, or frozen spinach, thawed and squeezed dry	½ cup heavy cream
	⅛ teaspoon cayenne pepper
16 oysters on the half shell	½ cup grated Parmesan cheese
½ cup dry white wine, divided	1 egg yolk
1 teaspoon plus 1 tablespoon finely chopped shallot, divided	⅛ teaspoon freshly grated nutmeg
	2 cups rock salt

Melt ½ tablespoon butter in a large, heavy skillet. Add spinach and sauté over high heat for 1 minute or until leaves wilt and release some of their water. Drain leaves in a colander, then coarsely chop to yield 1 cup.

Remove oysters from shells. Combine ¼ cup white wine, 1 teaspoon shallots and a pinch of salt in a large saucepan. Bring to a boil over medium-high heat. Reduce heat to medium-low, add oysters and simmer 2 minutes. Remove oysters with a slotted spoon when their edges begin to curl and look frilly. Continue to simmer poaching liquid until reduced to 2 tablespoons; remove from heat. Whisk in cream, cayenne pepper, cheese and egg yolk to form a smooth paste.

Melt remaining 1 tablespoon butter in a sauté pan over medium heat. Add remaining 1 tablespoon shallots and sauté 1 minute. Add spinach, remaining ¼ cup wine, salt and pepper and nutmeg. Cook 1 minute longer.

On individual ovenproof serving dishes, place 4 oyster shells in a layer of rock salt. Place a poached oyster in each shell. Add a tablespoon of spinach mixture and top with cheese paste. Broil oysters under a preheated boiler for 4 minutes or until golden and bubbling. Serve immediately. Repeat until all oysters are used. Yield: 4 servings.

Party Cheese Ball

2 (8-ounce) packages cream cheese, softened	2 teaspoons Worcestershire sauce
	¼ teaspoon celery salt
1⅓ cups flaked crabmeat	⅛ teaspoon curry powder
2 tablespoons grated onion	Dash of cayenne pepper
2 tablespoons chopped stuffed olives	1 cup grated coconut
2 slices bacon, cooked crisp and crumbled	

Combine all ingredients except coconut. Form mixture into a ball. Roll cheese ball in coconut. Refrigerate before serving.

Pickled Shrimp

5	pounds medium shrimp	1	(4-ounce) bottle capers, undrained
5	mild white medium onions, thinly sliced into rings (Vidalias are best)	¾	cup sugar
		¼	cup Worcestershire sauce
2	cups olive oil	1	teaspoon Tabasco sauce
1½	cups cider vinegar	1	teaspoon salt

Boil shrimp 3 minutes (no longer); drain immediately. Peel and devein; rinse and drain well. In a deep, flat pan, layer shrimp and onion rings repeatedly until all are used. Mix olive oil, vinegar, capers, sugar, Worcestershire sauce, Tabasco sauce and salt. Pour mixture evenly over shrimp and onions. Cover pan and refrigerate at least 12 hours, stirring occasionally.

To serve, lift onions and shrimp from marinade and place in a glass bowl or a large, lettuce-lined platter. Serve with cocktail picks.

Mix any leftover onions with mayonnaise to serve later as an hors d'oeuvre with crackers.

Pecan Praline Brie

2	pounds (about) dark brown sugar	1	pound chopped pecans
½-¾	cup butter	1	(14-ounce) wheel Brie cheese
2	tablespoons water		Fresh mint and strawberries for garnish

Combine sugar, butter and water in a saucepan. Bring to a boil. Stir in pecans. Cool. Cut Brie into serving-size wedges and separate slices. Pour sugar mixture between slices. Garnish with fresh mint and strawberries.

For individual servings, add kiwi fruit and figs, if desired.

To remove burned on food from your skillet, add a drop or two of dish soap and enough water to cover bottom of pan and bring to a boil on stovetop.

Salmon Spread

1	(1-pound) can salmon	1	tablespoon finely chopped parsley
1	tablespoon chopped capers	¼	cup mayonnaise
2	tablespoons prepared horseradish		Salt and pepper to taste
1	tablespoon lemon juice		

Carefully remove any bits of bone from salmon and flake into a large bowl. Add capers, horseradish, lemon juice, parsley and mayonnaise and mix well until blended. Season with salt and pepper. Refrigerate until serving. Yield: 2½ cups.

This can be molded in a fish mold. To mold, add 6 ounces of cream cheese to make the spread cohere. When time to unmold, run mold under hot water for a few minutes to loosen; turn out onto a decorative platter.

Salsa

4	large plum tomatoes (about 1 pound), diced to yield 2 cups	2	teaspoons jalapeño pepper, minced (remove seeds for less heat, wear rubber gloves)
¼	cup chopped Vidalia onion	1½	teaspoons fresh lime juice
3	tablespoons chopped fresh cilantro	¾	teaspoon kosher salt
		1	small clove garlic, minced

Combine all ingredients in a bowl. For a smoother texture, pulse half the salsa in a food processor, then combine it with remaining chunky salsa. Cover tightly and refrigerate up to 5 days. Yield: 4 to 6 servings.

Sausage Bacon Roll-Ups

4	tablespoons butter	1	egg, lightly beaten
½	cup water	4	ounces hot or mild bulk pork sausage
1½	cups packaged herb-seasoned stuffing	½-⅔	pound bacon, sliced

Melt butter in water in a saucepan. Add butter mixture to stuffing and mix well. Blend in egg and sausage. Chill 1 hour for easier handling. Shape chilled mixture into small oblong pieces, about the size of pecans.

Cut bacon slices into thirds. Wrap each stuffing piece with bacon and fasten with a wooden pick. Place on a rack in a shallow pan. Bake at 375 degrees for 35 minutes or until brown and crisp, turning halfway through cooking. Drain on paper towels and serve hot. These can be made ahead and frozen. Yield: About 3 to 4 dozen.

Shrimp Dip

2	pounds peeled, deveined and boiled shrimp	1	teaspoon prepared horseradish
½	cup butter, melted	½	cup mayonnaise
½	cup minced onion	1	teaspoon salt
	Juice of ½ lemon or lime	6	drops hot pepper sauce
		1	teaspoon monosodium glutamate

Drain and very finely chop shrimp, or put through a food grinder using a small knife plate. Place shrimp in a food processor. Pour butter over shrimp. Add onion, citrus juice, horseradish, mayonnaise, salt, pepper sauce and monosodium glutamate. Process until well mixed. Serve with crackers. Yield: 8 to 10 servings.

Dip may be packed into a mold and chilled.

Spinach Canapés

Pastry

1	cup self-rising flour	⅓	cup shortening
½	teaspoon salt	3-4	tablespoons ice water

Spinach Mixture

1	(10-ounce) package frozen chopped spinach, drained	2	ounces cream cheese, softened
4	slices bacon, cooked, drained and crumbled	2	tablespoons finely chopped onion
			Seasoned salt and pepper to taste

To make pastry, mix flour and salt. Cut in shortening. Sprinkle with water, 1 tablespoon at a time, adding only enough water to moisten mixture so it holds together. Shape dough into a ball. Lightly roll on a floured surface into a ⅛-inch thick rectangle.

Combine all spinach mixture ingredients. Spread mixture over pastry. Carefully roll into a log. Refrigerate log until firm. Cut chilled log into ¼-inch thick slices and place on a baking sheet. Bake at 400 degrees until pastry is golden. Serve immediately. Yield: 4 servings.

Smoked Salmon Log

6-8 ounces smoked salmon
12 ounces Cheddar cheese, shredded
1 (3-ounce) package cream cheese, softened

1 teaspoon Worcestershire sauce
Dash of garlic salt
Chopped fresh parsley or chopped nuts

Combine all ingredients except parsley or nuts and mix well. Form mixture into logs. Roll logs in chopped parsley or nuts. Wrap logs tightly in wax paper or plastic wrap. Refrigerate until needed. Serve with crackers or toast points. Yield: 4 servings.

Spinach Quiche Squares

½ cup butter
10 eggs, beaten
½ cup unsifted flour
1 teaspoon baking powder
1 teaspoon salt
1 bunch fresh spinach, chopped, or 1 (10-ounce) package frozen chopped spinach, thawed and squeezed dry

1 (8-ounce) can green chiles, seeded and chopped
2 cups fine curd cottage cheese
½ pound Cheddar cheese, shredded
½ pound Monterey Jack cheese, shredded

Melt butter in a 9x13-inch baking pan at 400 degrees for about 3 minutes. In a bowl, combine eggs, flour, baking powder and salt. Add spinach, melted butter, chiles and all cheeses. Return mixture to baking pan. Bake at 400 degrees for 15 minutes. Reduce heat to 350 degrees and bake 35 to 40 minutes. Remove from oven and let stand 5 minutes to set. Cut into squares. Yield: 60 squares.

May be cut into larger squares and served as a vegetable side dish.

Warm Goat Cheese Toasts

½ baguette
1 (11-ounce) log soft goat cheese

Olive oil for drizzling
1 (6-ounce) jar best-quality pesto

Cut baguette into sixteen ½-inch slices. Space slices evenly on a baking sheet. Cut cheese into 16 rounds and place a round atop each bread slice. Drizzle oil over cheese, letting it drip onto crusts. Bake at 425 degrees for 10 to 15 minutes or until undersides of bread slices are golden brown and cheese begins to brown. Top each toast with ½ teaspoon pesto. Serve warm. Yield: 16 servings.

Tomato Bouillon

¼	cup diced celery	½	teaspoon white pepper
¼	cup diced carrot	6	whole cloves
¼	cup diced onion	1	bay leaf
	Few sprigs fresh parsley, chopped	⅛	teaspoon dried thyme
4	cups tomato juice	2	cups chicken broth, heated

Simmer celery, carrot, onion, parsley, tomato juice, pepper, cloves, bay leaf and thyme in a covered saucepan for 1 hour. Strain to remove solids. Add chicken broth to liquid and reheat. Yield: 15 to 20 demitasse cups.

This is delicious on a cold day. I like to serve this in demitasse cups when guests arrive for lunch or dinner.

Cappuccino

3	cups brewed coffee	¼	cup rum
3	cups half-and-half	¼	cup brandy
½	cup dark crème de cacao		

Combine all ingredients and steam or heat in a saucepan. Serve immediately. Yield: 6 to 8 servings.

Frappucino

½	cup strong brewed coffee, espresso is perfect	¼-⅓	cup sugar
2	cups milk	1½	cups crushed ice

Combine all ingredients in a blender and blend well. Yield: 2 servings.

Irish Coffee

1	jigger Irish whiskey	1	cup strong coffee
1	teaspoon sugar	1	spoonful whipped cream

Place whiskey in a tall glass or mug. Add sugar and coffee and stir well. Heat in a microwave for 2 to 3 minutes or until heated through. Top with whipped cream. Yield: 1 serving.

Coffee Punch

8	tablespoons instant coffee	2	quarts half-and-half
2	cups sugar	1	tablespoon vanilla
1	(8-ounce) can chocolate syrup	2	quarts coffee ice cream, or vanilla if
3	quarts hot water		coffee flavor not available

Dissolve coffee, sugar and chocolate syrup in hot water. Add half-and-half and refrigerate until 30 minutes before serving. Add ice cream 30 minutes before serving. Yield: About 30 servings.

Champagne Punch

	Juice of 24 lemons or 24 ounces ReaLemon juice	3	cups sugar, boiled with 1 quart water for 3 minutes
8	(6-ounce) cans frozen orange juice concentrate	1	(29-ounce) can peaches, puréed
1	(3-ounce) package lemon gelatin	2	quarts water
1	(3-ounce) package orange gelatin	2	quarts Sauterne
1	(46-ounce) can pineapple juice	2	quarts white champagne

Combine all ingredients and serve. Yield: 50 servings.

For a nonalcoholic version, omit Sauterne and champagne and substitute 4 quarts ginger ale.

Cranberry Party Punch

3	(12-ounce) cans frozen lemonade concentrate, thawed and diluted	1	cup frozen orange juice concentrate, thawed and undiluted
1	quart cranberry juice cocktail	1	(1-liter) bottle ginger ale, chilled
		1	orange, thinly sliced

Combine all juices and chill. Add ginger ale just before serving. Garnish with orange slices. Yield: About 1½ gallons, 20 servings.

One of the cans of lemonade concentrate may be diluted and frozen to make an ice ring or cubes to use in the punch.

Georgia Peach Daiquiris

3	large ripe peaches, peeled and pitted	3	tablespoons sugar
2	tablespoons fresh lime juice	3	cups crushed ice
¼	cup light rum or vodka		

Place peaches and lime juice in a blender. Blend until smooth. Add liquor and sugar and blend. With blender running, add ice through opening in lid. Blend until slushy. Yield: 9 servings.

Hot Apple Cider Punch

1	gallon apple cider	2	cinnamon sticks
1	quart ginger ale	1½	teaspoons whole cloves
¾	cup cinnamon red hot candy	1	medium orange, sliced

Pour apple cider and ginger ale into a large electric percolator. Place candy, cinnamon sticks, cloves and orange slices in coffee basket. Perk. Yield: 20 servings.

Holiday Eggnog

6	eggs, separated	½	cup light rum
1	cup sugar	1½	quarts milk
1½	cups cognac or Grand Marnier, or combination	3	cups heavy cream, whipped Freshly grated nutmeg

Beat egg yolks until thick and light. Add sugar gradually, beating constantly. While beating, gradually add cognac and rum. Chill 1 hour, stirring occasionally.

Beat egg whites until stiff. Gradually add milk to cognac mixture. Fold in whipped cream and beaten egg whites. Store in covered jars in refrigerator for a day or so before serving.

To serve, ladle eggnog from a punch bowl, otherwise you will get too much fluff on one serving and not enough on the next. Provide freshly grated nutmeg for guests to use as desired. Yield: 8 to 10 servings.

Hot Buttered Rum

1	pound butter, softened	1	quart vanilla ice cream, softened
1	pound light brown sugar		Light rum
1	pound powdered sugar		Whipped cream
2	teaspoons cinnamon		Cinnamon sticks
2	teaspoons nutmeg		

Combine butter, both sugars, cinnamon and nutmeg and beat until light and fluffy. Add ice cream, stirring until well blended. Spoon mixture into a 2-quart freezer container; freeze.

To serve, thaw slightly. For each serving, place 3 tablespoons butter mixture and 1 jigger rum in a large mug. Fill with boiling water and stir well. (Refreeze any unused butter mixture.) Top each serving with whipped cream and serve with a cinnamon stick stirrer. Yield: About 25 servings.

Lime Punch

5	pounds sugar	3	(1-liter) bottles ginger ale
	Juice of 10-15 lemons	6	(3-ounce) packages lime gelatin
2	(46-ounce) cans pineapple juice	1	quart lime sherbet

Combine all ingredients except sherbet and chill. Just before serving, add sherbet. Yield: 100 servings.

Mint Julep

18	mint leaves on the stem, divided		Finely crushed ice
2	teaspoons water	1½	ounces bourbon
1	teaspoon sugar		

Partially tear 12 mint leaves, leaving them on the stem. Place leaves in a large glass or silver julep mug with water and sugar. Stir slowly until sugar is dissolved. Fill glass with ice. Add bourbon. Add more ice to fill as bourbon melts original ice. Stir. Tear remaining mint leaves and place on top of ice. Yield: 1 serving.

Orange Blossom Punch

6	(6-ounce) cans frozen orange juice concentrate, thawed and undiluted	3	(12-ounce) cans apricot nectar, chilled
9	cups water	3	(12-ounce) bottles ginger ale, chilled

Combine orange juice concentrate and water in a punch bowl; mix well. Pour in apricot nectar and ginger ale. Mix and add ice cubes. Yield: About 44 half-cup servings.

Party Raspberry Punch

1   (46-ounce) can unsweetened pineapple
    juice, chilled

2   (1-liter) bottles ginger ale, chilled
3   quarts raspberry sherbet, softened

Combine all ingredients in a punch bowl. Yield: 5½ quarts.

Pineapple-Lime Purée

½   pineapple, peeled, cored and chilled

Juice of 1 lime

Cut pineapple into medium-sized chunks and place in a blender or food processor. Add lime juice and purée. Serve immediately in chilled goblets. Yield: Four ½-cup servings.

Slush Punch

3½ cups sugar
6   cups water
2   (3-ounce) packages mixed fruit
    flavored gelatin

1   (46-ounce) can pineapple juice
1   quart orange juice
⅓   cup lemon juice
2   (1-liter) bottles ginger ale, chilled

Combine sugar and water in a large saucepan. Bring to a boil and simmer 3 minutes. Stir in gelatin, pineapple juice, orange juice and lemon juice. Ladle mixture into wide-topped freezer containers, leaving a 1-inch headspace. Cover tightly and freeze.

To serve, partially thaw juice mixture at room temperature for about 5 hours. Place mixture in a punch bowl. Stir with a fork to break up ice chunks. Add ginger ale. Yield: 1½ gallons.

Sparkling Punch

1   (6-ounce) can frozen lemonade
    concentrate, thawed and undiluted
1   (8-ounce) can crushed pineapple,
    undrained

1   (10-ounce) package frozen
    strawberries, partially thawed and
    undrained
3   (1-liter) bottles ginger ale, chilled

Combine all ingredients except ginger ale in a container or electric blender. Blend at high speed for 30 seconds or until smooth. Just before serving, stir in ginger ale. Yield: 4 quarts.

Tahitian Punch

1	(46-ounce) can pineapple juice, chilled	1	pint lemon or lime sherbet
1	(46-ounce) can orange-grapefruit juice, chilled		Sliced citrus fruit and mint sprig for garnish
1	(2-liter) bottle carbonated lemon-lime beverage, chilled		

In a large bowl, stir together both juices and carbonated beverage. Spoon sherbet into bowl. Garnish with slices of citrus and a sprig of mint. Yield: Thirty-eight ½-cup servings.

Tea Syrup for a Crowd

3	quarts water	7-8	cups sugar
4	ounces loose tea		

Bring water to a boil. Add tea and reduce heat to a simmer for 15 minutes. Strain into a bowl over sugar. Stir until dissolved. Transfer to a gallon jug.

To serve, combine 1 pitcher of tea with 3 to 4 pitchers of water.

Wassail

4	cups pineapple juice	2	sticks cinnamon
1½	cups apricot nectar	2	teaspoons whole cloves
4	cups apple cider	1	teaspoon nutmeg
1	cup orange juice		Bourbon to taste (optional)

Combine all fruit juices in a large saucepan. Tie cinnamon sticks, cloves and nutmeg in a cheesecloth bag and add to saucepan. Simmer mixture over medium heat for 30 minutes. Remove spice bag. Add bourbon, if desired. Serve hot. Yield: 2½ quarts.

Whiskey Sour Punch

2	cups bourbon	1	quart apple juice
2	(6-ounce) cans frozen lemonade concentrate, thawed and undiluted	1	quart ginger ale
			Ice ring

Combine all ingredients except ice ring and stir well. Place ice ring in a punch bowl. Pour bourbon mixture over ice ring. Yield: 3 quarts.

Breakfast, Brunch & Breads

Apple Walnut Breakfast Dessert Strudel

4	sheets puff pastry	1	tablespoon cinnamon
4	apples (mixed types such as Granny	1	teaspoon vanilla
	Smith, Rome, Gala), sliced	1	teaspoon nutmeg
¼	cup granulated sugar	1	cup walnuts, broken
½	cup brown sugar	1	egg
¼	cup flour		

Stack pastry in layers. Toss apples, sugars, flour, cinnamon, vanilla, nutmeg and walnuts together. Spread mixture down the center of pastry stack. Beat egg well, adding a splash of water. Fold long side of pastry into middle. Brush ends with egg and pinch together. Brush the other side with egg, bring to the middle and place against the first side. Pinch together to make a seam. Place seam-side down on a lightly greased baking sheet. Cut small diagonal slits in the top and brush thoroughly with remaining egg. Bake at 350 degrees for 35 to 40 minutes or until golden, puffed and starting to bubble. Cool about 10 minutes, then cut and serve with Spiced Cream Topping. Yield: 6 to 8 servings.

Spiced Cream Topping

1	cup heavy cream	1	teaspoon cinnamon
2	tablespoons powdered sugar	1	teaspoon vanilla

Beat cream with an electric mixer on high until starting to thicken. Add sugar and beat until almost whipped. Whip in cinnamon and vanilla.

Country Ham with Red-Eye Gravy

1	tablespoon butter	2	cups black coffee
2	(12-ounce) packages sliced country ham		

Heat butter in a large skillet or 2 skillets. When the butter is bubbling, add ham slices in a single layer and cook 2 to 3 minutes or until meat is slightly colored. Turn and cook on other side for 2 to 3 minutes. Pour off any excess fat from the skillet. Pour coffee over ham and cover. Simmer about 20 minutes or until gravy has thickened. Yield: 8 servings.

If I purchase the ham from a country store and it is very salty, I soak it for a few minutes in warm water with 1 tablespoon brown sugar added to remove some of the salt; then I cook as above.

Creamy Grits

2	cups water	1	cup quick grits
½	cup milk	½	cup heavy cream
¼	teaspoon salt	2	tablespoons butter

Combine water, milk and salt in a saucepan. Bring to a boil. Slowly add grits, stirring constantly. Boil slowly, stirring occasionally, until grits begin to thicken. When thick, stir in cream. Stir in butter. Cover and remove from heat. Serve with eggs and bacon or ham. Yield: 4 to 6 servings.

Crème Brûlée French Toast Casserole

⅓	cup butter, melted	8	eggs
2	tablespoons light corn syrup	1	cup milk
¾	cup light brown sugar	1	tablespoon vanilla
1	loaf French bread	1	tablespoon cinnamon

Combine butter, corn syrup and brown sugar in a saucepan and heat to a rapid boil. Spread mixture in a 9x13-inch pan. Cut bread into 1-inch thick slices and lay over mixture. Beat together eggs, milk, vanilla and cinnamon and pour over bread, allowing all slices to absorb the mixture. Refrigerate overnight. Bake at 350 degrees for 40 minutes. Serve with Warm Berry Compote. Yield: 6 servings.

Warm Berry Compote

2	cups sliced fresh strawberries	¼	cup fresh blackberries
½	cup fresh raspberries	3	cups maple syrup

Combine all ingredients in a 2-quart saucepan. Cook over low heat for 10 to 15 minutes or until warm. Pour over individual toast slices.

Your pancakes will be delicate and airy if the eggs are at room temperature when you add them to the milk and flour mixture. To make them very light, separate eggs and beat whites before adding to mixture. Be sure to let the batter rest for 15 minutes after it is mixed.

Dutch Baby

Pan Size	Butter	Eggs	Milk and Flour
2 to 3 quart	¼ cup	3	¾ cup each
3 to 4 quart	⅓ cup	4	1 cup each
4 to 4½ quart	½ cup	5	1¼ cups each
4½ to 5 quart	½ cup	6	1½ cups each

Place butter in a pan and set in 425 degrees oven until butter is melted and foamy. Meanwhile, quickly mix batter. In a blender or food processor, whirl eggs at high speed for 1 minute. With motor running, gradually pour in milk, then slowly add flour and continue to whirl 30 seconds longer. Remove pan from oven when butter is foamy and pour batter into pan. Return to oven and bake 20 to 25 minutes (depending on pan size) or until puffy and well browned. Serve immediately. Yield: 4 to 8 servings.

May be served with powdered sugar, fresh fruit, hot fruit or syrups.

French Toast

1	stick unsalted butter, cut into bits	4	cups corn flakes
8	eggs		Cinnamon sugar (2 tablespoons sugar mixed with ¼ teaspoon cinnamon)
4	cups milk		
2	tablespoons vanilla		Accompaniments: maple syrup, whipped cream, pecans or berries
2	tablespoons dark rum		
1	(1-pound) loaf challah, cut into 1-inch thick slices, ends discarded (or use to make bread crumbs)		

To clarify butter, melt butter in a small heavy saucepan over low heat. Remove pan from heat and let stand 3 minutes. Skim froth and pour butter through a sieve lined with a double thickness of rinsed and squeezed-dry cheesecloth into a bowl. Discard milk solids.

In a large bowl, whisk together eggs, milk, vanilla and rum. Pour half of mixture into a 9x13-inch baking dish. Place half of bread slices in mixture and soak 5 minutes. Turn slices and soak 5 minutes longer. In another large shallow dish, spread half of corn flakes. Coat soaked bread on each side with corn flakes and transfer to a tray. Soak and coat remaining slices with remaining egg mixture and corn flakes in same manner.

In a large heavy skillet, heat 2 tablespoons clarified butter over medium heat until hot but not smoking. Cook 2 to 3 bread slices, or as many as will fit in a single layer, for 3 minutes on each side or until puffed and golden brown. Transfer French toast as cooked to a baking sheet and keep warm in a 250 degree oven. Cook remaining slices in remaining butter in same manner. Sprinkle French toast with cinnamon sugar. Serve with accompaniments. Yield: 8 servings.

Ham and Cheese Strata

8	eggs	6	ounces Gouda cheese, cut into ¾-inch dice (1½ cups)
1½	cups milk		
½	teaspoon salt	½	cup julienne sun-dried tomatoes, drained
½	teaspoon freshly ground black pepper		
4	cups Italian bread cubes (1-inch)	¼	cup plus 1 tablespoon snipped fresh chives, divided
6	ounces Virginia ham, cut into ½-inch dice (1½ cups)	1	cup coarsely shredded Cheddar cheese (about 4 ounces)

Whisk together eggs, milk, salt and pepper in a large bowl. Stir in bread until evenly moistened. Stir in ham, Gouda cheese, tomato strips and ¼ cup chives until well-coated and evenly distributed. Pour mixture into a greased large baking dish. Sprinkle Cheddar cheese evenly over the top. Bake at 450 degrees for 20 minutes or until puffed and golden. Cool slightly. Sprinkle with remaining 1 tablespoon chives and serve. Yield: 4 servings.

Sausage Strata

6	slices white or whole wheat bread, crusts trimmed	1¼	cups milk
		¾	cup half-and-half
1	pound bulk pork sausage	1	teaspoon Worcestershire sauce
1	teaspoon prepared mustard	½	teaspoon salt
1	cup shredded processed Swiss cheese	½	teaspoon black pepper
3	eggs, lightly beaten		

Place bread slices in a greased 10x6x1½-inch baking dish. Brown sausage; drain well. Stir mustard into sausage. Spoon sausage mixture evenly over bread and sprinkle cheese on top. (Casserole may be refrigerated or frozen at this point. If frozen, remove from freezer the night before it is to be served and refrigerate until morning.)

Combine eggs, milk, half-and-half, Worcestershire sauce, salt, pepper and beat with a wire whisk until frothy. Pour mixture over cheese. Bake at 350 degrees for 30 minutes or until puffed and set. Yield: 4 to 6 servings.

Strawberry Fig Jam

4	(3-ounce) packages strawberry gelatin	6	cups sugar
½	cup water		Pinch of salt
7	cups peeled figs, mashed		

Dissolve gelatin in water in a saucepan. Add mashed figs, sugar and salt. Cook over low heat for 45 to 60 minutes, stirring occasionally. Pack in sterile jars and seal. Jam will keep for months.

Quiche Lorraine

Crust

1¾	cups all-purpose flour		1	egg
¼	teaspoon coarse salt		1	egg yolk
¼	cup coarsely chopped chives (optional)		3	tablespoons ice water
9	tablespoons unsalted butter, chilled and cut into small pieces			

Filling

10	ounces slab bacon, cut into ¾x½x¼-inch strips		2	cups heavy cream
3	eggs		¾	teaspoon salt
			¼	teaspoon freshly ground black pepper

Process flour, salt and chives in a food processor until combined. Add butter and process just until mixture resembles coarse meal. Whisk together egg, egg yolk and ice water in a small bowl. With processor running, pour in egg mixture and process until dough starts to come together. Shape dough into a disk. Wrap in plastic wrap and refrigerate at least 30 minutes.

On a lightly floured work surface, roll out dough to ¼-inch thick. Cut out a 13-inch circle and press circle into the bottom and up the sides of an 11-inch tart pan with a removable bottom. Trim dough flush with top edge of pan. Prick bottom all over with a fork. Place tart pan on a rimmed baking sheet and freeze 30 minutes or until firm.

Line tart shell with parchment paper and fill with pie weights or dried beans. Bake at 400 degrees for 20 minutes or until dough starts to feel firm on the edges. Remove parchment paper and weights and continue to bake 10 minutes or until crust is pale golden brown. Cool completely on a wire rack.

To make filling, cook bacon in a large skillet over medium heat for 10 minutes or until browned. Transfer with a slotted spoon to paper towels to drain. Whisk eggs, cream, salt and pepper together in a medium bowl. Pour mixture into baked crust. Scatter bacon strips on top. Bake at 400 degrees for 30 minutes or until puffed and pale golden brown. Cool at least 30 minutes before serving. Yield: 8 servings.

Very Good Grits

6	cups chicken broth		2	teaspoons salt
2	cups heavy cream		¼	teaspoon freshly ground black pepper
4	tablespoons unsalted butter		2	cups dry quick grits
2	large cloves garlic, minced			Tabasco sauce to taste

Combine broth, cream, butter and garlic in a large saucepan. Add salt and pepper and bring to a boil. Slowly whisk in grits and cook over low heat, whisking until thick and smooth, about 10 minutes. Season with Tabasco and extra salt and pepper and serve. Yield: 6 servings.

Sausage Grits Casserole

1	pound bulk sausage	½	teaspoon dry mustard
6	slices Swiss cheese	1	teaspoon Mrs. Dash seasoning
½	cup cooked grits	1	cup self-rising flour
2	cups milk, divided	4	tablespoons butter, melted
4	eggs		

Cook and crumble sausage and drain. Spread sausage in a 9x13-inch dish. Place cheese slices on top to cover. In a bowl, combine cooked grits, 1 cup milk, eggs, mustard and seasoning and beat with a hand mixer. Pour mixture over cheese slices. Mix flour, remaining 1 cup milk and butter. Pour over top of casserole to cover. Bake at 350 degrees for 40 minutes. Let stand before cutting. Yield: 6 generous portions.

Strata with Asparagus, Sausage and Fontina

10-12	slices French bread, cut into 1-inch cubes	4	roasted red bell peppers, peeled, seeded and thinly sliced
1	tablespoon extra virgin olive oil	1	pound asparagus, ends trimmed, stalks cut into 1-inch pieces and cooked until tender
10	ounces large link country sausages		
16	eggs		Salt and freshly ground pepper to taste
6	cup milk		
1	bunch green onions, light green portion only, finely chopped	4	cup shredded Fontina cheese, divided

Place bread cubes in a large bowl. Warm olive oil in a large skillet over medium heat. Add sausage and cook, turning occasionally, for 3 to 5 minutes total or until browned on both sides. Using a slotted spoon, transfer sausage to a plate. Cool and cut into thin slices. Transfer sausage to bowl with bread. In a separate large bowl, whisk together eggs and milk. Pour mixture over bread and sausage. Add green onions, bell peppers, asparagus, salt and pepper and 3 cups cheese. Stir until well blended. Transfer to a greased large baking dish. Cover with plastic wrap and refrigerate 4 hours or overnight.

When ready to bake, sprinkle remaining 1 cup cheese on top. Bake at 350 degrees for about 1 hour. Let stand 10 minutes before serving. Yield: 12 servings.

When boiling eggs, add a pinch of salt to the water to prevent eggshells from cracking.

Bran Muffins

3	cups sugar	1	quart buttermilk
5	cups all-purpose flour	4	eggs, beaten
5	teaspoons baking soda	1	cup vegetable oil
1½	teaspoons salt	1	(15-ounce) box raisin bran
8	ounces chopped dates		(preferably Post)

Combine all ingredients and mix well. Cover and refrigerate for up to 6 weeks. When ready to bake, spoon batter into well-greased muffin tins (papers will stick). Bake at 425 degrees for 15 minutes. Yield: About 6 dozen.

Sprinkle chopped walnuts on top before baking.

Cheddar Cheese Biscuits

2	cups self-rising flour, sifted	1	(8-ounce) carton sour cream
1	cup butter	1	cup shredded New York sharp cheese

Mix flour, butter and sour cream. Fold in cheese. Drop by teaspoonfuls into greased mini muffin tins. Bake at 350 degrees for 15 minutes. Serve warm or cold. Yield: 4 dozen.

Cornbread

¼	cup shortening	2	eggs, lightly beaten
1¼	cups self-rising cornmeal	2	cups buttermilk
1¼	cups self-rising flour		

Place shortening in a cast iron skillet or glass pie plate and put in oven while preheating oven to 425 degrees and while preparing batter. Sift cornmeal and flour together. Combine eggs and buttermilk in a bowl. Add dry ingredients to buttermilk mixture and mix with a fork; do not overmix. Pour hot shortening into batter, leaving a small amount of shortening in pan. Mix lightly and pour batter into hot skillet. Bake 25 minutes or until brown. Serve hot. Yield: 6 to 8 servings.

Cinnamon-Raisin Rolls

Dough

2¼	cups unbleached all-purpose flour	½	teaspoon salt
1	package active dry yeast	1	egg
1	cup milk	3	egg whites
4	tablespoons butter	2¼	cups whole-wheat flour
¼	cup sugar		

Filling

½	cup dark brown sugar	4	tablespoons butter
¼	cup whole-wheat flour	¾	cup raisins
1	tablespoon cinnamon		

Glaze

2	cups sifted powdered sugar	Milk

To prepare dough, combine unbleached flour and yeast in a large mixing bowl; set aside. In a small saucepan over low heat, combine milk, butter, sugar and salt. Stir just until butter starts to melt (120 to 130 degrees). Add warm milk mixture to dry ingredients and mix well. Add egg and egg whites and beat with an electric mixer on low speed for 30 seconds, scraping sides of the bowl constantly. Beat on high for 3 minutes. Using a spoon, stir in as much of whole-wheat flour as possible. Turn dough onto a lightly floured surface. Knead in enough of remaining whole-wheat flour as needed to make a soft dough that is smooth and elastic, kneading about 4 minutes. Shape into a ball and place in a bowl sprayed with cooking spray. Turn ball over once and allow to rise in a warm place for 1 hour or until doubled in bulk.

Prepare filling while dough is rising. Combine brown sugar, whole-wheat flour and cinnamon in a medium bowl and mix well. Cut in butter until crumbly using 2 knives or a pastry blender; set aside.

Punch dough down and turn onto a lightly floured surface. Cover and allow to rise 10 minutes. Roll dough out into a 12-inch square. Spread filling evenly over the dough. Top with raisins and roll up tightly like a jelly roll, pinching to seal the seam. Cut roll into eight 1½-inch slices. Arrange slices, cut-side up, in a 9x13-inch baking dish. Cover dish loosely with clear plastic wrap and allow to rise 45 minutes or until almost doubled in size. Remove plastic wrap and spray top of rolls with cooking spray, or brush with melted butter. Bake at 375 degrees for 25 to 30 minutes or until lightly browned. If the rolls start to get too brown, cover them with foil the last 5 to 10 minutes of baking. Remove from oven and allow to cool 2 minutes. Invert onto a wire rack and allow to cool slightly. Drizzle with glaze while warm.

To make glaze, combine powdered sugar with enough milk to reach a drizzle consistency. Yield: 8 rolls.

Cranberry Bread

4	cups flour	1	cup orange juice
2	cups sugar	¼	cup hot water
1	teaspoon salt	4	tablespoons butter, melted
1	teaspoon baking soda	1	tablespoon orange zest
1	tablespoon baking powder	2	cups chopped cranberries
2	eggs, lightly beaten	¾	cup chopped pecans or walnuts

Combine flour, sugar, salt, baking soda and baking powder in a large bowl. In a separate bowl, mix eggs, orange juice, hot water, butter and orange zest. Stir egg mixture into dry ingredients. Fold in cranberries and nuts. Spoon batter into 2 greased loaf pans. Bake at 325 degrees for 1 hour, 10 minutes. Remove bread from pans and cool on racks. Yield: 2 loaves.

French Bread

2	cups warm water, divided	6	cups sifted all-purpose flour
1	tablespoon dry yeast or cake yeast		Cornmeal
3	tablespoons shortening, softened	1	egg white
1	tablespoon salt	2	tablespoons water

Pour 1½ cups warm water into a large mixing bowl. Sprinkle yeast over remaining ½ cup warm water. Stir until dissolved, then add to water in large bowl. Add shortening, salt and 3 cups flour. Beat until smooth. Add remaining flour to form a stiff dough, working in with hands, if needed. Remove dough to a floured surface and knead 10 minutes or until smooth and elastic. Place dough in a greased bowl, turning to grease sides and top. Cover with a clean, dry cloth and set in a warm, draft-free place. Let rise 1½ to 2 hours or until doubled in bulk. Punch down and let rise again until almost doubled in bulk again. Punch down and divide dough into 3 equal parts. Shape each portion with hands into a long loaf, tapering the ends. Place each loaf on a separate greased baking sheet that has been lightly sprinkled with cornmeal. Make several gashes about ⅛-inch deep in each loaf. Let rise, uncovered, for 1 hour or until doubled in bulk. (For a crisp crust, place a shallow pan of water on the bottom of the oven.) Beat egg whites lightly with 2 tablespoons water and brush over loaves. Bake at 400 degrees for 20 minutes. Brush again with egg mixture and bake 20 minutes longer or until browned. Cool. Bread can be frozen to maintain freshness; reheat in foil. Yield: 3 loaves.

Dipping Sauces for Bread

Garlic Oil

1 cup extra virgin olive oil
1 tablespoon balsamic vinegar
1 tablespoon chopped fresh basil
1 tablespoon chopped fresh parsley
1 tablespoon chopped dried oregano
1-2 cloves garlic, minced

½ teaspoon salt
1 teaspoon freshly ground coarse black pepper
Dash of dried red pepper flakes
1 tablespoon finely chopped sun-dried tomatoes

Combine all ingredients and let stand at least 1 to 2 hours before serving to allow flavors to meld. Serve with crusty Italian bread cut into thick slices. Store in refrigerator for up to 2 to 3 days; garlic will become rancid after that.

Bread Oil

1 teaspoon dried red pepper flakes
1 teaspoon black pepper
1 teaspoon dried oregano
1 teaspoon dried rosemary
1 teaspoon dried basil

1 teaspoon dried parsley
1 teaspoon garlic powder
1 teaspoon minced fresh garlic
1 teaspoon kosher salt
¼-½ cup extra virgin olive oil

Combine all ingredients except olive oil on a deep plate or bowl. Pour olive oil over the top and allow to stand 30 minutes before serving. Serve with freshly baked bread for dipping.

Bread Dipping Oil II

1 cup aged balsamic vinegar
3 cups extra virgin olive oil

¼ teaspoon minced garlic
¼ cup pecorino, or pepper to taste

Combine all ingredients in a mixing bowl and whip thoroughly until fully incorporated. Store in refrigerator in an airtight container for up to 6 months. Use as a dipping sauce for any fresh crusty bread.

To determine whether an egg is fresh, immerse it in a pan of cool, salted water. If it sinks, it is fresh — if it rises to the surface, throw it away.

Foccacia Bread

1	tablespoon dry yeast	1	teaspoon canola oil
1	tablespoon sugar	2	tablespoons butter, melted
1	cup warm water	¼	cup chopped fresh rosemary, or
2½	cups white flour, divided		2 tablespoons dried
1	teaspoon salt, plus extra for sprinkling		

Place yeast, sugar and warm water in a large bowl or food processor and allow mixture to become bubbly. Mix in 2 cups flour and 1 teaspoon salt. Knead about 10 minutes or process in food processor for 15 seconds or until smooth and elastic, adding flour as needed. Form dough into a ball and place in a bowl greased with canola oil. Cover with a towel and let dough rise in a warm place for 1 hour or until doubled. Punch down dough and divide in half. Let dough rest for a few minutes. Press dough into 2 greased 9-inch square cake pans. Brush butter over the top of the loaves. Sprinkle with rosemary and lightly press into the surface. Let dough rise another 45 minutes or until doubled in size. Lightly sprinkle loaves with salt. Bake at 450 degrees for 20 to 25 minutes or until lightly browned. Wonderful with Dipping Sauces (page 37). Yield: 2 loaves.

Fried Cornbread

¾	cup self-rising cornmeal	½	cup milk, or more if needed
¼	cup self-rising flour		Oil for frying

Mix cornmeal and flour. Add milk. (Add a little more milk if you want mixture to drop from the spoon.) Drop from a tablespoon into about 1 to 2 inches of hot oil. When bottom is browned, turn and brown on other side. Drain on paper towels. Yield: 4 servings.

Sprinkle top with Parmesan cheese.

My mother used plain cornmeal mixed with water for these. I prefer the above recipe.

Garlic Bread

1	loaf French or Italian bread	2	cloves garlic, crushed
½	cup butter, melted, or olive oil	1	tablespoon minced parsley

Cut bread in half horizontally. Mix butter with garlic and parsley. Spread mixture over cut sides of bread. Brown in a 450 degree oven or under the broiler. Yield: 6 to 8 servings.

To make croutons: cube French or Italian bread. Place in a bowl and pour butter mixture over bread cubes. Mix with a fork and spread coated cubes over a baking sheet. Bake at 275 degrees until browned.

Helen's Tea Biscuits

½ cup butter, softened
1 (8-ounce) package cream cheese,
    softened

2 cups biscuit baking mix

Cut butter and cream cheese into baking mix. Roll out dough and cut with a small biscuit cutter. Bake at 400 degrees until lightly browned. Serve with jam for tea.

Hushpuppies

1 cup self-rising cornmeal
1 cup self-rising flour
1 teaspoon baking powder
1 small onion, finely chopped

¾ cup buttermilk
1 egg, lightly beaten
    Vegetable oil or shortening for frying

Combine cornmeal, flour, baking powder and onion. Add buttermilk and egg and stir just until combined; do not overmix. Carefully drop batter by tablespoonfuls into deep hot oil (370 degrees). Cook only a few at a time. Fry, turning once, for 3 to 5 minutes or until golden brown. Drain well on paper towels. Yield: About 2 dozen.

I keep a cup of water nearby when frying these so I can rinse my spoon off occasionally.

Morning Glory Muffins

4 cups all-purpose flour
2½ cups sugar
4 teaspoons baking soda
4 teaspoons cinnamon
1 teaspoon salt
4 cups grated carrots
1 cup raisins

1 cup chopped pecans
1 cup sweetened shredded coconut
2 tart apples, such as Granny Smith,
    peeled and grated
6 eggs
2 cups vegetable oil
4 teaspoons vanilla

Sift together flour, sugar, baking soda, cinnamon and salt in a bowl. Mix in carrots, raisins, pecans, coconut and apples. Add eggs, oil and vanilla and stir just until combined. Spoon batter into well-greased muffin tins, filling all the way to the top. Bake at 350 degrees for 35 minutes for large muffins, or about 20 minutes for mini muffins. Cool in tins 5 minutes. Turn out onto a rack and cool completely. Yield: 30 large or 90 mini muffins.

New Orleans Beignets

1½	cups warm water (100 to 115 degrees)	1	cup evaporated milk
1	package active dry yeast	7	cups flour, divided
½	cup sugar, divided	¼	cup vegetable shortening
1	teaspoon salt		Oil for deep frying
2	eggs		Powdered sugar for dusting

Pour warm water into a large bowl. Sprinkle yeast over water and add a couple teaspoons of sugar. Stir until dissolved. Let stand 10 minutes. Add remaining sugar, salt, eggs and milk. Gradually stir in 4 cups flour and beat with a wooden spoon until smooth and thoroughly blended. Beat in shortening. Add remaining flour, ⅓ cup at a time, beating in with spoon until it becomes too stiff to stir; work in the rest of flour with your hands. Place dough in a greased bowl, turning to grease top. Cover with plastic wrap and refrigerate overnight.

Roll dough out on a floured board or marble pastry surface to ⅛-inch thick. Cut into 2½x3½-inch rectangles with a sharp knife. Heat oil in a deep fryer to 360 degrees. Fry beignets, about 3 to 4 at a time, for 2 to 3 minutes or until they are puffed out and golden brown on both sides. Turn them over in oil with a tongs once or twice while frying to brown evenly, since they rise to the surface as soon as they begin to puff out. Drain each batch, place on a paper towel-lined platter, and keep warm in a 200 degree oven until all are cooked. Sprinkle heavily with powdered sugar and serve hot with coffee. Yield: 3 to 4 dozen.

Popovers

3	eggs	1¼	cups flour
1¼	cups milk, room temperature		Pinch of salt

Hand beat eggs with a whisk until lemon colored and foamy. Add milk and stir until well blended; do not overbeat. Add flour and salt all at once. Hand beat until foamy and smooth on top. Grease popover tins; if you do not have popover tins, you may use muffin tins. Pour batter into a pitcher. Pour batter into tins, filling every other one so that popovers do not touch as they rise. Bake at 450 degrees for 15 minutes. Reduce heat to 350 degrees and bake 30 minutes longer. Do not open oven door to check popovers or they will fall. Remove from tins with a sharp knife and serve hot. Yield: 10 popovers.

Poppy Seed Bread

3¾ cups biscuit baking mix	1 egg, beaten
1¼ cups shredded Cheddar cheese	1½ cups milk
1 tablespoon poppy seeds, plus extra for sprinkling	

Combine baking mix, cheese and poppy seeds. Add egg and milk and mix just until blended. Beat vigorously for 1 minute. Pour batter into a well-greased 9x5-inch loaf pan. Sprinkle with additional poppy seeds. Bake at 350 degrees for 50 to 60 minutes or until done. Remove from pan and cool before slicing. Yield: 1 loaf.

Potato Bread with Starter

Starter

2 packages dry yeast	⅔ cup sugar
1½ cups warm (105 to 115 degrees) water, divided	3 tablespoons potato flakes

Starter "Feed" (repeat for each "feeding")

1 cup warm water	3 tablespoons potato flakes
⅔ cup sugar	

Dissolve yeast in ½ cup warm water. Add remaining 1 cup warm water, sugar and potato flakes. Let mixture sit out all day, then refrigerate for 2 to 5 days.

Remove from refrigerator and "feed" it with 1 cup warm water, ⅔ cup sugar and 3 tablespoons potato flakes. Let sit out all day or overnight. Now you are ready to use 1 cup starter to make your first batch of bread.

To replenish starter, "feed" with 1 cup water, ⅔ cup sugar and 3 tablespoons potato flakes. Let sit out 12 to 24 hours, then refrigerate. Starter will hold for about 1 week.

Bread

1 cup starter	1 teaspoon salt
1½ cups warm water	⅔ cup sugar
½ cup vegetable oil	6-7 cups unsifted all-purpose flour

Combine all ingredients with a wooden spoon. Knead for 8 minutes or until satiny. Turn dough into a greased bowl, cover and let rise until doubled. Punch down dough and shape into 2 loaves. Place loaves in lightly greased loaf pans, or form into rolls and arrange on lightly greased baking sheets. Let rise until doubled in size. Bake at 350 degrees for 18 minutes for rolls or 30 to 40 minutes for loaves. Yield: 2 loaves.

Potato Rolls

1½	cups warm water
1	package dry yeast
⅔	cup sugar
1½	teaspoons salt
⅔	cup shortening

2	eggs, beaten
7-7½	cups all-purpose flour
1	cup freshly cooked and mashed potatoes, warm
	Melted butter

Combine warm water and yeast in a very large mixing bowl. Stir until yeast dissolves. Add sugar, salt, shortening, eggs, flour and potatoes. Mix by hand until dough is easy to handle. Turn out onto a lightly floured surface. Knead until dough is smooth and elastic. Place dough in a large greased bowl and turn to grease top of dough. Cover with plastic and refrigerate until 2 hours before baking. Make rolls slightly larger than a large egg and place on baking sheets. Bake at 350 degrees until golden; watch carefully as they tend to burn quickly. Brush rolls with melted butter. Yield: About 3 dozen.

Pumpkin Walnut Bread

2	cups all-purpose flour
1	teaspoon baking soda
1	teaspoon baking powder
1	teaspoon salt
½	teaspoon cinnamon
½	teaspoon ground cloves
½	teaspoon ground ginger
½	cup unsalted butter, softened

¾	cup plus 1 tablespoon sugar
2	eggs, room temperature
1	cup canned or fresh pumpkin purée
1½	teaspoons lemon zest
1	teaspoon vanilla
½	cup sour cream
½	cup whole milk
1½	cups chopped walnuts

Combine flour, baking soda, baking powder, salt, cinnamon, cloves and ginger in a bowl; set aside. Beat butter in a separate large bowl with an electric mixer until light. Gradually beat in ¾ cup sugar. Beat in eggs, one at a time. Beat in pumpkin, lemon zest and vanilla. Whisk sour cream and milk in a small bowl. Alternately, in 2 additions, beat dry ingredients and sour cream mixture into batter. Fold in walnuts. Transfer batter to 2 greased loaf pans and smooth top. Sprinkle remaining 1 tablespoon sugar over loaves. Bake at 325 degrees on center rack of oven for 1 hour, 10 minutes or until a tester inserted in the center comes out clean. Cool in pan 10 minutes. Turn out onto a rack and cool. Can be make 2 days ahead, wrapped in foil and stored at room temperature. Yield: 2 loaves.

Sally Wilson's Quick Rolls

1	cup milk	1	package dry yeast (1 tablespoon)
2	tablespoons sugar	¼	cup lukewarm water
3	tablespoons butter	4	cups flour, divided
1½	teaspoons salt		

Combine milk, sugar, butter and salt in a saucepan and heat until scalded. Cool until lukewarm. Mix yeast with ¼ cup lukewarm water and let stand until dissolved. Add yeast mixture to lukewarm milk mixture. Mix in half the flour. Add remaining half of flour, or enough to form a ball of dough. Let rise in a warm place for 1 hour or more. Roll out dough to ¼ inch thick and cut with biscuit cutter. Fold over and place in pan ½ inch apart and let rise 1 hour. Bake at 475 degrees. If kept more than 2 days, use 2 tablespoons yeast. Yield: 2 dozen.

Savory Corn Muffins

1	(14¾-ounce) can creamed corn	1	cup all-purpose flour
2	cups yellow cornmeal, divided	1	tablespoon sugar
1	cup buttermilk	1½	teaspoons salt
2	eggs	2	teaspoons baking powder
½	cup butter, melted	⅓	teaspoon baking soda

Adjust oven rack to center position and heat oven to 450 degrees. Put a 12-cup muffin tin in oven to heat while preparing batter.

Microwave creamed corn in a 1-quart glass measuring cup to a full boil. Stir in 1 cup cornmeal to make a very thick, pasty mush. If the mush is not stiff, microwave about 30 seconds longer. Whisk in buttermilk, then eggs and finally butter. In a separate medium bowl, mix remaining 1 cup cornmeal with flour, sugar, salt, baking powder and baking soda. Add corn mixture to dry ingredients and stir just until combined.

Remove muffin tin from oven and coat with cooking spray. Divide batter evenly among cups. Bake at 450 degrees for 15 minutes or until golden brown on sides and bottom. Turn out onto a wire rack and cool 5 minutes. Yield: 12 muffins.

Southern Biscuits

2	cups self-rising flour	1	cup buttermilk
½	cup shortening		

Sift flour. Blend shortening into flour with fingers or a pastry blender. Make a well in the center of the flour mixture and pour in buttermilk. Mix lightly with fingers or a fork to make a dough. Roll out dough on a floured surface. (I use the palm of my hand, but not everyone has the knack.) Cut into circles with a biscuit cutter and place on a greased pan. Bake at 450 degrees until golden brown. Yield: About 12 biscuits.

Spicy Cheese Biscuits

3½	cups all-purpose flour	1	cup shredded sharp Cheddar cheese
2	tablespoons baking powder	1	cup grated sharp Romano cheese
1	tablespoon sugar	⅔	cup vegetable shortening, chilled and cut into small pieces
2	teaspoons cayenne pepper		
½	teaspoon salt	1¼	cups chilled buttermilk

Sift together flour, baking powder, sugar, cayenne pepper and salt twice into a medium bowl. Mix in cheeses. Add shortening and blend by rubbing with fingertips until mixture resembles coarse meal. Add buttermilk and stir until dough begins to form clumps. Turn dough out onto a lightly floured surface. Knead gently about 8 turns or until smooth. Roll out dough to ¾-inch thickness. Cut into biscuits using a 3-inch cutter. Gather dough scraps and roll to ¾-inch thickness. Cut out additional biscuits. Transfer biscuits to a large greased baking sheet. Bake at 450 degrees for 15 minutes or until puffed and golden brown. Serve warm. Yield: 9 biscuits.

Toasted Cheese Sticks

1	loaf unsliced white bread	1	(4-ounce) package processed American cheese product
¾	cup butter		
		½	cup melted butter

Remove crusts from bread. Cut crosswise into seven 1-inch thick slices. Cut each slice into 3 pieces and place on a wire rack to dry out for 30 minutes. Melt ¾ cup butter in a small saucepan. Stir in cheese. Brush all sides of bread strips with butter mixture. When mixture becomes difficult to spread, add remaining ½ cup melted butter to cheese mixture and continue to brush on bread. Skewer bread pieces lengthwise and broil on all sides until lightly browned. Serve hot with a salad. Yield: 21 cheese sticks.

Yeast Rolls

2	tablespoons yeast (2 packages)	½	cup shortening
1	cup lukewarm water	1½	teaspoons salt
¾	cup sugar, divided	2	eggs, beaten
1	cup boiling water	6	cups all-purpose or bread flour
½	cup butter		Melted butter

Dissolve yeast in 1 cup lukewarm water with 1 teaspoon sugar and let stand until it bubbles. In a separate bowl, pour boiling water over ½ cup butter, shortening, remaining sugar and salt. When cool, add dissolved yeast mixture and eggs to shortening mixture. Mix in flour and knead a few times. Place dough in a greased bowl and refrigerate overnight.

About 3½ hours before using, roll out dough on a floured surface and cut with a biscuit cutter. Dip rolls in melted butter and fold over on a baking sheet, leaving enough room to allow for rising of dough. Let rise until doubled in size. Bake at 425 degrees until brown. Brush with melted butter. Yield: 2½ dozen.

Vidalia Onion Custard Bread

2	tablespoons butter	½	teaspoon salt
1	large onion, halved and sliced	1½	cups milk
1¼	cups all-purpose flour	1	egg, lightly beaten
4	teaspoons baking powder	½	cup shredded Cheddar cheese

Topping

| ¼ | cup shredded Cheddar cheese | 1 | tablespoon poppy seeds |
| 2 | tablespoons reserved caramelized onion | 1 | tablespoon butter, melted |

Melt butter in a large skillet over medium heat. Add onion and sauté 10 to 15 minutes or until golden brown. Reserve 2 tablespoons onion for topping.

In a large bowl, combine flour, baking powder and salt. Stir in milk, egg and cheese. Add remaining onions. Pour batter into a greased 9-inch deep dish pie plate.

For topping, sprinkle cheese, reserved onion and poppy seeds over batter. Drizzle with melted butter. Bake at 400 degrees for 25 to 35 minutes or until golden brown. Cool slightly. Cut into wedges and serve warm. Yield: 6 to 8 servings.

Yummy Sweet Rolls

1	cup sour cream, scalded and hot	½	cup warm water (105 to 115 degrees)
½	cup butter, melted	2	eggs, beaten
½	cup sugar	4	cups all-purpose flour
1	teaspoon salt		Filling (recipe below)
2	packages dry yeast		Glaze (recipe below)

Combine sour cream, butter, sugar and salt and mix well. Let mixture cool to lukewarm. Dissolve yeast in warm water in a large mixing bowl. Stir in sour cream mixture. Mix in eggs. Gradually stir in flour; dough will be soft. Cover tightly and chill overnight. Divide dough into 4 equal portions. Turn each portion out onto a lightly floured surface and knead 4 to 5 times. Roll each portion into a 12x8-inch rectangle. Spread one-fourth of filling over each rectangle, leaving a ½-inch border around edges. Carefully roll up jelly-roll fashion, beginning at long side. Firmly pinch edge and ends to seal. Cut each roll into 1½-inch slices. Place slices, cut-side down, 2 inches apart on greased baking sheets. Cover and let rise in a warm (85 degrees), draft-free place for 1½ hours or until doubled in bulk. Bake at 375 degrees for 12 minutes or until golden brown. Drizzle glaze over each roll. Yield: About 2½ dozen.

Filling

2	(8-ounce) packages cream cheese, softened	1	egg
		2	teaspoons vanilla
¾	cup sugar	½	teaspoon salt

Combine all ingredients in a food processor or electric mixer. Process or mix until well blended. Yield: About 2 cups.

Glaze

2	cups powdered sugar, sifted	2	teaspoons vanilla
¼	cup milk		

Combine all ingredients and mix well. Yield: About 1 cup.

Salads

Apple and Poppy Seed Slaw

8	cups shredded green cabbage (about 1 small head)	2	tablespoons apple cider vinegar
3	medium carrots, coarsely grated (about 2½ cups)	⅔	cup sour cream
3	medium Granny Smith apples, peeled, cored and coarsely grated	½	cup mayonnaise
4	green onions, thinly sliced	¼	cup frozen apple juice concentrate, thawed
		2	tablespoons poppy seeds
			Salt and pepper to taste

8 cups shredded green cabbage (about 1 small head)
3 medium carrots, coarsely grated (about 2½ cups)
3 medium Granny Smith apples, peeled, cored and coarsely grated
4 green onions, thinly sliced

2 tablespoons apple cider vinegar
⅔ cup sour cream
½ cup mayonnaise
¼ cup frozen apple juice concentrate, thawed
2 tablespoons poppy seeds
Salt and pepper to taste

Mix cabbage, carrots, apples and green onions in a large bowl. Add vinegar and toss to coat.

In a medium bowl, whisk sour cream, mayonnaise, apple juice concentrate and poppy seeds to blend. Add to cabbage mixture and toss to blend. Season with salt and pepper. Cover and refrigerate at least 1 hour, or up to 1 day ahead. Keep refrigerated until ready to serve. Toss to blend before serving. Yield: 8 to 10 servings.

Apple Salad

2 cups diced peeled apples
3 tablespoons lemon juice
1 cup diced celery
¾ cup pecans

¾ cup mayonnaise
½ cup white raisins, optional
Salt to taste
Lettuce leaves

Toss apples with lemon juice to prevent browning; drain. Mix apples with celery, pecans, raisins (if using) and mayonnaise. Season with salt. Serve on lettuce leaves. Yield: 4 to 6 servings.

Asheville Salad

1 (10¾-ounce) can condensed tomato soup
4 (8-ounce) packages cream cheese
2 (¼-ounce) envelopes unflavored gelatin
½ cup cold water

½ cup minced bell pepper
½ cup minced celery
¼ cup mayonnaise
¼ teaspoon salt
Lettuce leaves

Bring soup to a boil. Remove from heat and add cream cheese. Beat until smooth. Soften gelatin in ½ cup cold water and add to soup mixture. Chill 4 minutes. Add bell pepper, celery, mayonnaise and salt. Pour mixture into molds or a glass dish and chill. Unmold or cut. Serve on lettuce leaves. Yield: 6 servings.

Beet Salad

2   pounds red baby beets, scrubbed well
       and trimmed
3   tablespoons olive oil
2   tablespoons red wine vinegar

Salt and freshly ground black pepper
       to taste
⅓   cup small fresh mint leaves for garnish

Wrap groups of 2 or 3 beets together in little packets of foil. Place packets on a baking sheet. Bake at 350 degrees for 1 hour or until very tender. When the beets are cool enough to handle, slip off and discard skins, wearing rubber gloves. Halve beets lengthwise and place in a bowl. Whisk together oil, vinegar and salt and pepper. Add to beets and toss to coat. Sprinkle with mint leaves. Yield: 6 servings.

Bellini Salad

1   (¼-ounce) envelope unflavored gelatin
½   cup cold water
¾   cup white grape juice
¼   cup sugar
⅛   teaspoon salt

¼   teaspoon lemon juice
½   cup sparkling wine (see note below)
¾   cup sliced fresh peaches
¾   cup pitted fresh cherries

Soak gelatin in ½ cup cold water for 5 minutes. Bring grape juice to a boil and pour over gelatin mixture. Add sugar and salt and whisk gently until dissolved. Add lemon juice and wine and refrigerate until slightly thickened. Fold in peaches and cherries. Pour mixture into a mold or individual glasses and refrigerate 4 hours or until firm.
Yield: 4 to 6 servings.

Don't use an expensive champagne for the sparkling wine, but do use a drinkable wine; perhaps Christallino Brut caba.

Blue Cheese Dressing

4   cups mayonnaise
       Dash of Tabasco sauce
¾   tablespoon finely chopped onion
1   teaspoon white pepper

1½   teaspoons garlic salt
¼   cup buttermilk
¾   cup vinegar
6   ounces blue cheese, crumbled

Mix all ingredients and serve.

Betty's Ambrosia Mold

1	(8-ounce) can crushed pineapple in juice, undrained	1¾	cups frozen whipped topping, thawed
2	cups boiling water	1	(11-ounce) can Mandarin orange segments, drained
1	(6-ounce) package orange gelatin, or two 3-ounce packages	1½	cups miniature marshmallows
		½	cup coconut

Drain pineapple, reserving liquid. Add cold water to reserved liquid to measure 1 cup. Pour boiling water over gelatin in a large bowl and stir 2 minutes or until dissolved. Stir in pineapple liquid. Refrigerate 1¼ hours or until slightly thickened to the consistency of unbeaten egg whites. Stir in whipped topping with a wire whisk until smooth. Refrigerate 10 minutes or until mixture will mound. Stir in pineapple, oranges, marshmallows and coconut. Spoon into a 6-cup mold. Refrigerate 4 hours or until firm. Unmold onto a serving dish. Yield: 10 servings.

Bing Cherry Salad

2	(¼-ounce) envelopes unflavored gelatin	3	(3-ounce) packages raspberry gelatin
½	cup cold water	1	teaspoon salt
4	(17-ounce) cans pitted Bing or other dark sweet cherries in heavy syrup, undrained	1½	cups port wine
		2	cups chopped pecans
			Lettuce leaves

Dissolve unflavored gelatin in ½ cup cold water. Drain cherries, reserving liquid. Add water to reserved liquid to measure 3 cups. Bring cherry liquid to a boil. Stir in dissolved unflavored gelatin, raspberry gelatin, salt and wine. Cool and pour into a greased dish so that the salad is about 1½ inches in depth. Refrigerate until thickened enough to suspend cherries and pecans. Stir in cherries and pecans and return to refrigerator until set, or up to 3 days ahead. Slice into squares and serve each square on a lettuce leaf. Yield: 14 to 16 servings.

Broccoli Salad

½	cup mayonnaise	1	medium-size red onion, sliced
2	teaspoons sugar	½	cup raisins
2	teaspoons vinegar	10-12	slices bacon, cooked crisp and crumbled
2	large heads broccoli, cut into florets, stem discarded		

Mix mayonnaise, sugar and vinegar in a small bowl. In a large bowl, combine broccoli, onion and raisins. Pour mayonnaise dressing over salad and refrigerate 2 hours. Garnish with bacon before serving. Yield: 4 to 6 servings.

Congealed Cranberry Salad

1	pound fresh cranberries, ground	1	cup boiling water
1	fresh orange, ground	1	cup chopped celery
2	cups sugar	1	(9-ounce) can crushed pineapple
2	(3-ounce) packages lemon gelatin	1	cup chopped nuts

Mix cranberries, orange and sugar and let stand overnight.

Dissolve gelatin in boiling water. Stir in celery, pineapple, nuts and cranberry mixture. Pour mixture into a greased mold and refrigerate overnight. Unmold onto a serving plate just before serving. Yield: 8 to 10 servings.

Cucumber Salad

2	cups sour cream		Salt and pepper to taste
½	cup chopped green onions	3	cucumbers, peeled and sliced into thin
2	tablespoons chopped fresh dill		rounds
	Dash of Tabasco sauce		

Combine sour cream, onions, dill, Tabasco and salt and pepper. Spoon mixture over cucumbers. Yield: 4 servings.

Cranberry Dream Salad

1	(16-ounce) can whole-berry cranberry sauce (not jellied)	1	(8-ounce) can crushed pineapple, drained
1	tablespoon mayonnaise	1	cup chopped walnuts or pecans
1	(8-ounce) package cream cheese	1	cup heavy cream, whipped
2	tablespoons sugar		

Place cranberry sauce in a blender and process on high until smooth. Add mayonnaise, cream cheese and sugar and process until well blended. Fold pineapple and nuts into whipped cream. Fold cranberry mixture into whipped cream and pour into a pan. Freeze. To serve, let stand 15 minutes at room temperature before slicing. Yield: 6 to 8 servings.

Cobb Salad

1⅓	cups salad oil	½	bunch watercress, chopped
⅔	cup red wine vinegar	1	bunch chicory, chopped
1	clove garlic, minced	1	head romaine lettuce, torn
1	teaspoon salt	1½	tablespoons minced fresh chives
½	teaspoon black pepper	3	tomatoes, chopped
1	teaspoon sugar	2½	cups diced cooked chicken breast
1	teaspoon dry mustard	6	slices bacon, cooked and crumbled
1	teaspoon paprika	2	hard-cooked eggs, diced
1	teaspoon Worcestershire sauce	3	ounces blue cheese, crumbled
½	head iceberg lettuce, chopped	1	avocado, diced

Early in the day, combine salad oil, vinegar, garlic, salt, pepper, sugar, mustard, paprika and Worcestershire sauce in a jar. Cover dressing, shake well and refrigerate.

When ready to serve, place iceberg lettuce, watercress, chicory, romaine lettuce, chives, tomatoes, chicken, bacon, eggs, blue cheese and avocado in a large salad bowl. Gently mix well, or arrange ingredients in an attractive pattern around the sides of the salad bowl. Pour desired amount of dressing over salad. Serve immediately. Yield: 6 servings.

Creamy Potato Salad

My sister, Betty, makes this on the Fourth of July.

9	medium potatoes	¼	teaspoon black pepper
3	hard-cooked eggs	11	slices bacon, cooked and crumbled
⅔	cup mayonnaise	¼	cup chopped green onions
1	teaspoon prepared mustard	½	cup chopped celery
¾	cup sour cream	¼	cup commercial Italian salad dressing
1	teaspoon salt		

Cook potatoes in boiling salted water for 30 minutes or until tender. Drain well and cool slightly. Peel and cut potatoes into ¾-inch cubes. Halve hard-cooked eggs and remove yolks. Mash yolks; chop whites and set aside. Mix mashed yolks with mayonnaise, mustard, sour cream, salt and pepper.

In a large bowl, combine potato cubes, chopped egg whites, bacon, green onions, celery and Italian dressing. Fold in mayonnaise mixture. Chill at least 2 hours. Yield: 12 servings.

 Rub a raw potato on stained fingers to remove stains. Rinse with water.

Chicken Salad

5	cups cooked, diced chicken
2	cups finely chopped celery
5	hard-boiled eggs, diced
1	cup diced sweet pickles, or sweet pickle relish, drained
1	tablespoon grated onion
1	cup toasted almonds (Use ¾ cup in salad. Save ¼ cup for garnish.)
1½-2	cups Hellmann's mayonnaise

Boil one hen or two large fryers with celery, onion, carrots, peppercorns and salt until tender. Remove skin and bones. Discard vegetables. Strain and save broth for another use.

Mix all ingredients and chill. Yield: 8 to 10 servings.

French Dressing

½	(10¾-ounce) can condensed tomato soup
¾	cup vinegar
½	cup salad oil
¼	cup sugar
1	tablespoon Worcestershire sauce
3	tablespoons grated onion
1	tablespoon salt
1	tablespoon paprika
1	teaspoon dry mustard

In order listed, place soup, vinegar, oil, sugar, Worcestershire sauce and onion in a jar and mix. Combine salt, paprika and mustard and add to jar. Cover and shake well. Store indefinitely in refrigerator.

French Wine Dressing

1	clove garlic, minced
½	teaspoon dry mustard
⅓	cup ketchup
¼	cup olive oil
⅓	cup red port wine
1	tablespoon sugar
1	teaspoon salt
½	teaspoon Worcestershire sauce
⅓	cup wine vinegar
¾	cup salad oil

Combine all ingredients and refrigerate.

Fresh Spinach Salad

Salad

1	pound fresh spinach
1	(8-ounce) can sliced water chestnuts, drained
2	hard-cooked eggs, sliced

8	slices bacon, cooked crisp and crumbled
1	small onion, thinly sliced and separated into rings
10	fresh mushrooms, sliced

Dressing

1	cup salad oil
½	cup wine vinegar
½	cup sugar

⅓	cup ketchup
	Dash of salt

Wash spinach, dry and tear into bite-size pieces. Add water chestnuts, eggs, bacon, onion and mushrooms. Lightly toss together.

Combine all dressing ingredients in a small jar. Shake until well blended. Serve dressing over salad. Yield: 6 to 8 servings.

Dijon Vinaigrette

1½	cups vegetable oil or olive oil
⅓	cup red wine vinegar

5	tablespoons Dijon mustard
¼	teaspoon black pepper

Whisk all ingredients together in a bowl. Serve immediately or cover and refrigerate for up to 1 week. Use as a dressing for salad greens. Yield: 2 cups.

Grace's Fruit Marinade

1	cup wine vinegar
2	cups sugar
2	teaspoons dry mustard

2	cups vegetable oil
1	teaspoon poppy seeds

Mix vinegar, sugar and mustard in a saucepan. Bring to a boil. Cool thoroughly. Add oil and poppy seeds and whip well. Pour marinade over a mixture of fresh fruit and marinate about 10 minutes before serving. This will marinate a large punch bowl of fruit.

Frozen Fruit Nut Salad

2	(3-ounce) packages cream cheese, softened	1	teaspoon salt
2	tablespoons lemon juice	1	(29-ounce) can fruit cocktail, drained
½	cup mayonnaise	½	cup coarsely chopped nuts
¼	cup sugar	1	cup heavy cream, whipped
			Watercress or other greens for garnish

Blend cream cheese, lemon juice and mayonnaise until smooth. Add sugar and salt and mix well. Stir in fruit cocktail and nuts. Fold in whipped cream. Pour mixture into a mold or other freezer-proof dish. Freeze until firm. Dip mold in hot water and quickly unmold onto a serving plate. Garnish with watercress and cut into slices to serve. Yield: 10 servings.

You can freeze this in individual molds. Very good and pretty for a bridesmaid luncheon when frozen in flower molds. Yield: 6 to 8 servings.

German Potato Salad

6	large new red potatoes	3	tablespoons sugar
8	ounces bacon	¼	cup vinegar
2	small onions, chopped	¾	cup water
2	tablespoons flour	1	cup buttermilk

Cook unpeeled potatoes in enough boiling water to cover until tender; drain and cool slightly. Peel and slice potatoes; set aside.

Cook bacon in a skillet until crisp. Drain, reserving bacon drippings. Crumble bacon and set aside. Add onions to reserved drippings in skillet and sauté. Stir in flour and sugar. Cook, stirring constantly, until thickened. Stir in vinegar and water. Add extra water if needed to reach desired consistency. Remove from heat and stir in buttermilk. Add potatoes and bacon. Toss lightly to coat potatoes with sauce. Spoon into a serving bowl. Yield: 8 servings.

Green Goddess Dressing

1	clove garlic, chopped	½	cup sour cream
3	tablespoons chopped anchovies	1	cup mayonnaise
3	tablespoons finely chopped chives or green onion tops	⅓	cup chopped fresh parsley
3	tablespoons lemon juice		Salt and freshly ground black pepper to taste
3	tablespoons tarragon vinegar		

Mix together ingredients in order listed in a jar. Cover with lid and shake.

Salads

Homemade Mayonnaise

3 eggs
1 tablespoon salt
1 tablespoon sugar
1 tablespoon dry mustard

Several dashes Tabasco sauce
Dash of cayenne pepper
1 (1-quart, 6-ounce) bottle salad oil
Juice of ½ lemon

Combine eggs, salt, sugar, mustard, Tabasco and cayenne in a food processor and mix. With motor running, add half of the oil, ½ cup at a time. Mix in lemon juice. Add remaining half of oil, ½ cup at a time with processor running.

Marinated Cucumbers

4 large cucumbers, peeled and thinly sliced
2 teaspoons salt
3 green onions with tops, sliced
1 tablespoon chopped fresh dill
1 tablespoon chopped fresh parsley

1 lemon, thinly sliced
½ cup white wine or cider vinegar
1 tablespoon sugar
1 tablespoon fresh lemon juice
1 tablespoon olive or salad oil
¼-½ teaspoon black pepper

Layer cucumbers in a bowl, sprinkling with salt between layers. Cover and refrigerate several hours. Drain, rinse with cold water and drain again. Add green onions, dill, parsley and lemon slices. Toss to mix lightly. Combine vinegar, sugar, lemon juice, oil and pepper. Pour dressing over cucumber mixture and toss. Chill 1 hour or until ready to serve or pack for a picnic. Yield: 6 to 8 servings.

Overnight Cabbage Slaw

1 medium head cabbage, shredded
1 small onion, grated
1 medium-size green, red or yellow bell pepper, or combination, finely chopped
¾ cup sugar

¾ cup vinegar
½ cup vegetable oil
1 teaspoon celery seeds
1 teaspoon dry mustard
1 teaspoon salt
⅛ teaspoon black pepper

Combine cabbage, onion and bell pepper in a large bowl. Sprinkle with sugar. Combine vinegar, oil, celery seeds, mustard, salt and black pepper in a medium saucepan. Boil 3 minutes. Pour hot dressing over vegetables and stir well. Chill overnight. Yield: 8 to 10 servings.

Mediterranean Pasta Salad

1	pound dry rotini spirals or rotelle pasta	¼	cup red wine vinegar
1	bunch broccoli	1	clove garlic
1	(6-ounce) can tuna in oil, drained and flaked	2	teaspoons salt
		1	teaspoon oregano
1½	cups diced red bell pepper	¾	teaspoon freshly ground black pepper
¼	cup capers	¾	cup olive or salad oil

Cook pasta according to package directions for al dente; drain and place in a large bowl; set aside.

Cut broccoli into florets, discarding stems or save for another use. Blanch broccoli florets, then plunge into cold water and drain. Add drained broccoli to pasta in bowl along with tuna and bell pepper.

Make a vinaigrette by combining capers, vinegar, garlic, salt, oregano and pepper in a blender or food processor. With motor running, add oil slowly and blend until smooth. Pour vinaigrette over pasta mixture and toss well. Yield: 12 servings.

To serve as a side salad, you may omit the tuna.

Orange Walnut Salad

½	cup chopped walnuts	4	oranges, peel and white pith removed, sectioned
2	teaspoons butter		
6	cups mixed fresh greens (I use a combination of romaine, iceberg and spinach)	1	white or red onion, sliced and separated into rings
			Dressing (recipe below)

Toast walnuts in butter until lightly browned; cool on paper towels. In a large bowl, combine fresh greens, orange segments and onion slices. Toss to mix. Just before serving, toss lightly with dressing (you will not need all of dressing) and top with toasted walnuts. Yield: 6 to 8 servings.

Dressing

1	cup vegetable oil	1	teaspoon dry mustard
½	cup vinegar	1	teaspoon paprika
½	cup sugar	1	teaspoon grated onion
1	teaspoon salt	1	teaspoon celery seeds

Combine oil, vinegar, sugar, salt, mustard, paprika and onion in a blender. Process until smooth. Stir in celery seeds. Cover and chill. Yield: 1¾ cups.

One of my favorite salads for entertaining.

Poppy Seed Dressing

¾	cup sugar	⅓	cup vinegar
1	teaspoon dry mustard	½	medium onion, grated
1	teaspoon salt	1⅓	teaspoons poppy seeds
1	cup salad oil		

Mix sugar, mustard and salt. Add to oil and vinegar in a blender, beating constantly. Add onion and poppy seeds. If dressing separates after it has been chilled, shake vigorously. Store for several weeks in refrigerator in a covered jar. Yield: 1 pint.

Pressed Chicken Salad

Chicken

1	(5-pound) hen		Carrot
	Celery		Salt and pepper to taste
	Onion		

Salad

	Chopped chicken (from above)	2	(¼-ounce) packages unflavored gelatin
2	cups chopped celery		(2 tablespoons)
1	cup almonds	½	cup cold water
2	tablespoons capers	1	cup reserved hot broth (from above)
4	hard cooked eggs, chopped	2	cups mayonnaise-type salad dressing
			Lettuce

To prepare chicken, cook chicken in boiling water with celery, onion, carrot and salt and pepper until done. Drain chicken; reserve 1 cup broth and keep hot. Finely chop chicken.

For salad, mix chopped chicken with celery, almonds, capers and eggs. Soften gelatin in ½ cup cold water, then dissolve in reserved hot broth. Cool. Add cooled gelatin mixture to mayonnaise. Stir mayonnaise mixture into chicken salad. Pour into a loaf pan. Chill and serve in slices on lettuce. Yield: 6 servings.

Surrounded by fresh fruit, this makes a good ladies luncheon entrée.

Potato Salad

2	pounds white Idaho potatoes, peeled and cubed	1	cup sweet pickle relish
1	cup finely chopped celery	1	teaspoon prepared mustard
1	tablespoon grated onion	¼	cup pimento
½	cup finely chopped red, green or yellow bell pepper	4	hard-cooked eggs
		¾-1	cup mayonnaise

Cook potatoes in boiling salted water for 20 minutes or until tender; drain and cool. Combine potatoes with celery, onion and bell pepper in a large bowl. Add pickle relish, mustard and pimento. Chop hard-cooked eggs, removing 1 yolk to mash and use for garnish. Add chopped egg to salad. Mix in mayonnaise. Arrange salad in a serving bowl. Sprinkle mashed egg yolk on top for garnish. Yield: 8 servings.

I sometimes use a combination of Idaho and Golden potatoes.

Roquefort Dressing

½	cup Roquefort cheese	½	cup mayonnaise
1	(3-ounce) package cream cheese	1	tablespoon lemon juice
½	cup heavy cream	1	tablespoon cider vinegar

Blend cheeses, cream and mayonnaise in a blender for 4 to 5 minutes. Add lemon juice and vinegar and blend for a second. Chill before use. Dressing will keep in refrigerator 3 to 4 days. Yield: About 2 cups.

Red Raspberry Salad

2	(10-ounce) packages frozen raspberries, thawed	¾	cup boiling water
1	(20-ounce) can crushed pineapple	1	(6-ounce) package raspberry flavored gelatin
1	(6-ounce) can frozen orange juice concentrate, thawed and undiluted		Lettuce (optional)

Drain raspberries and pineapple, reserving juices. Combine fruit juices and orange juice concentrate. (There should be about 2½ cups liquid.) Combine boiling water with 1 cup fruit juice and bring to a boil. Add hot liquid to gelatin and stir to dissolve. Add remaining fruit juice. Chill until gelatin is the consistency of unbeaten egg white. Fold in raspberries and pineapple. Pour mixture into a greased 6-cup ring mold and chill until firm. Unmold onto lettuce. Yield: 8 to 10 servings.

Romaine with Apple, Pecans and Blue Cheese

4½	cups torn romaine lettuce hearts	¼	cup pecan pieces, toasted
1	large apple, unpeeled and chopped	½	cup Creamy Blue Cheese Dressing
1	avocado, cubed		(recipe below)
½	cup chopped red onion		

Combine lettuce, apple, avocado, onion and pecans in a large bowl. Toss with dressing. Yield: 4 servings.

Creamy Blue Cheese Dressing

⅓	cup blue cheese	⅓	cup orange juice
2	tablespoons vinegar	8	ounces plain non-fat yogurt
1	teaspoon Dijon mustard		

Mash cheese with a fork in a small bowl. Add vinegar, mustard, juice and yogurt. Stir to combine thoroughly. Yield: 1½ cups.

Shoe Peg Corn Salad

5	stalks celery, chopped	½	cup salad oil
½	green bell pepper, chopped	2	tablespoons vinegar
1	small onion, chopped	1	teaspoon salt
2	tablespoons chopped pimento	1	teaspoon dry mustard
1	(16-ounce) can shoe peg corn, drained	1	teaspoon sugar

Combine celery, bell pepper, onion, pimento and corn in a bowl. In a separate bowl, mix salad oil, vinegar, salt, mustard and sugar. Pour oil mixture over vegetables. Refrigerate at least 12 hours before serving. Keeps well in refrigerator for up to several days. Yield: 4 to 6 servings.

Special Fruit Salad Dressing

¼	cup sugar	1	egg
½	teaspoon salt	2	tablespoons vinegar
1½	tablespoons flour	¾	cup pineapple juice

Mix all ingredients, in order listed, in a saucepan, stirring well after each addition. Cook over low heat, stirring constantly, until thick and smooth. Chill. Serve with your favorite combination of fruit on a bed of lettuce.

Shrimp Salad

8	cups whole cooked, peeled shrimp (see below)	1	tablespoon grated onion
2	cups diced celery	2	cups mayonnaise
5	hard-cooked eggs, diced		Zest of 2 lemons
1	cup diced drained sweet pickles		Salt and white pepper to taste

Combine all ingredients. Refrigerate overnight before serving. Yield: 8 servings.

Boiling Shrimp

Add water to a large pot in an amount at least 2 times the volume of shrimp. Add salt and a lemon slice and bring to a good boil. Drop in unpeeled shrimp. When water returns to a boil, remove from heat. Leave shrimp in hot water 2 to 3 minutes. Drain and peel.

Crisp cooked asparagus cut on the diagonal into 1-inch pieces may be added to the salad.

Spinach and Apple Salad with Bacon

2	apples	3	tablespoons oil
	Fresh lemon juice	4	ounces spinach, carefully washed, stems removed
4	ounces sliced bacon	12	black olives, chopped
1	tablespoon Dijon mustard	2	hard-cooked eggs, cut into wedges
1-2	tablespoons balsamic vinegar		
	Salt and white pepper to taste		

Peel apples, if desired, then core and chop. Place chopped apple in a bowl and sprinkle with a few drops of lemon juice. Toss lightly and set aside.

Cook bacon in a skillet over high heat for 5 minutes or until crisp. Drain on paper towels and crumble, set aside.

In a small bowl, stir together mustard, vinegar and salt and pepper until well mixed. Add oil and stir vigorously until blended. Set dressing aside for a few minutes to allow flavors to blend.

Place spinach in a salad bowl. Add apples, bacon, olives and mustard dressing and toss well. Garnish with egg wedges and serve. Yield: 4 servings.

Spinach Pecan Salad

1	tablespoon butter	1	large Granny Smith apple, thinly sliced
½	cup pecan halves	½	cup crumbled blue cheese
1	tablespoon brown sugar	2	tablespoons olive oil
1	(6-ounce) package fresh baby spinach	2	tablespoons vinegar

Melt butter in a small skillet over low heat. Add pecans and brown sugar and cook, stirring constantly, for 2 to 3 minutes or until caramelized. Cool on wax paper.

Place spinach in a large serving bowl. Toss in cooled pecans, apple and blue cheese. Add oil and vinegar and toss to coat. Yield: 4 servings.

Spinach Vidalia Onion Strawberry Salad

1	pound fresh spinach, washed and patted dry, stems removed	2	tablespoons sesame seeds
1	pint fresh strawberries, sliced	1	tablespoon poppy seeds
1	medium Vidalia onion, very thinly sliced and separated into rings	¼	teaspoon Worcestershire sauce
		¼	teaspoon paprika
¼	cup sugar	½	cup olive oil
		¼	cup cider vinegar

Tear spinach into bite-size pieces into a large bowl. Add strawberries and onions and toss. Combine sugar, sesame seeds, poppy seeds, Worcestershire sauce, paprika, olive oil and vinegar in a blender. Process 30 seconds. Drizzle over salad and toss gently. Yield: 4 to 6 servings.

Thousand Island Salad Dressing

4	cups mayonnaise (store-bought or homemade)	2	hard-cooked eggs, diced
½	cup sweet pickle relish, drained	¼	cup ketchup
⅓	cup dill pickle relish, drained	¼	cup chopped fresh parsley or green onions, or combination
⅓	cup chili sauce		

Combine all ingredients in a large bowl and mix carefully by hand with a wooden spoon.

Spring Greens with Roasted Beets Salad

Salad

6	cups mixed spring greens	Roasted Beets (recipe below)
3	Vidalia onions, thinly sliced	Shallot Vinaigrette (recipe below)

Combine spring greens, onions and beets in a large bowl. Toss with vinaigrette. Yield: 6 servings.

Roasted Beets

12 small beets, scrubbed
2   tablespoons olive oil
    Salt

Cut off beet tops, leaving a 1-inch stem to prevent bleeding. Place beets and oil in an ovenproof dish. Sprinkle with salt and cover dish with foil. Roast at 325 degrees for 1 hour. Cool, peel and slice, or leave whole if beets are small. Beets can be roasted the night before.

Shallot Vinaigrette

3	tablespoons balsamic vinegar	1	tablespoon finely chopped shallots (squeeze out juice by twisting in a tea towel)
1	tablespoon lemon juice		
1	teaspoon dry mustard	¾	cup olive oil
1	teaspoon salt		
½	teaspoon freshly ground black pepper		

Combine vinegar, lemon juice, mustard, salt, pepper and shallots in a small bowl. Slowly whisk in oil. Adjust seasoning as needed. Let stand 1 hour before using. Dressing can be made up to 3 days in advance.

Winter Spinach Salad

1	bunch spinach, roughly chopped	¼	cup walnuts, coarsely chopped
½	cup seedless grapes	2	tablespoons apple cider vinegar
3	green onions, thinly sliced	2	tablespoons olive oil
1	Granny Smith apple or ripe pear, thinly sliced		Salt and pepper to taste
		¼	cup goat or feta cheese, crumbled

Place spinach on a large plate. Combine grapes, green onions, apple slices and walnuts and sprinkle over spinach. Whisk together vinegar and oil and season with salt and pepper. Pour vinaigrette over salad and toss in cheese. Arrange on individual salad plates. Yield: 6 servings.

Tomato Aspic

1¾ cups tomato juice or V-8 juice, divided	½ teaspoon Worcestershire sauce
1 (¼-ounce) envelope unflavored gelatin	½ teaspoon grated onion
1 tablespoon lemon juice	¼ teaspoon salt
½ teaspoon sugar	Few drops of Tabasco sauce

Combine ½ cup tomato juice with gelatin in a small saucepan. Cook over low heat, stirring constantly, until gelatin dissolves. Remove from heat and stir in remaining 1¼ cups tomato juice. Add lemon juice, sugar, Worcestershire sauce, onion, salt and Tabasco. Pour mixture into a lightly greased 2-cup mold. Chill until firm. Yield: 4 servings.

You may add 1 cup diced celery, ½ cup sliced water chestnuts and ½ cup chopped artichoke hearts to this salad.

Tomato Vodka Aspic

4 cups fresh or canned tomato juice	½ teaspoon freshly ground black pepper
½ cup lemon juice	2 (¼-ounce) envelopes unflavored gelatin
½ cup vodka, or substitute ½ cup additional tomato juice	¼ cup minced celery
	¼ cup minced green onions
1 tablespoon horseradish	2 tablespoons minced fresh basil, tarragon or parsley
1 teaspoon celery salt	
2 teaspoons hot pepper sauce	¼ cup thinly sliced olives (optional)
½ teaspoon salt, or to taste	

In a large bowl, combine tomato juice, lemon juice, vodka, horseradish, celery salt, hot pepper sauce, salt and pepper. Pour ½ cup of tomato juice mixture into a small bowl. Sprinkle gelatin over surface of juice gently, scattering it evenly to prevent clumps. Let gelatin soften in bowl about 5 minutes. Place remaining tomato mixture in a nonreactive saucepan and warm gently; do not boil. Add softened gelatin to warmed juice mixture and stir to dissolve. Remove from heat and cool to room temperature. Evenly divide celery, onions, herbs and olives into 6 to 8 martini glasses. Pour cooled aspic mixture over the vegetables and refrigerate until firm.

If using a larger mold or bowl, chill aspic mixture until slushy, then fold in vegetables and herbs. Pour mixture into a greased 6-cup mold and chill until firm. Yield: 6 to 8 servings.

Sunday Dinner

Crown Roast of Fresh Pork, page 134

Potato Salad, page 59

Place Setting

Baked Stuffed Yellow Squash, page 103

Southern Fried Chicken, page 151

Light Sweet Potato Pie, page 228

Candied Sweet Potatoes, page 105

*Marzipan Pumpkins, page 258, with
Mrs. Middleton's Caramel Cake, page 183,
with Chocolate Leaves, page 257*

German Chocolate Roulage, page 178

Five Cakes: Carrot Cake (back) page 172; Lemon Chiffon Cake (left) page 181; Sixteen Layer Chocolate Fudge Cake, page 184; Lemon Coconut Cake (right) page 182; Mrs. Middleton's Caramel Cake, page 183, with Chocolate Ribbons (back right) page 260

Lemon Chiffon Cake, page 181, with Sugared Pansies, page 256

Strawberries in Tuxedos, page 243

Lemon Tart Brûlée, page 233

Fresh Cherry Pie, page 231

Creamy Cheesecake, page 170, with Raspberry Sauce, page 254

Soups & Sandwiches

Ann's Chicken Velvet Soup

5 tablespoons butter	1 cup warm cream
¾ cup flour	1½ cups finely diced cooked chicken
6 cups warm chicken broth, divided	½ teaspoon salt
1 cup warm milk	Black pepper to taste

Melt butter in a saucepan. Add flour and cook and stir over low heat until well blended. Slowly add 2 cups broth, milk and cream. Cook slowly, stirring frequently, until thickened. Add remaining 4 cups broth and chicken and bring to a boil. Season with salt and pepper. Yield: 6 to 8 servings.

Artichoke Cream Soup

1 (14-ounce) can artichoke hearts	3 egg yolks
2 tablespoons minced onion	½ cup heavy cream
4 tablespoons butter	¼ teaspoon nutmeg
2 tablespoons all-purpose flour	1 teaspoon lemon juice
½ cup cold milk	Salt to taste
2-3 cups chicken consommé	

Drain and chop artichoke hearts, reserving liquid; set both aside. In a 3-quart saucepan, sauté onion in butter until transparent. Blend in flour and milk, stirring constantly. Add reserved artichoke liquid and consommé and bring to a boil. Remove 1 cup of hot liquid. Combine egg yolks and cream and stir into extracted 1 cup hot liquid. Return mixture to saucepan and stir well. Add chopped artichokes, nutmeg, lemon juice and salt. Serve hot or cold. Yield: 6 to 8 servings.

Baked Potato Soup

1 cup sliced celery	1 teaspoon (or 1 cube) chicken bouillon
¾ cup chopped onion	½ teaspoon salt
2 tablespoons butter	¼ teaspoon black pepper
2 tablespoons flour	4 large baking potatoes, baked and cubed
2 cups half-and-half, divided	Garnishes of choice: shredded Cheddar cheese, sour cream, chopped fresh chives, bacon bits
½ cup water	
1 tablespoon chopped fresh parsley	

Sauté celery and onion in butter until tender. Blend flour with ¼ cup half-and-half and add to sautéed mixture. Stir well. Add water, parsley, bouillon, salt and pepper. Simmer until heated through; do not boil. Add remaining 1¾ cups half-and-half and heat through; do not boil. Stir in potatoes. Serve with garnishes. Yield: 2 to 4 servings.

Cheese and Potato Soup

1	medium onion, chopped	1	(10¾-ounce) can condensed cream of
1	clove garlic, pressed		chicken soup
4	tablespoons butter	1	pound processed cheese, thinly sliced
6-7	medium potatoes, peeled and cut into small cubes	1½	cups heavy cream
	Salt and pepper to taste		Chopped fresh chives or shredded sharp cheese for garnish

Sauté onion and garlic in butter. Add potatoes and barely cover with hot water. Season with salt and pepper. Cook until potatoes are mushy. If desired, mash potatoes with a potato masher in the pot. Stir in soup and sliced cheese. Cook and stir until cheese melts. Mix in cream. Do not boil. Garnish individual servings with chives or shredded cheese. Yield: 6 servings.

Chestnut Soup

6	cups rich chicken stock		Sea salt and freshly ground pepper
6-8	whole star anise	4-6	tablespoons crème fraîche or heavy
1	pound peeled chestnuts		cream

Bring chicken stock and anise to a boil in a covered large saucepan over medium-high heat. Reduce heat to a simmer and cook 30 minutes. Discard anise. Add chestnuts to stock and bring to a boil. Reduce heat to a simmer and cover. Cook 20 minutes or until chestnuts are tender throughout and falling apart.

Remove one-third of chestnuts from the soup and reserve. Purée remaining soup. Add reserved chestnuts to purée and heat until hot but not boiling. Season with salt and pepper. Ladle into warmed soup bowls. Add 1 tablespoon crème fraîche to each bowl. Serve immediately. Yield: 4 to 6 servings.

Crab Bisque

1	pound blue crabmeat, fresh or pasteurized	1	teaspoon salt
2	tablespoons finely chopped onion	¼	teaspoon paprika
2	tablespoons finely chopped celery		Dash of white pepper
4	tablespoons butter, melted	1	quart light cream
3	tablespoons all-purpose flour	¼	cup chopped fresh parsley

Pick over crabmeat to remove any shell or cartilage. Cook onion and celery in butter until softened. Blend in flour, salt, paprika and white pepper. Cook and stir until thickened. Stir in cream gradually and cook until thickened. Add crabmeat and cook until heated. Just before serving, sprinkle with parsley. Yield: 6 servings.

Cauliflower Soup

1	head cauliflower, broken into florets	1	teaspoon plus 2 tablespoons olive oil,
3	quarts water		divided
1	(16-ounce) package thin spaghetti		Salt and pepper to taste

Crumb Topping

½	cup butter	2	cups soft plain bread crumbs

Boil cauliflower in 3 quarts water for 15 minutes or until starting to soften but still firm. Add spaghetti and 1 teaspoon olive oil. Cook until spaghetti is tender. Add remaining 2 tablespoons olive oil. Season with salt and pepper. Serve immediately in soup bowls. Sprinkle crumb topping over top before serving. Yield: 6 to 8 servings.

To make crumb topping, melt butter in a saucepan. Add bread crumbs and stir over medium heat until golden. Add more crumbs if needed to reach the consistency of buttered graham cracker crumbs for a pie crust.

Cream of Broccoli Soup

1½	bunches broccoli	5	cups chicken broth
2	stalks celery	1½	teaspoons salt
6	tablespoons butter	¼	teaspoon freshly ground black pepper
1	small onion, chopped		Pinch of nutmeg
1	medium leek, chopped	¾	cup milk
1½	cups sliced mushrooms	1	cup heavy cream
2	tablespoons flour		Zest of 1 lemon

Separate broccoli florets from stems. Set aside florets, reserving 2 cups for garnish. Shred broccoli stems with celery in a food processor. Melt butter in a 5-quart Dutch oven. Add shredded broccoli and celery, remaining florets (those not reserved for garnish), onion, leek and mushrooms and sauté 7 minutes. Sprinkle with flour. Cook 3 minutes longer, stirring occasionally. Add broth, salt, pepper, nutmeg and milk. Simmer 25 minutes. Purée soup in batches in a blender or food processor until smooth. Return to Dutch oven over low heat. Add cream, reserved broccoli florets and lemon zest. Simmer 7 minutes. Taste and adjust seasoning as needed. Yield: 7½ cups.

To add body to the base for a sauce, "mash" as many as possible of the cooked vegetables you've used to make the stock through the sieve as you strain it. The resulting "vegetable purée" will thicken the liquid.

Corn and Cheese Chowder

2	cups water	1	(17-ounce) can cream style corn
2	cups diced potatoes	2	cups milk
¼	cup chopped onion	1	cup canned tomatoes, chopped
½	cup diced celery	2	teaspoons salt
2	tablespoons margarine	⅛	teaspoon black pepper
½	teaspoon dried basil	½	cup shredded Cheddar cheese
1	large bay leaf	1	tablespoon minced fresh parsley

Combine water, potatoes, onion, celery, margarine, basil and bay leaf in a large Dutch oven. Bring to a boil. Reduce heat and simmer 10 minutes or until potatoes are tender. Discard bay leaf. Stir in corn, milk, tomatoes, salt and pepper and heat thoroughly. Add cheese and cook and stir until cheese melts. Mix in parsley. Yield: 8 to 10 servings.

Gazpacho

1-2	cloves garlic, crushed	1½	stalks celery, diced
2	tablespoons olive oil	⅓	medium cucumber, diced
3	tablespoons red wine vinegar	⅓	cup diced onion
1	teaspoon salt	⅓	(0.75-ounce) package fresh chives, chopped
1	teaspoon Worcestershire sauce		
¼	teaspoon black pepper	2	tablespoons chopped fresh parsley
6	dashes Tabasco sauce	2	cups tomato juice
2	tomatoes, peeled and diced		

Combine all ingredients and refrigerate overnight. If soup becomes too thick, add more tomato juice. Soup improves with age. Recipe doubles easily. Yield: 6 to 8 servings.

Iced Raspberry Soup

2	cubes chicken bouillon	½	cup pineapple juice
1¼	cups boiling water	2	tablespoons sugar
2	(10-ounce) packages frozen raspberries, thawed	½	cup sour cream
		2	tablespoons chopped toasted almonds

Dissolve bouillon in boiling water. Press raspberries through a food mill or sieve into a bowl. Add dissolved bouillon, pineapple juice and sugar and stir until sugar is dissolved. Chill. Top each serving with a spoonful of sour cream and sprinkle with almonds. Yield: 5 servings.

Homemade Vegetable Soup

Stock
1	pound beef bones	3	stalks celery
1	large onion	1½	quarts water
2	carrots		

Soup
1	large onion, cubed	¼	cup dry rice or elbow macaroni
1	large potato, cubed	1	cup tomato sauce, or 2 cups tomato juice
2	carrots, chopped		Salt and pepper to taste
2	stalks celery, chopped		

Place all stock ingredients except water in a roasting pan. Bake, uncovered, at 350 degrees for 45 minutes. For a darker stock, leave onion unpeeled. Place the contents of pan in a large stock pot, making sure to scrape pan drippings into pot (add water to pan to help loosen drippings from bottom, if needed). Add 1½ quarts water to pot and cook 30 to 60 minutes. Strain stock into a container; discard bones and vegetables.

To make soup, transfer stock to a pot. Add onion, potato, carrots, celery, rice and tomato sauce. Season with salt and pepper. Cook 30 to 45 minutes or until vegetables are tender. Yield: 6 to 8 servings.

You may add any leftover vegetables you have in the refrigerator, such as corn, beans, peas, etc.

Mushroom Soup

¾	pound fresh mushrooms, chopped	1	cup heavy cream
½	cup chopped onion	1	cup light cream or half-and-half
2	tablespoons unsalted butter		Salt and white pepper to taste
2	cups beef broth		

Sauté mushrooms and onion in a saucepan in butter until onion is tender and most of the liquid given off by the mushrooms has evaporated. Purée mixture in a food processor or blender and return to saucepan. Add broth, cover and bring to a boil. Reduce heat and simmer 10 minutes. Add both creams and heat until soup is very hot, but do not boil. Season with salt and pepper. Yield: 4 to 6 servings.

Onion Soup

5	medium onions	5	cups beef broth or consommé
4	tablespoons butter		Toasted rounds French bread
1	tablespoon flour		Shredded Guryère cheese

Thinly slice onions and separate into rings. Heat butter in a large saucepan. Add onion rings and cook gently over low heat, stirring constantly with a wooden spoon, until rings are golden brown. Sprinkle flour over onions and stir until blended. Gradually pour in broth. Cook, stirring constantly, until soup begins to boil. Reduce heat to a simmer. Cover and simmer 20 minutes. Adjust seasoning as needed. Serve in individual tureens, each containing a bread round and heaped with cheese. Sprinkle extra cheese on top and broil until cheese is brown and sizzling. Yield: 8 servings.

Quick Beefy Vegetable Soup

1	pound ground beef	2	cups beef broth
1	(16-ounce) package frozen mixed vegetables	2	cups cubed potato
		½	teaspoon salt
2	cups tomato juice	¼	teaspoon black pepper

Brown beef in a 3-quart saucepan, stirring to crumble. Drain off drippings and discard. Return beef to saucepan. Add frozen vegetables, tomato juice, broth, potato, salt and pepper. Bring to a boil. Reduce heat to a simmer and cook 20 to 25 minutes or until potatoes are tender. Yield: 4 servings.

Sausage Potato Soup

1	pound bulk pork sausage	1½	teaspoons salt
5	cups sliced raw potatoes	¼	teaspoon celery seeds
2	medium onions, sliced	3	tablespoons finely chopped parsley
1½	cups water	2½-3 cups milk	

Brown sausage, stirring to crumble; drain and set aside. Combine potatoes, onions, water, salt and celery seeds in a large Dutch oven. Cover and bring to a boil. Reduce heat and simmer about 20 to 25 minutes or until potatoes are tender. Slightly mash potatoes. Add sausage, parsley and milk. Cook until heated. Yield: 6 to 8 servings.

If you want to speed up this dish, you may use frozen hash browns for the raw potatoes.

Turkey and Wild Rice Soup

2	tablespoons butter	1	(6-ounce) package long-grain and wild rice mix
1	medium onion, chopped		
4	ounces mushrooms, sliced	2	tablespoons dry sherry (optional)
2⅓	cups water	2	cups diced cooked turkey
2	cups chicken broth	1	cup heavy cream
		1	egg yolk

Melt butter in a large saucepan over medium heat. Add onion and mushrooms and cook 2 minutes or until onion is translucent. Add water and broth. Stir in rice mix with seasoning packet and bring to a boil. Reduce heat, cover and simmer 20 to 25 minutes or until rice is tender. Add sherry and boil 1 minute. Add turkey. Reduce heat to low.

Mix cream with egg yolk. Stir a few spoonfuls of hot soup into cream mixture, then slowly add back into soup in a steady stream, stirring constantly. Cook only until slightly thickened and hot; do not boil. Yield: 4 servings.

Turkey Vegetable Soup

4	tablespoons butter	2	tablespoons chopped fresh parsley
2	medium onions, chopped	½	teaspoon sage or poultry seasoning
2	tablespoons all-purpose flour	2	cups cubed cooked turkey
1	teaspoon curry powder	1½	cups half-and-half
3	cups chicken broth	1	(10-ounce) package frozen chopped spinach
1	cup chopped potato		
½	cup thinly sliced carrot		Salt and freshly ground pepper to taste
½	cup sliced celery		

Melt butter in a large saucepan over medium-high heat. Add onions and sauté 10 minutes or until translucent. Stir in flour and curry powder and cook 2 to 3 minutes. Add broth, potato, carrot, celery, parsley and sage and bring to a boil. Reduce heat to low and cover. Simmer 10 minutes. Add turkey, half-and-half and spinach. Cover and simmer 7 minutes or until heated through. Season with salt and pepper. Serve hot. Yield: 6 to 8 servings.

I make this to use leftover turkey after Thanksgiving or Christmas.

Vichyssoise

2	tablespoons butter	4	teaspoons salt
3	leeks, white part only, cut into ⅓-inch slices	2	teaspoons Accent
2	medium-size white onions, diced	¼	teaspoon white pepper
5	white potatoes, peeled and sliced ¼-inch thick	2	cups hot milk
3	cups hot water	2	cups half-and-half
1	(14½-ounce) can chicken broth	1	cup heavy cream
			Finely chopped chives for garnish

Melt butter in a large heavy pot. Add leeks and onions. Cover and cook slowly, stirring occasionally with a wooden spoon, until tender but not brown. Add potato slices, hot water, broth, salt, Accent and white pepper. Cover and simmer 45 minutes. Strain. Discard vegetables. Add hot milk and half-and-half. Bring to a boil. Remove from heat and add heavy cream. Chill. Serve cold, garnished with chives. Yield: 6 to 8 servings.

White Bean Soup

2	cups dried great Northern beans	8	cloves garlic, chopped
3	tablespoons olive oil	3	slices bacon, chopped
1	large onion, chopped	10½	cups (or more) chicken broth
1	cup chopped leek, white and pale green parts only	1	tablespoon chopped fresh thyme
1	large tomato, seeded and chopped	1	teaspoon chopped fresh rosemary
½	cup chopped carrot	½	cup heavy cream
½	cup chopped celery		Salt and pepper to taste
			White truffle oil (optional)

Place beans in a large heavy pot. Add enough water to cover by 2 inches and soak overnight. Drain and set aside.

Heat olive oil in same pot over medium-high heat. Add onion, leek, tomato, carrot, celery, garlic and bacon and sauté 6 minutes or until vegetables are tender. Add drained beans, broth, thyme and rosemary and bring to a boil. Reduce heat to medium-low and cover. Simmer, stirring occasionally, for 1 hour or until beans are very tender. Purée soup in a blender, in batches, until smooth. Return soup to pot. Add cream. Add more broth, ¼ cup at a time, as needed to reach desired consistency. Season with salt and pepper. Ladle soup into 8 bowls. Lightly drizzle each serving with truffle oil, if desired. Yield: 8 servings.

Truffle oil is available at specialty food stores.

I like to purée half of this soup and leave half with whole beans in it and mix the two.

Watercress Soup

1½ cups chopped onion	⅛ teaspoon freshly grated nutmeg
2 large cloves garlic, minced	Salt and pepper to taste
1 tablespoon vegetable oil	2 cups packed watercress, rinsed and
¼ cup dry white wine	spun dry, coarse stems discarded
1 cup chicken broth	1 cup half-and-half
3 cups water	2 tablespoons fresh lemon juice
1½ pounds russet baking potatoes, peeled and ½-inch diced	

In a kettle, cook onion and garlic in vegetable oil over medium-low heat, stirring occasionally, until onion is softened. Add wine and cook and stir until the wine is nearly evaporated. Add broth, water, potatoes, nutmeg and salt and pepper. Bring to a boil. Reduce heat and simmer 10 minutes or until potato is tender. Add watercress. Cook and stir 1 minute. Remove from heat and stir in half-and-half. Allow soup to cool. Purée in a blender in batches until smooth. Transfer puréed soup to a bowl. Add lemon juice and season with salt and pepper. Serve warm or chilled. To chill soup, cover and refrigerate 1 hour or until cold, then transfer to a large thermos. The soup may be made 1 day in advance and stored in refrigerator. Yield: 4 to 6 servings.

White Bean and Vegetable Soup

1 pound dried white beans, such as great Northern	1 pound potatoes, diced
	4 cups chicken broth
4 ounces salt pork, rind discarded, meat cut into ¼-inch cubes	6 cups water
	6 cups packed fresh spinach leaves, washed, spun dry and coarsely shredded
2 cups finely chopped onion	
2 large cloves garlic, minced	
4 stalks celery, cut crosswise into ¼-inch slices (2 cups)	1 cup dry white wine
	Salt and pepper to taste
4 large carrots, cut crosswise into ¼-inch slices (2 cups)	Freshly grated Parmesan cheese

Soak beans in enough cold water to cover by 2 inches overnight. (Or quick soak according to package directions.) Drain and set aside.

In a large heavy pot, cook salt pork over medium-low heat, stirring, until crisp. Transfer cracklings with a slotted spoon to paper towels; set aside. Add onion and garlic to pan drippings and cook and stir until onion is softened. Add drained beans, celery, carrots, potatoes, broth and 6 cups water. Cover, stirring occasionally, for 1½ to 2 hours or until beans are tender. Stir in spinach and wine. Add extra broth or water, if needed, to reach desired consistency. Season with salt and pepper. Simmer, stirring, for 5 minutes. Sprinkle individual servings with cheese and cracklings. Yield: 6 to 8 servings.

Chicken 'N Artichoke Crescent Sandwich

1	boneless, skinless whole chicken breast, cut into bite-size pieces	⅛	teaspoon hot pepper sauce
½	teaspoon salt	1	(6-ounce) jar marinated artichoke hearts, drained and chopped
⅛	teaspoon black pepper	1	(2-ounce) jar chopped pimento, drained
1	(2½-ounce) jar sliced mushrooms, drained	1	(8-ounce) can refrigerated crescent roll dough
1	tablespoon butter		
1	tablespoon oil	1	egg white, lightly beaten
⅓	cup mayonnaise or mayonnaise-type salad dressing	1	tablespoon sesame seeds
			Sour cream (optional)
⅛-¼	teaspoon garlic powder		

Sprinkle chicken with salt and pepper. Cook chicken and mushrooms in butter and oil, stirring occasionally, for 3 to 5 minutes or until chicken is tender and lightly browned; set aside. In a medium bowl, combine mayonnaise, garlic powder and hot pepper sauce. Stir in artichoke hearts, pimento and chicken mixture. Blend well.

Separate dough into 4 rectangles, firmly pressing perforations to seal. Spoon about ⅓ cup chicken mixture on half of each rectangle to within ¼ inch of edges. Fold dough in half over filling. Place on an ungreased baking sheet. Press edges together to seal. Brush with egg white and sprinkle with sesame seeds. Bake at 350 degrees until lightly browned. Serve warm with sour cream, if desired. Yield: 4 servings.

Crab Sandwich

1	cup crabmeat, flaked		Seasoned salt
2	hard-cooked eggs, diced	6	slices white toast
¼	cup French dressing		Mayonnaise
¼	cup sweet pickle relish	4	slices American cheese
¼	teaspoon salt	4	slices avocado for garnish
6	thick slices tomato		

Combine crab, eggs, dressing, pickle relish and salt. Sprinkle both sides of tomato slices with seasoned salt. Spread toast with mayonnaise. On a wooden board or baking sheet, make 2-decker sandwiches, using tomatoes for filling of bottom layer and crab mixture for second layer. Top each sandwich with 2 slices cheese. Halve diagonally. Bake at 400 degrees for 7 to 10 minutes or until cheese is melted and sandwiches are golden brown. Garnish with avocado slices. Yield: 2 sandwiches.

Easy Going Reuben Sandwich

2   large or 4 small slices rye bread
1   tablespoon Thousand Island dressing
1   (2½-ounce) package sliced corned beef
     or pastrami

2   (¾- to 1-ounce) slices Swiss cheese
½   cup sauerkraut, rinsed and drained
1-2 tablespoons butter

Spread half of bread slices with Thousand Island dressing. Top beef, cheese and sauerkraut. Place remaining bread on top. Spread outside of bread with butter and grill on both sides until browned. If bread is large, cut in half to make 2 sandwiches. Yield: 2 servings.

Egg Salad Sandwiches

12   slices bacon
8   hard-cooked eggs, peeled and coarsely
     chopped
⅓   cup finely chopped celery
¼   cup chopped pimento-stuffed green
     olives

½   cup mayonnaise, divided
1   tablespoon Dijon mustard
     Salt and pepper to taste
12   slices white sandwich bread, toasted
12   red leaf lettuce leaves

Sauté bacon in a large heavy skillet over medium heat 8 minutes or until brown and crisp. Using a slotted spoon, transfer bacon to paper towels to drain. Cut bacon slices in half crosswise.

Combine eggs, celery and olives in a bowl. Mix in ¼ cup mayonnaise and mustard. Season with salt and pepper. Place toast slices on a work surface. Spread toast lightly with remaining ¼ cup mayonnaise. Divide egg salad among 6 slices toast. Place 4 bacon pieces, then 2 lettuce leaves atop egg salad on each sandwich. Cover with remaining toast slices, mayonnaise-side down. Cut sandwiches in half diagonally. Yield: 6 servings.

 Use air freshener to clean mirrors. It does a good job and smells better.

Ham and Cheese Sandwiches in Beer Batter

12	slices white bread	3	eggs, lightly beaten
	Mayonnaise	¼	cup beer
12	slices Swiss cheese		Butter
6	(⅛- to ¼-inch thick) slices baked ham		

Spread 1 side of each slice of bread with a small amount of mayonnaise. Make 6 sandwiches, using 2 slices cheese and 1 slice ham for each. Trim crusts and filling and cut sandwiches in half with a sharp knife.

Mix eggs and beer. Melt butter in a skillet over medium-low heat. Dip each sandwich in beer batter and place in skillet. Cook sandwiches in butter over low heat until lightly browned on both sides and cheese is slightly melted. Yield: 6 servings.

Ham-Chicken Club Sandwich

2	(3-ounce) packages cream cheese, softened	8	thin slices boiled ham
2	tablespoons milk	4	lettuce leaves
¼	cup finely chopped candied ginger or chopped chutney	4	thick slices cooked chicken or turkey breast
4	large poppy seed hard rolls	4	circular slices avocado
			Salt and pepper to taste

Blend cream cheese and milk. Stir in ginger. Slice each hard roll into 3 layers. Spread bottom and middle layers with cream cheese mixture. Place 2 ham slices on bottom layer and top with a lettuce leaf. Place center roll layer on lettuce, cream cheese-side up. Arrange chicken slices and avocado on cream cheese. Sprinkle with salt and pepper. Close with top slice of roll. Cut each roll in half to serve. Yield: 4 servings.

Ham Salad

½	pound cooked ham, ground	2	tablespoons mayonnaise
2	tablespoons minced green bell pepper	1	tablespoon minced onion
1	teaspoon prepared mustard		

Combine all ingredients and refrigerate until ready to use. Yield: about ¾ cup sandwich filling.

Grilled Cheese Sandwich

4	tablespoons butter, softened	4	green onions, minced
8	slices sourdough bread	1	teaspoon Old Bay seasoning
9	ounces Gruyère cheese, shredded	12	strips bacon, cooked crisp
⅔	cup mayonnaise		

Spread butter over one side of each slice of bread. Combine cheese, mayonnaise, green onions and Old Bay seasoning in a medium bowl. Let stand at room temperature for 20 minutes. Divide mixture evenly among unbuttered side of 4 slices of bread. Top each with 3 slices bacon. Place remaining bread, buttered-side up, on sandwiches.

Place a nonstick pan or griddle over medium-high heat. Cook sandwiches in pan until bread starts to brown and crisp. Turn sandwiches over, pressing each with a spatula to flatten slightly. Cook until bottom is golden brown. Reduce heat to medium and cover pan until cheese melts, checking frequently. (You may have to flip sandwiches again to prevent excess browning of the bread.) Remove from heat. Cut each sandwich into quarters and serve. Yield: 4 servings.

Hot Brown Sandwich

⅓	cup butter	¼	cup shredded Cheddar cheese
1	medium onion, minced	½	cup grated Parmesan cheese
⅓	cup all-purpose flour	6-8	slices bread
3	cups hot milk		Sliced turkey, chicken or ham
1	teaspoon salt		(or a combination is great!)
	Cayenne pepper		Bacon strips, cooked crisp (optional)
3	tablespoons chopped fresh parsley		Mushroom caps, sliced and sautéed
	Nutmeg to taste		(optional)
2	egg yolks, beaten		

Melt butter in the top of a double boiler. Add onion and cook until softened. Blend in flour to make a smooth paste. Add milk, salt, cayenne, parsley and nutmeg. Cook, stirring constantly, until sauce is thick and smooth. Add a little of hot cream sauce to yolks to temper them. Stir yolks into sauce and set pan over hot water. Add both cheeses and stir until melted.

To assemble sandwiches, trim crust from 2 slices of bread per serving. Toast bread and lay in an ovenproof dish. Spread bread with a thin coating of sauce. Cover generously with meat, then a large portion of sauce so that all of toast is covered. Broil until sauce browns and puffs up. Garnish with bacon strips and mushrooms, if desired. Yield: 3 to 4 servings.

Hot Chicken and Cheese

4	chicken breast halves	¼	cup flour
2	cups chicken broth	4	slices white bread, toasted
	Salt and pepper to taste	1	cup shredded sharp Cheddar cheese,
4	tablespoons butter		or to taste

Cook chicken in broth seasoned with salt and pepper. Reserve broth for making sauce. Slice chicken and set aside.

Melt butter in a saucepan. Stir in flour until smooth. Stir in reserved broth and adjust seasoning as needed. Cook sauce slowly, stirring often, for 10 minutes.

Arrange toasted bread in a casserole dish. Place chicken on toast. Pour sauce over chicken and top with cheese. Broil 4 to 5 minutes. Serve very hot. Yield: 4 servings.

To turn this sandwich into a Hot Brown, use Parmesan cheese instead of Cheddar and add a slice of tomato and 2 slices of half-cooked bacon on top before broiling. A little sherry in the sauce is also good.

Monte Cristo Sandwich

8	slices white bread	3	eggs
4	tablespoons butter, softened, divided	⅓	cup milk
2	tablespoons prepared mustard	½	teaspoon salt
4	(1-ounce) slices Swiss cheese, halved	1	cup cranberry-orange relish
8	ounces sliced cooked turkey		(from a jar), stirred to soften
4	(1-ounce) slices boiled ham		

Spread bread slices on one side with 2 tablespoons butter and mustard. Top each of 4 slices, buttered-side up, with a half slice of cheese, 2 ounces of turkey, 1 slice of ham and another half slice of cheese. Cover with remaining bread slices, buttered-side down. Cut each sandwich into 2 triangles.

In a shallow dish, beat eggs, milk and salt with a fork. Dip both sides of each sandwich in egg mixture, letting excess drip off. In a large skillet, melt remaining 2 tablespoons butter over medium heat. Add sandwiches without crowding and cook 3 minutes per side or until golden. Serve hot with relish as a dipping sauce. Yield: 4 servings.

Spray your Tupperware with nonstick cooking spray before pouring in tomato based sauces to prevent stains.

Pimento Cheese

5	tablespoons mayonnaise		Dash of white pepper
1	(3-ounce) package cream cheese, softened		Dash of Tabasco sauce
1	clove garlic	1	(2-ounce) jar diced pimentos, drained and chopped
1	tablespoon grated onion	12	ounces extra-sharp Cheddar cheese, shredded

Process mayonnaise, cream cheese, garlic, onion, white pepper and Tabasco sauce in a food processor until smooth. Mix in pimentos and cheese by hand. Do not process. Refrigerate at least 1 hour.

Add finely chopped pecans for extra texture.

Tuna Salad Sandwiches

1	small onion, quartered	3	tablespoons sweet pickle relish
3	stalks celery, outer layer peeled with a potato peeler	⅓	cup mayonnaise
3	(6-ounce) cans water-packed tuna, drained	3	tablespoons cider vinegar
		12-16	slices whole wheat or wheat berry bread

Using the steel blade of a food processor, chop onion and celery until medium-fine. Remove steel blade and insert the plastic mixing blade. Add tuna, relish, mayonnaise and vinegar. Process until well combined. You may mix this by hand for a chunky texture. Spread between slices of bread. Yield: 6 to 8 sandwiches.

Turkey Tomato Melts

2	tablespoons butter	4	teaspoons Parmesan cheese, or four ½-ounce strips
8	(2-ounce) slices raw turkey breast		Farmer's cheese
4	slices tomato	4	slices French bread
4	green bell pepper rings		

Melt butter in a skillet over medium heat. When butter just begins to brown, add turkey. Cook 3 minutes and turn. Top half of the turkey slices with a tomato slice, bell pepper ring and Parmesan and farmer's cheeses. Cover skillet and cook 2 minutes longer. Place a plain turkey slice on each slice of French bread. Top with a turkey slice with toppings. Serve open-faced. Yield: 4 servings.

Side Dishes

Artichoke and Fresh Asparagus Quiche

1	(8-ounce) package cream cheese	1	cup fresh asparagus, stalks and tip broken into 1½-inch pieces
1	cup milk	1	cup chopped artichoke hearts
4	eggs	1	pie shell, baked
1½	cups shredded Monterey Jack cheese		Blanched asparagus stalks for garnish

Combine cream cheese, milk, eggs, Monterey Jack cheese, asparagus pieces and artichoke hearts. Pour mixture into baked pie shell. Bake at 350 degrees for 20 to 30 minutes or until firm and golden brown. Garnish with asparagus spears. Yield: 4 to 5 servings.

Baked Cheese and Garlic Grits

4	cups water	½	cup butter
½	teaspoon salt	½	cup milk
1	cup dry quick-cooking grits	1	clove garlic, minced
1½	cups shredded sharp Cheddar cheese	2	eggs, beaten

Bring water with salt to a boil. Stir in grits and cook according to directions on package until done. Remove from heat. Add cheese, butter, milk and garlic and stir until butter and cheese melt. Add a small amount of hot grits to eggs and stir well. Stir egg mixture back into grits. Pour grits into a lightly greased 2-quart baking dish. Bake at 325 degrees for 1 hour. Yield: 8 servings.

Baked Oysters

4	tablespoons butter	1½	pints select oysters, drained, juice reserved
2	cups saltine cracker crumbs		
½	cup chopped fresh parsley	½	cup light cream
1	teaspoon salt	½	teaspoon Tabasco sauce
¼	teaspoon paprika		

Melt butter in a saucepan. Remove from heat and stir in cracker crumbs, parsley, salt and paprika. Sprinkle a third of crumb mixture into a greased 9-inch pie pan. Layer half the oysters on top. Top with half the remaining crumbs and remaining oysters. Combine reserved oyster juice, cream and Tabasco and pour over the top. Sprinkle with remaining crumb mixture. Bake at 350 degrees for 35 minutes or until golden brown. Yield: 4 to 6 servings.

Black Beans with Andouille Sausage

1	pound dried black beans	1	red onion, diced
2	bay leaves	1	red bell pepper, diced
1	whole onion	1	small green bell pepper, diced
1	whole carrot	2	jalapeño peppers, fresh or canned
1	stalk celery	1½	teaspoons salt
2	cloves garlic	½	teaspoon black pepper
1	pound andouille, kielbasa or chorizo		Sour cream for garnish
	sausage		Sliced green onions for garnish

Wash beans, cover with cold water and soak overnight. (For quick soak method, add beans to 6 cups water. Heat to boiling and boil 2 minutes. Remove from heat and let stand, covered, for 1 hour.) Drain.

In a 5-quart Dutch oven, combine beans with enough water to cover. Add bay leaves, whole onion, carrot, celery and garlic. Bring to a boil. Reduce heat and cover. Simmer 1½ hours or until beans are tender. Make sure there is about ½ inch of liquid above the beans while cooking; add more water as needed. Remove vegetables from beans and discard. Add sausage, red onion, red and green bell peppers, jalapeño peppers, salt and black pepper. Simmer 30 minutes. Remove sausage, dice and return to pot. Adjust seasonings as needed. Serve hot with sour cream and green onions. Yield: 6 to 8 servings.

To serve this as a cold salad, make vinaigrette and add to drained beans while still hot. Toss and cool to room temperature.

Vinaigrette

⅔	cup salad oil	½	teaspoon salt
⅓	cup vinegar	⅛	teaspoon black pepper
1	tablespoon Dijon mustard		

Combine all vinaigrette ingredients in a jar with a tight-fitting lid. Cover and shake.

To easily and quickly peel tomatoes or peppers, place them in a very hot oven and sear until blackened. Then put them in a paper bag to steam so that the skin loosens and can be removed by a gentle rubbing.

Brandied Peaches

3	cups sugar	2	quarts halved or whole fresh peaches, peeled
1	cup water		
¾	cup brandy		

Sterilize 4 pint jars in boiling water; leave in hot water until ready to fill. Combine sugar and 1 cup water in a large saucepan. Over medium heat, bring to a boil, stirring until sugar is dissolved. Add peaches. Reduce heat and simmer 10 minutes or just until peaches are tender. Remove from heat.

Meanwhile, put 1 tablespoon brandy in each hot sterilized jar. Half fill jars with peaches. Add another tablespoon brandy to each jar. Fill jars with remaining peaches and top each with 1 tablespoon brandy. Cover with syrup and seal as directed by jar manufacturer. Yield: 4 pints.

Brenda's Brittle Cake Pickles

2	cups pickling lime	5	pounds sugar
2	gallons water	10	cups cider vinegar
7	pounds cucumbers, sliced about ⅛-inch thick	7	teaspoons pickling spices

Mix lime with 2 gallons water thoroughly; strain water. Add cucumbers to water and soak 24 hours. Drain and rinse cucumbers. Soak cucumbers in fresh water for 4 hours, changing water every hour. Drain.

Combine sugar, vinegar and pickling spices in a saucepan. Bring to a boil. Pour syrup over drained cucumbers and let stand overnight. The next day, bring syrup and cucumbers to a simmer. Remove from heat. Transfer to canning jars and seal. Yield: 8 pints.

 Wrap celery in aluminum foil before putting in the refrigerator to keep longer.

Cucumber Cinnamon Rings

2	gallons large cucumber rings, peeled and seeded (use a long corer to remove seeds)	8½	quarts water
		1	cup vinegar
		1	tablespoon alum
2	cups lime	1	bottle red food coloring

Syrup

2	cups vinegar	2	cups water
10	cups sugar	8	sticks cinnamon
1	(3-ounce) package red hot cinnamon candies		

Combine cucumbers, lime and 8½ quarts water and let stand 24 hours. Drain, then rinse cucumbers with clear running water. Soak cucumbers 3 hours in enough cold water to cover; drain. Simmer cucumbers with vinegar, alum, food coloring and enough water to cover for 2 hours; drain.

To make syrup, combine vinegar, sugar, candies, water and cinnamon sticks in a saucepan. Bring to a boil and pour over drained cucumbers. Let stand overnight. Drain cucumbers, reserving syrup. Reheat syrup and pour over cucumbers again. Let stand overnight. Drain cucumbers, reserving syrup. Pack cucumbers tightly into hot, sterilized jars. Heat syrup and pour over rings. Seal. Yield: 8 pints.

These are very good and colorful. They are very attractive on luncheon plates or for garnish during the holidays.

Fried Vidalia Onion Rings

3-4	large Vidalia onions	1	egg, separated
1	cup all-purpose flour	¾	cup milk
1	teaspoon salt	1	tablespoon salad oil, plus extra for deep-frying
1½	teaspoons baking powder		

Slice onions into rings. In a bowl, mix together flour, salt and baking powder. In a separate bowl, beat egg yolk. Stir milk and 1 tablespoon salad oil into yolk. Add milk mixture to dry ingredients and stir until smooth. In another bowl, beat egg white until soft peaks form. Fold whites into batter until smooth. Dip onion rings into batter. Deep-fry in hot oil until golden brown. Yield: 4 servings.

Dutch Oven Beans for a Crowd

1	(16-ounce) package dry navy beans	3	tablespoons brown sugar
1	cup dry baby lima beans		Salt to taste
1	cup dry red kidney beans	¼	teaspoon black pepper
18	cups water, divided	¼	teaspoon ground cloves
2	tablespoons salad oil	1	(28-ounce) can tomatoes, undrained
2	medium-size green bell peppers, cut into 1-inch wide strips	1	(12-ounce) can tomato paste
2	medium onions, diced	1½	pounds kielbasa sausage, cut into ½-inch chunks
3	cloves garlic, minced		

About 3½ hours before serving, rinse all beans in cold running water and discard any stones or shriveled beans. In an 8-quart Dutch oven, bring beans and 12 cups water over high heat to a boil. Cook 3 minutes. Remove Dutch oven from heat, cover and let stand 1 hour. Drain and rinse beans, set aside.

In same Dutch oven over medium-high heat, heat salad oil. Add bell peppers, onions and garlic and cook, stirring occasionally, until tender. Return beans to Dutch oven. Stir in brown sugar, salt, black pepper, cloves and remaining 6 cups water. Bring to a boil over high heat. Reduce heat to low and cover. Simmer 1 hour, stirring occasionally. Stir in undrained tomatoes, tomato paste and kielbasa, stirring well to break up tomatoes. (I put tomatoes in the blender.) Cover and simmer 30 minutes longer or until beans are tender. Skim off fat. Yield: 12 servings.

I add 2 chunks of streak of lean to the pot and leave off the ground cloves. I have made this both ways and like the flavor of the meat better.

Hot Brandied Fruit

1	(36-ounce) can apricot halves	½	cup butter, melted
1	(29-ounce) can pear halves	¾	cup brown sugar
1	(29-ounce) can peach halves	½	cup brandy
1	(20-ounce) can pineapple slices	10	whole cloves
1	(10-ounce) jar maraschino cherries	4	sticks cinnamon

Drain fruit, reserving juice. Combine fruits in a 2½-quart casserole dish; set aside. Stir together juices and measure out 1 cup of juice mixture; set aside. Combine butter and sugar and stir until smooth. Add reserved juice mixture, brandy, cloves and cinnamon. Stir until blended and pour over fruit in casserole dish. Bake at 350 degrees for 30 minutes or until bubbly. Yield: 8 to 10 servings.

Fresh Spinach Pie

1	pound fresh spinach, washed, coarse stems removed	1	cup heavy cream
1	tablespoon water	3	eggs, beaten
½	teaspoon salt	8	ounces fresh mushrooms, sliced
⅛	teaspoon black pepper	1	(1-inch) pie shell, unbaked
⅛	teaspoon nutmeg	2	cups shredded Swiss or Gruyère cheese
5	tablespoons butter, divided	3	slices bacon, cooked crisp and crumbled
2	tablespoons flour		

Chop spinach and place in a large saucepan with 1 tablespoon water. Steam 3 to 5 minutes or until tender; drain well. Place drained spinach in a bowl and season with salt, pepper and nutmeg. In a small saucepan, melt 4 tablespoons butter. Stir in flour. Cook, stirring constantly, for 2 minutes. Gradually add cream and cook until thickened. Add spinach mixture.

In a medium skillet, melt remaining 1 tablespoon butter. Add mushrooms and sauté 4 to 5 minutes. Prick the pie shell with a fork. Layer cheese, bacon, spinach mixture and mushrooms in pie shell. Bake at 375 degrees for 40 minutes. Turn oven off and leave in oven 5 to 8 minutes. Remove from oven and serve. Yield: 4 to 6 servings.

Rosemary Mushroom Grits

3½	cups beef broth	1	tablespoon olive oil
¾	cup dry grits	1	sprig rosemary, chopped
2	cloves garlic, minced, divided	2	cups fresh shiitake mushrooms
¾	cup Parmigiano-Reggiano cheese	2	tablespoons chopped fresh parsley
2½	tablespoons butter		Salt and pepper to taste
1	teaspoon freshly ground black pepper		

Bring broth to a boil in a saucepan. Stir in grits and 1 clove garlic. Reduce heat and cover. Cook, stirring occasionally, for 20 minutes or until thickened. Remove from heat. Stir in cheese, butter and pepper. Cook over low heat, stirring frequently, until cheese and butter melt.

Sauté remaining clove of garlic in olive oil in a skillet until tender but not browned. Stir in rosemary and mushrooms. Cook over medium heat for 8 to 10 minutes or until brown, stirring frequently. Remove from heat. Stir in parsley and season with salt and pepper. Let stand until cool. Spoon half of grits mixture into a large baking dish. Spread mushroom mixture over grits and top with remaining grits mixture. Cover and chill several hours or overnight. Cut into squares or desired shapes. Yield: 8 servings.

If you prefer to serve hot, arrange squares on a baking sheet and broil until light brown.

Homemade Pizza

Pizza Crust

1	cup boiling water	1	package dry yeast
2	tablespoons shortening	3-4	cups all-purpose flour
¼	teaspoon salt		

Sauce

2	(14½-ounce) cans tomatoes, undrained and chopped	2	teaspoons salt
2	small green bell peppers, chopped	2	teaspoons sugar
2	small onions, chopped	2	teaspoons dried oregano
2	bay leaves	⅛	teaspoon black pepper

Toppings

1½	pounds ground beef	1	(4-ounce) can sliced mushrooms, drained (optional)
1	teaspoon salt		
1	(3½-ounce) package sliced pepperoni (optional)	3	cups shredded mozzarella cheese
		1	cup shredded Cheddar cheese
1½	cups sliced black olives (optional)	½	cup grated Parmesan cheese

Combine water, shortening and salt in a large mixing bowl. Stir until shortening is melted. Cook to lukewarm (105 to 115 degrees). Sprinkle yeast over water mixture and stir until dissolved. Gradually add flour and stir until dissolved. Turn dough out onto a lightly floured surface and knead until smooth and elastic. Shape dough into a ball and place in a greased bowl, turning once to grease top. Cover and let rise in a warm, draft-free place (85 degrees) for 1 hour or until doubled. Punch down dough and divide in half. Lightly grease hands and pat dough evenly into two 12-inch pizza pans.

Meanwhile, combine all sauce ingredients in a large saucepan. Simmer over low heat for 1 hour or until thickened, stirring occasionally. Remove bay leaves. Spread sauce evenly over each pizza crust, leaving a ½-inch border around the edges.

For toppings, cook beef with salt in a skillet over medium heat until meat is no longer pink, stirring to crumble. Drain well on paper towels. Spoon meat over tomato sauce. Top with pepperoni, olives and mushrooms, if desired. Bake at 450 degrees for 10 minutes. Sprinkle with mozzarella and Cheddar cheese and bake 10 minutes longer. Remove from oven and sprinkle with Parmesan cheese. Yield: two 12-inch pizzas.

Sausage Mushroom Stuffing

1	pound sweet Italian sausage	½	teaspoon dried thyme, crumbled
4	cups sliced raw mushrooms	5	cups stale whole wheat bread cubes
2½	cups chopped celery		(about 10 slices)
2	cups chopped onion	5	cups stale white bread cubes
3	cloves garlic, finely chopped		(about 10 slices)
1	teaspoon salt	⅓	cup chopped fresh parsley
⅛	teaspoon black pepper		Chicken broth
1	teaspoon dried sage leaves		

Remove casings and break sausage into small pieces. In a large saucepan, cook sausage over medium heat, stirring frequently, until browned. With a slotted spoon, remove sausage from pan and reserve. Discard all but 2 tablespoons fat in pan. Add mushrooms, celery, onion, garlic, salt, pepper, sage and thyme. Cook, stirring occasionally, for 15 minutes or until celery and onion are soft but not brown. Mix vegetable mixture with reserved sausage, bread cubes, parsley and enough chicken broth to moisten well. Transfer to a greased casserole dish. Bake at 350 degrees until done. Yield: 6 to 8 servings.

Potato and Pasta Gratin

1	(12-ounce) russet potato, peeled and	1	pound onions, sliced
	cut into ½-inch slices (about 2 cups)	¾	cup heavy cream
8	ounces dry small pasta, such as elbow,	¾	cup milk (do not use low-fat or nonfat)
	bowtie or other	1½	cups shredded Swiss cheese
2	tablespoons butter		

Cook potato in boiling salted water in a large pot for 10 minutes or until tender. Using a slotted spoon, transfer potato to a large bowl. Add pasta to same pot of boiling water and cook until just tender, but still firm to bite. Drain and add pasta to bowl with potato.

Meanwhile, melt butter in a large heavy skillet over medium heat. Add onion slices and sauté 15 minutes or until tender. Add sautéed onion, cream, milk and cheese to potato mixture and mix well. Season with salt and pepper. Transfer to a greased 8-inch square baking dish. Bake at 350 degrees for 20 minutes or until heated through and cheese melts. Serve hot. Yield: 6 servings.

Roasted Garlic

4   whole garlic bulbs
2   teaspoons olive oil
¼   teaspoon salt

¼   teaspoon herb of choice, such as
      oregano, rosemary or tarragon

Cut the very tip off garlic bulbs and gently remove the loose papery outer layers. Leave bulbs intact. Place bulbs in a small baking pan and drizzle with oil. Sprinkle with salt, pepper and herb of choice. Fill bottom of pan with water to cover about one-fourth of bulbs. Seal pan with foil. Bake at 450 degrees for 1 hour or until bulbs are soft. Break off clove and squeeze pulp. Yield: 4 servings.

Spiced Peaches

5   quarts peaches
3   cups sugar
1½ cups vinegar

2   tablespoons mixed spices, enclosed in
    a cheesecloth bag

Peel peaches. Add sugar and let stand overnight. The next morning, add vinegar and spice bag. Cook peaches until tender. Lift peaches out of syrup and place in sterilized jars. Boil syrup until thickened. Pour syrup over peaches and seal.

Stuffed Deviled Eggs

12 hard-cooked eggs
1   teaspoon salt
½   teaspoon prepared mustard

1   tablespoon vinegar
    Mayonnaise
¼   teaspoon paprika

Peel eggs and cut in half lengthwise. Remove yolks, reserving white halves. Mash yolks in a bowl with salt, mustard, and vinegar. Blend well. Mix in mayonnaise. Spoon yolk filling into a pastry bag. Pipe filling into white halves. Sprinkle with paprika. Yield: 24 halves.

I add a small sprig tip of parsley to each egg half to add color.

Wine Jelly

2   cups sherry or port wine
3   cups sugar

½   (4-ounce) package Certo

Combine wine and sugar in the top of a double boiler over boiling water. Stir constantly until thoroughly heated. Remove from heat and add Certo. Pour into jars and cover with wax. Serve jelly with pork or chicken.

Pasta & Rice

A Brief History of Wild Rice

The Indian word for wild rice is Mahnomen. It has been harvested from the lakes and rivers of northern Minnesota by natives in canoes since long before the white man set foot in this land. When wild rice comes off the lakes and rivers, it is in a dark green hull and moist. The moisture is roasted out of the grain by a parching process and results in a firm, nonperishable grain. The hull is then removed, followed by a careful cleaning and grading process before the grain becomes the gourmet delight known throughout the world.

Today there are two types of wild rice on the market; naturally grown wild rice and commercially grown paddy rice.

Basic Wild Rice

Wild rice is a delicious side dish. Wash thoroughly in running water, put in a saucepan and add boiling salted water at a rate of 4 cups water to 1 cup wild rice. Cook about 40 minutes or until rice "blooms", which is where the grains split lengthwise and butterfly so white is exposed on the side of each grain. Drain rice and transfer to a dish. Cover dish to allow rice to steam until serving time. Add butter and season with salt and pepper to taste.

Black Beans and Rice

1	(12-ounce) package dried black beans	4	teaspoons salt
7	cups water	1	teaspoon black pepper
8	cloves garlic, minced	3	tablespoons vinegar
2	large onions, chopped	2	cups cooked rice
2	green bell peppers, chopped	½	cup chopped onion or scallions for garnish
⅓	cup olive oil		
1	smoked ham hock, or bone leftover from a baked ham		

Place beans in a large container. Add enough water to cover beans by 1 to 2 inches. Soak beans overnight. Drain beans and place in a soup pot. Add 7 cups water, garlic, onions, bell pepper, olive oil, ham hock, salt and pepper. Simmer 3 to 4 hours or until beans are tender and liquid is thick. Add vinegar just before serving. Serve over cooked rice and garnish with chopped onion. Yield: 8 servings.

Cabin Bluff Rice

1 cup dry wild rice
8 slices bacon

½ cup sliced onion

Wash rice thoroughly in cold water, pouring off chaff and foreign matter. Cook 30 to 40 minutes in gently boiling salted water; use a lot of water, at least 4 cups to 1 cup of rice. Cook to almost done; do not overcook. Drain thoroughly in a colander for about 1 hour.

Cook bacon until crisp in a large heavy skillet. Remove bacon and crumble when cooled. Remove all but about 1 tablespoon bacon drippings from skillet. Add onion to bacon drippings and sauté until tender but not browned. Add drained rice and crumbled bacon and cook over low heat, turning with a fork, until all flavors are blended and rice is done. Yield: 6 to 8 servings.

After combining ingredients and lightly cooking in skillet, dish can be finished in a covered casserole dish in a 250 degree oven.

Buttered Noodles with Chives

10 ounces dry egg noodles
2 tablespoons unsalted butter, cut into
   pieces
½ cup chicken broth, heated

¼ cup chopped fresh chives
¾ teaspoon salt
¼ teaspoon black pepper

Cook noodles in a large pot of boiling salted water for 10 to 12 minutes or until tender, stirring occasionally. Drain in a colander and transfer to a large bowl. Immediately add butter, broth, chives, salt and pepper and toss. Yield: 8 servings.

Green Rice

2 tablespoons oil
2 green onions with tops, chopped
1 green bell pepper, chopped
2¼ cups chicken broth

1 cup dry rice
½ teaspoon salt
Chopped fresh parsley for garnish

Heat oil in a skillet. Add green onions and bell pepper and sauté until limp but not brown. In a saucepan, bring broth to a boil. Add broth, rice and salt to skillet. Stir and pour mixture into a casserole dish. Cover and bake at 350 degrees for 45 minutes or until rice is tender. When done, fluff with a fork and sprinkle with parsley. Yield: 4 servings.

Fettuccine Alfredo

3	tablespoons butter	½	cup shredded provolone cheese
2	tablespoons all-purpose flour	⅛	teaspoon cayenne pepper
1	cup evaporated milk	1	(9-ounce) package fettuccine
½	cup chicken broth		Freshly ground black pepper
½	cup freshly grated Parmesan cheese		

Melt butter in a medium saucepan. Stir in flour. Gradually add milk and broth, stirring constantly until mixture comes to a boil and thickens. Stir in cheeses and cayenne until cheese is melted.

Prepare fettuccine according to package directions; drain. Toss cooked fettuccine with cheese sauce. Season with black pepper. Yield: 4 servings.

Fettuccine with Shrimp and Asparagus

1	cup sliced fresh mushrooms	¼	cup yogurt
2	cloves garlic, minced	½-¾	cup milk
1	tablespoon olive oil	½	cup grated Parmesan cheese
1	cup diagonally sliced asparagus	1	pound dry fettuccine, cooked, drained
18	large shrimp, peeled, deveined and cooked		and kept warm
			Salt and pepper to taste
1	egg white	2	tablespoons minced fresh parsley

Sauté mushrooms and garlic in olive oil in a medium skillet for 3 to 4 minutes. Add asparagus and sauté 3 to 4 minutes or until asparagus is crisp-tender. Add shrimp and cook 2 to 3 minutes or until warm. Cover skillet and remove from heat.

Mix egg white, yogurt, milk and cheese in a saucepan. Cook over medium-low heat for 3 to 4 minutes or until sauce is warm and smooth. Spoon sauce over fettuccine and toss. Add shrimp mixture and toss. Season with salt and pepper and sprinkle parsley on top. Yield: 6 servings.

Macaroni and Cheese

½	cup unsalted butter, plus more to grease casserole dish
6	slices firm white bread, crusts removed, torn into ¼- to ½-inch pieces
5½	cups milk
½	cup all-purpose flour
2	teaspoons salt, plus more for cooking water
¼	teaspoon freshly ground black pepper
¼	teaspoon cayenne pepper
4½	cups shredded sharp white Cheddar cheese, divided
2	cups shredded Gruyère cheese, or 1¼ cups Pecorino Romano cheese, divided
1	pound dry elbow macaroni

Place bread pieces in a food processor and process to make crumbs. In a small saucepan over medium heat, melt 2 tablespoons butter. Pour melted butter over bread crumbs and toss; set aside.

Warm milk in a saucepan over medium heat, or in a microwave. Melt remaining 6 tablespoons butter in a high-sided skillet or heavy saucepan over medium heat. When butter bubbles, stir in flour. Cook and stir 1 minute. Whisk in hot milk a little at a time to keep mixture smooth. Continue cooking, whisking constantly, for 8 to 12 minutes or until mixture bubbles and thickens. Remove from heat. Stir in salt, black pepper, cayenne, 3 cups Cheddar cheese and 1½ cups Gruyère cheese. Set sauce aside.

Cover a large pot of salted water and bring to a boil. Cook macaroni in boiling water for 3 to 4 minutes or until outside of pasta is cooked and inside is underdone. Drain macaroni in a colander. Stir well drained macaroni into reserved cheese sauce.

Use butter to grease a casserole dish. Pour half of macaroni mixture into dish. Sprinkle half of both remaining cheeses on top. Add remaining macaroni mixture and top with remaining cheeses. Sprinkle bread crumbs on top. Bake at 375 degrees for about 30 minutes. Yield: 12 servings.

You can use all sharp Cheddar cheese instead of the mixture of cheeses.

Pecan Rice

1	cup pecans	3	cups hot cooked long-grain rice
1	tablespoon unsalted butter		Salt and pepper to taste

Spread pecans on a baking sheet. Toast nuts at 250 degrees for about 15 minutes. Coarsely chop.

Melt butter in a large skillet. Add toasted pecans, stirring to coat. Add hot rice and toss with pecans. Season with salt and pepper. Yield: 6 to 8 servings.

Penne in Cream Sauce with Sausage

1	tablespoon butter	1	cup heavy cream
1	tablespoon olive oil	6	tablespoons chopped fresh Italian
1	medium onion, thinly sliced		parsley, divided
3	cloves garlic, minced		Salt and pepper to taste
1	pound sweet Italian sausage, casings	1	pound dry penne pasta
	removed	1	cup freshly grated Parmesan cheese,
⅔	cup dry white wine		divided
1	(14½-ounce) can diced peeled		
	tomatoes with juice		

Melt butter with oil in a large heavy skillet over medium-high heat. Add onion and garlic and sauté 7 minutes or until golden brown and tender. Add sausage and sauté 7 minutes or until golden brown and cooked through, breaking up sausage with the back of a spoon. Drain any excess drippings from skillet. Add wine to skillet and bring to a boil. Cook 2 minutes or until all liquid evaporates. Add tomatoes with juice and simmer 3 minutes. Add cream and simmer 5 minutes or until sauce thickens slightly. Stir in 4 tablespoons parsley. Season with salt and pepper. Remove sauce from heat.

Cook pasta in a large pot of boiling salted water until tender but still firm to bite. Drain pasta and transfer to a large bowl. Bring sauce to a simmer and pour over pasta. Add ¾ cup cheese and toss to coat. Sprinkle remaining ¼ cup cheese and 2 tablespoons parsley on top. Yield: 4 to 6 servings.

Red Beans and Rice

1	pound dry red beans, picked over	3	cloves garlic, minced
2	ham hocks	2	bay leaves
3	onions, chopped		Salt and pepper to taste
2	stalks celery, chopped	½	cup butter
2	green bell peppers, chopped		Hot cooked rice

Place beans in a container and cover with water. Soak overnight. The next day, drain beans and place in a soup pot. Add ham hocks, onions, celery, bell pepper, garlic and bay leaves. Cover with cold water and place lid on pot. Bring to a boil. Reduce heat to a simmer. Cook over low heat for 2½ to 3 hours, adding more water as needed to keep beans from sticking to pot. After beans are tender, remove some beans from pot and mash. Return mashed beans to whole beans and stir. Season with salt and pepper. Add butter and heat until butter is melted. Serve over hot rice. Yield: 6 servings.

Rice Supreme

½	cup butter	1	(10¼-ounce) can beef onion soup
1	cup dry rice		Salt and pepper to taste
1	(10¼-ounce) can beef broth or consommé	1	(4-ounce) can mushrooms

Melt butter in a casserole dish. Add rice, broth and soup. Season with salt and pepper. (Remember, the soups are salted.) Cover dish and bake at 375 degrees for 1 hour. Remove from oven and top with mushrooms. Bake, uncovered, for 15 minutes longer. Yield: 4 to 6 servings.

If recipe is doubled, do not double the butter.

I use one cup of chopped fresh mushrooms instead of the canned. Add fresh mushrooms with the rice. Mushrooms will rise to the top while baking. I still uncover and bake for the 15 minutes.

Risotto

1	cup dry rice, preferable converted (not instant)	1¾	cups rich chicken broth, barely simmering
2	tablespoons olive oil	1	teaspoon loosely packed saffron
¼	cup finely chopped onion	2	tablespoons warm water
¼	cup finely minced prosciutto or ham		Salt to taste
⅔	cup dry white wine	2	tablespoons butter
⅛	teaspoon dried hot pepper flakes	½	cup freshly grated Parmesan cheese

Rinse rice and drain well. Heat olive oil in a heavy saucepan. Add onion and sauté until lightly browned. Add prosciutto and cook and stir about 1 minute. Add rice and cook over high heat, stirring and scraping from the bottom, for 5 minutes or until rice starts to brown. Stir in wine and pepper flakes. Cook, stirring occasionally, for 4 minutes or until wine is almost all absorbed. Add ½ cup of broth and cook 2 minutes. Meanwhile, combine saffron and warm water; set aside. Add another ½ cup broth to rice mixture and cook over medium-high heat for 5 minutes, stirring gently and shaking the pan so liquid is evenly absorbed. Add remaining broth, salt and saffron in water. Cook over high heat about 6 to 7 minutes, stirring occasionally and shaking pan. Stir in butter and remove from heat. Gently fold in cheese and serve. Yield: 2 to 4 servings.

Rice and Sausage Stuffing

½ pound sweet or hot sausage	2½ cups mushrooms, cut into ½-inch cubes
1 cup finely chopped onion	1 teaspoon finely chopped fresh or dried
1 tablespoon finely minced garlic	rosemary
½ cup finely chopped celery	3 cups cooked rice (recipe below)
1 cup finely chopped green bell pepper	Salt and freshly ground pepper to taste

Cook sausage and onion in a saucepan, stirring to break up chunks, until meat loses its raw look and onion is wilted. Add garlic, celery, bell pepper and mushrooms. Cook, stirring occasionally, for about 5 minutes. Drain if desired and return to saucepan. Add rosemary and stir to blend. Stir in cooked rice and season with salt and pepper. Cook briefly. Yield: 8 to 10 servings or about 6 cups (enough for a 12-pound bird).

Cooked Rice

5 tablespoons butter, divided	2 sprigs parsley
¾ cup minced onion	2 sprigs thyme, or ½ teaspoon dried
½ teaspoon minced garlic	1 bay leaf
2 cups dry rice	¼ teaspoon cayenne pepper, or Tabasco
3 cups chicken broth	sauce to taste

Melt 2 tablespoons butter in a heavy saucepan. Add onion and garlic and cook, stirring with a wooden spoon, until onion is wilted. Add rice and stir briefly over low heat until rice is coated with butter. Stir in broth, making sure there are no lumps of rice. Add parsley, thyme, bay leaf and cayenne. Cover with a tight-fitting lid. Cook exactly 17 minutes on stovetop or bake at 400 degrees. Remove cover and discard parley and thyme sprigs and bay leaf. Using a two-pronged fork, stir in remaining 3 tablespoons butter. If rice is not to be served immediately, keep covered in a warm place. Yield: 8 to 12 servings.

Rice Pilaf

2 cups dry rice	¾ cup chopped fresh parsley
⅔ cup butter	½ cup chopped green onion
4 cups chicken broth	1 cup chopped pecans or almonds
¾ cup chopped celery	Salt to taste
¾ cup shredded carrot	

Sauté rice in butter until lightly browned. Add broth and transfer to a casserole dish. Bake at 350 degrees for 30 minutes. Add celery, carrot, parsley, green onion, nuts and salt. Bake 30 minutes longer. Excellent with chicken, ham or roast. Yield: 6 to 8 servings.

Spicy Pasta, Bean and Sausage Soup

2	(15- to 16-ounce) cans garbanzo beans	¼	cup tomato paste
2	tablespoons olive oil	5	cups canned chicken broth
1	pound hot Italian sausage, casing removed	8	ounces (about 2⅓ cups) dry orecchiette (small ear shaped) pasta, or other small pasta
4	teaspoons chopped fresh rosemary	1½	cups grated Romano cheese, divided
2	large cloves garlic, chopped		Salt and pepper to taste
¼	teaspoon dried red pepper flakes		

Strain liquid from beans into a blender. Add 1 cup drained beans and purée until smooth. Heat olive oil in a large pot over medium heat. Add sausage, rosemary, garlic and pepper flakes. Sauté 8 minutes or until sausage is cooked, breaking up sausage with a fork. Mix in tomato paste. Add bean purée, remaining beans, broth and pasta. Simmer, stirring occasionally, for 30 minutes or until pasta is tender and mixture is thick. Mix in ¼ cup cheese. Season with salt and pepper. Serve, passing remaining 1¼ cups cheese on the side. Yield: 4 to 6 servings.

Wild Rice and Chestnut Dressing

3	cups water	1	teaspoon dried thyme
¾	cup dry jumbo grade wild rice, rinsed and drained	1	pound sliced whole wheat bread, 2-3 days old, toasted and cut into cubes
3	teaspoons salt, divided	1	(15-ounce) jar steamed chestnuts
½	cup unsalted butter, plus extra for greasing dish	3	eggs
2	cups finely chopped onion	2½	cups turkey or chicken broth
2	cups finely chopped celery	¼	cup finely chopped fresh flat-leaf parsley
1	tablespoon poultry seasoning	1½	teaspoons freshly ground black pepper

Bring 3 cups water to a boil in a heavy pot over high heat. Add rice and 1 teaspoon salt. Reduce heat to low and cover partially. Cook, stirring occasionally, for 45 minutes or until rice is tender. Drain and cool.

Use butter to generously grease a large, shallow baking dish. Melt ½ cup butter over medium heat in a large skillet. Add onion, celery, poultry seasoning and thyme. Cover and cook, stirring once or twice, for 15 minutes or until vegetables are tender. Cool.

In a large bowl, combine bread, chestnuts, vegetable mixture and rice. In a separate bowl, whisk eggs until blended. Whisk broth into eggs, then stir egg mixture into bread stuffing. Stir in parsley, remaining 2 teaspoons salt and pepper. Spoon dressing into prepared dish and cover tightly with foil. Bake at 325 degrees for 1 hour. Uncover and bake 20 to 30 minutes longer or until dressing is lightly browned on top. Yield: 10 servings.

Wild Rice with Mushrooms

1	cup wild rice	1	tablespoon finely chopped green bell pepper
4	tablespoons butter		
1	tablespoon grated onion	8	ounces fresh mushrooms, finely sliced
1	tablespoon finely chopped fresh parsley		Salt and pepper to taste
			Generous dash of nutmeg
1	tablespoon finely chopped fresh chives		

Cook rice; drain well. Melt butter in a skillet. Add onion, parsley, chives and bell pepper and sauté 3 minutes. Add mushrooms and cook 5 minutes over medium-low heat, stirring frequently. Season with salt and pepper and nutmeg. Stir in drained rice. If desired, press into a greased mold. Serve with wild game. Yield: 4 to 6 servings.

Wild Rice Dressing

1	cup wild rice	1	egg, lightly beaten
1	cup chopped onion	¼	teaspoon sage
1	cup chopped celery		Salt and pepper to taste
⅓	cup butter		

Cook rice in boiling salted water, or pour boiling water over rice and let stand overnight. Drain and transfer to a bowl. Sauté onion and celery in butter until tender. Add vegetables to rice along with egg, sage and salt and pepper.

This is a good dressing for ducks; it will stuff 2 duck cavities.

To add a bit of color to homemade pasta, use a puree of fresh vegetables, such as spinach or beets, to give the dough an inviting and original hue.

Vegetables & Casseroles

Asparagus

Basic Preparation

A pound of asparagus has 12 to 15 spears and serves 2 to 4 people. Cook asparagus until barely fork tender. Do not overcook or asparagus will absorb water and break down. Wash asparagus and break off woody ends. It will break off at the right place if you bend the stalk. There are various ways to cook asparagus, I have listed some of my favorites.

Blanch: Bring water to a boil in a skillet. Add salt to taste. Place asparagus in water to cover and boil, uncovered, for 5 to 8 minutes or until barely cooked through. Immediately remove asparagus and place on paper towels to cool. When ready to serve, heat butter to cover bottom of a skillet. Add asparagus and shake pan to heat. Sprinkle with salt and pepper and squeeze lemon juice, if desired. Fresh garlic may also be added to the butter.

Microwave: You may also cook asparagus in the microwave with excellent results. Place in a glass loaf pan with the ends on the outside and the tips in the middle. Add 2 to 4 tablespoons of water and salt to taste. Microwave 3 to 6 minutes or until crisp-tender; drain. Add butter and garlic and reheat 30 seconds.

Steam: Place whole trimmed asparagus on a steamer rack in a large saucepan over boiling water. Cover and steam 4 to 8 minutes.

Stir-Fry: Cut asparagus spears at an angle into 1-inch lengths. Stir-fry in hot oil or butter, stirring constantly, for 3 to 7 minutes.

Grilled: Brush spears (blanched if jumbo size) with olive oil and place directly on the grill. Cook 3 to 6 minutes, turning several times.

Oven-Roasted: Place washed and trimmed asparagus on a baking sheet. Add 2 tablespoons olive oil or vegetable oil for each pound of asparagus. Toss to coat and arrange asparagus into a single layer. Roast at 450 degrees for 7 to 10 minutes or until crisp-tender.

Freshly grated Parmesan cheese or French feta cheese may be added after asparagus is removed from oven but while still hot.

Basil Butter for Asparagus

⅓	cup fresh basil leaves	1	teaspoon salt
2	tablespoons chopped fresh parsley	⅛	teaspoon ground nutmeg
6	tablespoons unsalted butter, cut into pieces		Freshly ground black pepper to taste

Process basil and parsley in a food processor. Add butter, salt, nutmeg and pepper and process until blended. Store in refrigerator. Soften at room temperature for about 30 minutes before serving. This butter is also good served on steaks and other green vegetables. Yield: Enough for 3 pounds asparagus.

Autumn Acorn Squash

2	small acorn squash, washed and dried		Nutmeg to taste
2	tablespoons butter		Curry powder to taste
	Salt and pepper to taste	6	teaspoons water

Halve squash lengthwise and scoop out seeds. Remove a small slice from the bottom of each half so it will rest firmly in pan. Butter the flat rim of each top cut side and divide remaining butter among the scooped out hollows. Season each hollow with salt and pepper, nutmeg and curry powder. Place each half in a small baking dish. Add a quarter inch of water in the bottom of the dish. Spoon 1½ teaspoons water into each hollow. Bake at 350 degrees for 45 minutes or until pierced easily with a fork. Serve with extra butter. May be prepared ahead and baked before serving. Yield: 4 servings.

Baked Stuffed Yellow Squash

Yellow squash, about 5 to 6 inches
long, 1 per serving
While onions
(¼ volume of squash stuffing)

Butter
Salt and white pepper
Paprika (optional)

Wash squash and carefully trim off stem and blossom end. Place whole squash in a pot and cover with water. Bring to a boil and cook gently until just tender; do not overcook. Scoop squash out of hot water and cool on a towel. When cool enough to handle, slice each squash horizontally with 1 side larger than the other. Scoop out pulp of the larger side. Place empty shells in a single layer in an ungreased shallow casserole dish, alternating the large end with the stem end.

For stuffing, place removed pulp in a bowl. Dice remaining smaller halves and add to bowl. Dice onions to equal one-fourth of the volume of stuffing. Sauté onions in 4 tablespoons butter for 8 squash; do not overbrown. Add squash centers and diced squash to onions. Cook and stir together until squash is very tender and most of the liquid has cooked out. Season with salt and pepper. Fill stuffing into squash shells, rounding the top. Sprinkle with paprika, if desired. Bake at 325 degrees for 20 minutes or until heated through.

Freeze left over wine into ice cubes to use in casseroles and sauces.

Baked Tomatoes

4	large firm ripe tomatoes, halved horizontally	2	tablespoons finely chopped green bell pepper
¼	cup all-purpose flour	1	teaspoon Worcestershire sauce
½	teaspoon salt	4	strips lean bacon, halved crosswise
½	teaspoon dry mustard	⅓	cup shredded sharp Cheddar cheese
¼	teaspoon paprika		Parsley for garnish
2	tablespoons finely chopped onion		

Arrange tomatoes, cut-side up, in a shallow baking dish. Combine flour, salt, mustard, paprika, onion, bell pepper and Worcestershire sauce. Spread mixture evenly over each tomato half. Lay a piece of bacon over each tomato half and sprinkle with cheese. Bake at 350 degrees for 25 to 30 minutes. Yield: 8 servings.

Black-Eyed Peas with Ham Hocks

1	(1½-pound) package dried black-eyed peas	1	medium onion, peeled
3	small ham hacks, or 2 large	4	teaspoons salt
10	cups water	½	teaspoon white pepper

Wash peas thoroughly in cold running water and remove any faulty peas or other foreign matter. Soak peas overnight in water.

Place ham hocks in a heavy pot with 10 cups water. Simmer about 30 minutes. Drain peas and add to pot with ham hocks along with whole onion. Simmer 45 minutes or until peas are done. Add salt and pepper. Discard onion and serve. Yield: 10 to 12 servings.

Boiled Corn

Corn on the cob, shucked, 1 cob per serving	Salt and pepper to taste
	Butter

Bring a large pot of unsalted water to a boil. Cook freshly picked corn, uncovered, in boiling water for just 2 minutes. Cook store-bought corn, which might have been sitting around a few days, for 3 to 4 minutes. Cover with a lid and let stand 5 minutes longer. Drain. Season with salt and pepper. Add butter and leave corn in pot, covered, until ready to serve.

Broccoli with Sour Cream Sauce

1	bunch broccoli, cut into large pieces	½	teaspoon poppy seeds
2	tablespoons butter	¼	teaspoon salt
2	tablespoons minced onion		Dash of cayenne pepper
1½	cups sour cream	½	teaspoon paprika
2	teaspoons sugar	⅓	cup broken pecans, toasted
1	teaspoon white vinegar		

Cook broccoli just until tender; drain. Melt butter in a saucepan. Add onion and sauté. Remove from heat and add sour cream, sugar, vinegar, poppy seeds, salt, cayenne and paprika. Pour sauce over broccoli. Sprinkle with pecans. Yield: 4 servings.

Candied Sweet Potatoes

6	sweet potatoes	Vanilla flavoring
½	cup white granulated sugar	White corn syrup

Bake sweet potatoes in their skins until just tender. Peel and split down the middle and place in an ovenproof casserole dish. Sprinkle with sugar. Mix vanilla and corn syrup and pour over potatoes to barely cover.

Bake at 375 degrees for 30 minutes or until potatoes are bubbly and slightly brown on top. Yield: 6 servings.

Collard Greens

2-3	small bunches collard greens (12 cups coarsely chopped)	1	ham hock or smoked neck bones
2	tablespoons oil	½	cup cider vinegar
1	cup diced onion	9	cups chicken broth
1	tablespoon minced garlic	1	teaspoon Tabasco sauce, or to taste
			Kosher or sea salt and black pepper

To prepare collard greens, grasp the stalk and strip the leaves off in a downward motion. Wash, discard stems and coarsely chop.

Heat oil in a large stock pot over medium heat. Add onion and garlic and sauté 2 to 3 minutes or until the onion is translucent. Add ham hock and vinegar. Gradually add the collard greens. Cook over medium heat, stirring occasionally, until greens wilt. Add broth and Tabasco. Bring to a boil. Reduce heat to a simmer and cook about 2 hours. Add more broth if needed while cooking. Season with salt and pepper and more Tabasco, if desired. Keep warm until ready to serve. Yield: 6 to 8 servings.

I use my pressure cooker for these and cook for 30 minutes. If I am serving for a holiday, I prepare ahead of time and freeze. Remove from the freezer to thaw the night before you plan to serve them. Place in a large pot and simmer.

Creamed Field Corn

2	dozen ears field corn		1	cup half-and-half
¼	cup cold water			Salt and pepper to taste
½	cup butter			

Remove shucks and silks from corn. With a sharp knife, remove just the tips of the corn kernels into a bowl. With the duller side of the knife, scrape the kernels until only the husk remains. After you have scraped all of the corn, add cold water to the corn.

Melt butter in a heavy skillet or saucepan over low heat; do not allow butter to brown. Add corn to the pan and cook, stirring occasionally, until the corn begins to thicken. Add half-and-half and continue to cook and stir for 20 minutes or until the corn is done. Season with salt and pepper. Yield: 4 to 6 servings.

Do not use sweet corn. Sweet corn does not have enough starch for this dish.

Eggplant Parmigiano American

Beef Patties

1½	pounds ground beef chuck		¼	teaspoon black pepper
1	teaspoon onion salt		2	tablespoons salad oil

Eggplant and Assembly

1	medium eggplant, washed		2	(8-ounce) cans tomato sauce
⅓	cup flour		1	cup shredded sharp American cheese
1	teaspoon salt		¼	teaspoon dried oregano
⅛	teaspoon black pepper			Snipped fresh parsley
¼	cup salad oil			

To make patties, combine ground beef, onion salt and pepper. Form mixture into 8 patties. Heat salad oil in a skillet. Add patties and sauté until brown on both sides but rare inside; set aside.

Cut eggplant into eight ½-inch thick slices. Combine flour, salt and pepper and sprinkle over eggplant slices. Heat salad oil in a skillet. Sauté slices in hot oil until golden on both sides.

To assemble, arrange half the eggplant slices in a 13x9-inch baking dish. Top with half the meat patties. Spread 1 can of tomato sauce over the top and sprinkle with half the cheese and oregano. Repeat layers. Bake, uncovered, at 350 degrees for 30 minutes or until cheese is bubbly. Top with parsley. Yield: 4 servings.

Fresh Mustard Greens

8   ounces salt pork, sliced
12 cups fresh mustard greens, washed and
      stemmed

Salt
Hot pepper sauce

Fry salt pork in a large saucepan. Remove half the meat; set aside. Add mustard greens and water to pot. There should be enough water on greens; if they are too dry, add about ½ cup. Place reserved salt pork on top of greens. Cover and cook 40 minutes or until tender. Season to taste with salt. Lift greens out of juices and place in a bowl. Using 2 knives, slightly slice. Serve with hot pepper sauce. Yield: 6 to 8 servings.

Young tender greens need no water added, but more mature greens need ½ to 1 cup added so they will not stick to pot.

Fresh Squash

½   cup butter
2-3 pounds yellow squash, sliced ¼-inch
      thick

1   large Vidalia onion, sliced
    Salt and pepper to taste

Melt butter over medium heat in a heavy saucepan. Add a layer of squash, then a layer of onion. Alternate layers until all is used. Cover and simmer until mixture creates its own juices. After juices are created, cook over medium heat until tender. Season with salt and pepper. Yield: 4 to 6 servings.

Fresh Turnip Greens

8   ounces salt pork, sliced
12 cups fresh turnip greens, washed and
      stemmed

6-8 turnip roots
     Salt

Fry salt pork in a large saucepan. Remove half the meat; set aside. Add 2 cups water to the pot. Add turnip greens. Peel and cut turnip roots into quarters and place on top of turnip greens. Place reserved salt pork on top of roots. Cover and cook until tender. Season to taste with salt. Lift greens and roots out of juices and place in a bowl. Using 2 knives, slightly slice and transfer to a serving dish. Yield: 6 servings.

Fried Okra

Fresh garden okra (small and tender),
thoroughly washed and drained
Corn meal and flour, mixed in equal
parts

Salt and pepper
Bacon fat

Trim tops and tails of okra and slice into ⅜-inch pieces. Toss okra with a mixture of corn meal, flour and salt and pepper. Fry in hot bacon fat until crisp and golden brown.

I buy about 6 small or 4 large pods of okra per serving.

Garlic Mashed Potatoes

5	pounds russet potatoes, peeled and cut into 1-inch pieces	1	(8-ounce) carton sour cream
½	cup butter	1	(8-ounce) package cream cheese, softened
½	cup milk	2	teaspoons salt
2-4	cloves garlic, minced	1	teaspoon white pepper

Place potatoes in a large pot and add water to cover. Cover pot and bring to a boil over high heat. Boil 13 to 15 minutes or until fork-tender; drain. In a 4-cup glass bowl, combine butter, milk and garlic. Microwave on high for 3 to 4 minutes or until mixture boils. Mash milk mixture into potatoes along with sour cream, cream cheese, salt and pepper. Place in a 9x13-inch baking dish and cover. Bake at 350 degrees for 35 to 40 minutes or until heated through. Yield: 8 to 10 servings.

Glazed Carrots

3	cups carrots, cut into strips, quarters or circles	¼	cup brown sugar
2	tablespoons butter	1	tablespoon water

Precook carrots until almost done. Combine butter, brown sugar and water in a heavy skillet over low heat. Add precooked carrots. Cook over low heat, turning carrots several times, for 5 to 10 minutes or until syrup is thick and carrots are tender and look glazed. Use low heat to prevent scorching. Yield: 6 servings.

For a sweet-sour combination, substitute 1 tablespoon lemon juice for the water. If a more tart glaze is preferred, increase lemon juice to suit your taste.

Green Beans with Walnuts

2	pounds green beans, trimmed and cut on diagonal into 1½-inch pieces	2	large cloves garlic, minced
2	tablespoons unsalted butter	½	cup walnuts, coarsely chopped
			Salt and pepper to taste

Cook beans in boiling salted water for 5 minutes or until barely tender; drain. In a large heavy skillet, heat butter over medium heat until foam subsides. Add garlic and walnuts and cook until garlic begins to turn pale golden. Add beans and cook and stir 3 minutes or until crisp-tender. Season with salt and pepper. Yield: 8 servings.

Hashed Cream Potatoes

4½	cups peeled and finely diced potatoes, cooked and cooled	⅓	cup light cream
		1½	teaspoons salt
¼	cup flour	⅛	teaspoon black pepper
2	tablespoons minced onion	4	tablespoons butter

Combine potatoes, flour, onion, cream, salt and pepper and toss well. Heat butter in a skillet. Add potatoes and pat into a large round cake using a spatula. Cook, without stirring, over low heat for 25 to 30 minutes or until brown on underside. Run spatula around edge of pan several times to prevent sticking. Invert pan over a serving plate. To serve, cut potato cake into 6 pie-shaped wedges. Yield: 6 servings.

This is a good way to use leftover baked potatoes.

Herbed New Potatoes

12	small new potatoes	4	teaspoons minced fresh chives
4	teaspoons butter		Fresh parsley sprigs for garnish
4	teaspoons minced fresh parsley		

Peel a ½-inch strip around the center of each potato and immediately place in a medium saucepan of cold water. Add enough additional water to pan to cover the potatoes by 2 inches. Bring to a boil over medium-high heat. Boil 20 minutes or until potatoes are easily pierced with a fork, but still firm; drain. Do not overcook. Cover to keep warm.

Place butter in a microwave-safe bowl. Microwave on high 5 to 10 seconds or until melted. Stir in parsley and chives and pour mixture over potatoes. Toss to coat. Spoon potatoes into a large serving bowl. Garnish with sprigs of parsley. Serve immediately. Yield: 4 servings.

You may also add chopped cooked bacon and/or finely minced green onions.

Marinated Vegetables

2	cups broccoli florets	½	cup chopped green bell pepper
2	cups cauliflower florets	½	cup sliced celery
2	cups sliced carrots	½	cup sliced black olives
1	medium zucchini, sliced		Dressing (recipe below)
1	medium cucumber, sliced	8	cherry tomatoes, halved
½	cup chopped red bell pepper	1	cup halved mushrooms

Combine broccoli, cauliflower, carrots, zucchini, cucumber, bell peppers, celery and olives in a large bowl. Pour dressing over vegetables and toss gently. Cover and chill at least 12 hours. Add tomatoes and mushrooms just before serving. Yield: 8 to 12 servings.

Dressing

1¼	cups vegetable oil	2	cloves garlic, crushed
⅔	cup vinegar		Salt and pepper to taste
½	cup sugar		

Combine all dressing ingredients in a jar. Cover tightly and shake well.

Navy Beans with Ham Hocks

1	(16-ounce) package navy beans	Salt and pepper
1	ham hock	

Soak beans overnight in enough water to cover. (Short soaking method: bring beans and water to a boil. Boil 2 minutes, then soak 1 hour.) Drain beans and place in a large pot. Add water to pot to cover beans by 2 inches. Add ham hock. Simmer 2 to 3 hours or until beans are tender. Season with salt and pepper. Remove ham hock and cut ham from bone. Discard bone and add ham to beans. Serve over rice with corn bread. Yield: 6 to 8 servings.

Pickled Carrots

1	cup vinegar	1	tablespoon kosher dill pickle spice mix
1	cup water	1	tablespoon salt (non-iodized)
1	tablespoon sweet pickle spice mix	2	(1-pound) bags baby carrots

Combine vinegar, water, spice mixes and salt in a nonreactive saucepan. Bring to a boil. Add carrots and cook until tender. Pack carrots into sterilized jars. Add vinegar and water mixture from saucepan to cover carrots. Seal with clean lids and turn upside down to cool. Pickled carrots will be ready to eat after 7 to 9 days.

Quick Cooked Cabbage

| 2 | tablespoons bacon fat or butter | ¾-1 | teaspoon salt |
| 5 | cups finely shredded cabbage | | Dash of black pepper |

Heat bacon fat in a 10-inch skillet. Add cabbage, salt and pepper. Toss several times or until cabbage is coated with fat. Cover and cook about 3 minutes. Yield: 4 servings.

A peeled and diced Granny Smith apple may be added to the cabbage before it is added to the skillet.

Seasoned Pole Beans

2	pounds fresh green pole beans	1	medium-size white onion
6	cups water		Salt and pepper to taste
1	(4-inch square) white salt bacon, sliced		

Wash beans in cold running water. With a sharp knife or potato peeler, remove the string edges from each bean and cut off ends. (I cut off the ends with a knife and use a potato peeler to remove the side strings.) Place the beans in a zip-lock bag in the refrigerator crisper drawer.

Bring 6 cups water to a boil. Add bacon and onion and reduce heat. Cover and simmer about 1 hour. Remove bacon and onion. Cool stock and refrigerate until fat rises to the top; remove the fat. Adjust stock seasoning with salt and pepper. Bring stock to a boil. Add beans, all lying in the same direction. Cover and reduce heat to low. Boil beans 15 to 20 minutes or until tender. Yield: 6 to 8 servings.

Snow Peas with Water Chestnuts

| ½ | (6-ounce) cans water chestnuts, thinly sliced | 2 | (7-ounce) packages frozen snow peas, thawed to room temperature |
| 2 | tablespoons butter | | |

Heat water chestnuts slightly in butter. Boil peas in lightly salted water for 1 minute. Drain peas and toss with water chestnuts and butter. Yield: 4 servings.

Spinach Squares

3	tablespoons butter	¼	cup grated Parmesan cheese, divided
1	small onion, chopped	¼	teaspoon black pepper
4	ounces mushrooms, sliced	¼	teaspoon dried basil
4	eggs	¼	teaspoon dried oregano
¼	cup fine dry bread crumbs	2	(10-ounce) packages frozen chopped
1	(10¾-ounce) can condensed cream of		spinach, thawed and squeezed dry
	mushroom soup		

Melt butter in a wide skillet over medium heat. Add onion and mushrooms and cook and stir until soft. In a large bowl, lightly beat eggs. Stir in onion mixture, bread crumbs, soup, 2 tablespoons cheese, pepper, basil, oregano and spinach. Transfer to a well-greased 9-inch square baking pan. Sprinkle with remaining 2 tablespoons cheese. Bake, uncovered, at 325 degrees for 35 minutes or until edges are beginning to brown. Serve warm. Or, once cooked, cover and refrigerate; serve cold. To reheat, bake at 325 degrees for 10 to 12 minutes. Yield: 8 servings.

Squash Rings with Honey Soy Glaze

2	(1¼- to 1½-pound) acorn squash	1½	teaspoons minced fresh ginger
3	tablespoons honey	1	clove garlic, minced
1	tablespoon reduced-sodium soy sauce		Salt and pepper to taste
2	teaspoons rice vinegar		

Cut off both ends of each squash. Cut each squash crosswise into 4 rings. Scoop out seeds and discard. Place squash rings in a single layer on a large baking sheet lined with foil and sprayed with cooking spray. Cover tightly with foil. Bake at 450 degrees for 15 minutes or until squash begins to soften.

Meanwhile, whisk together honey, soy sauce, vinegar, ginger and garlic in a bowl. Remove foil from squash after baking initial 15 minutes and brush half of honey mixture over squash. Sprinkle with salt and pepper and bake, uncovered, 10 minutes. Brush remaining honey mixture over squash and bake 10 minutes longer or until squash is brown, tender and glazed. Yield: 8 rings.

Stir-fry Snow Peas

2	tablespoons vegetable oil	8	ounces snow pea pods, strings removed
2	cloves garlic, chopped	3	tablespoons soy sauce
8	ounces mushrooms, sliced	1	teaspoon sugar
1	(8-ounce) can water chestnuts, sliced	½	teaspoon salt

Heat oil in a wok or heavy skillet until very hot, almost smoking. Add garlic and sauté. Add mushrooms, water chestnuts and pea pods. Stir-fry 2 minutes or until vegetables are crisp-tender. Combine soy sauce, sugar and salt. Add mixture to pea pods and toss to coat. Yield: 4 servings.

Stuffed Baked Potatoes

8	medium baking potatoes	¼	cup chopped green onion tops or chives
1	cup half-and-half, slightly heated		
4	tablespoons butter	6	slices bacon, cooked crisp and crumbled
⅓	cup sour cream		
	Salt and pepper to taste	1	cup shredded Cheddar cheese

Wash potatoes, poke a few times with a fork and grease lightly. Bake at 425 degrees for 1 hour or until potatoes are fully cooked. Cut off a slice from the top of each potato and scoop out inside pulp. Place potato shells in an ovenproof casserole dish. Mash potato pulp well. Mix in half-and-half, butter, sour cream, salt and pepper and onions. Fill mixture into potato shells. Sprinkle bacon and cheese on top. Bake at 350 degrees for 15 to 20 minutes or until cheese is melted and potatoes are hot. Serve with steaks. Yield: 8 servings.

Stuffed Green Peppers

12	green bell peppers	½	teaspoon black pepper
2	pounds ground beef	5	large tomatoes, chopped
1	cup chopped onion	1	cup cooked rice
2	tablespoons Worcestershire sauce	1	cup shredded Cheddar cheese
1½	teaspoons salt		

Cut off top of peppers and remove seeds. Precook peppers in boiling water for 5 minutes; drain. Arrange peppers in a 3-quart rectangular baking dish.

Cook beef and onion in a large heavy skillet until browned. Drain off excess fat. Stir in Worcestershire sauce, salt and pepper. Add tomatoes and rice. Spoon beef filling into peppers. Bake at 350 degrees for 20 minutes. Top with cheese and return to oven until cheese melts. Yield: 12 servings.

Stuffed Zucchini

6	medium zucchini	¼	cup dried bread crumbs
½	cup chopped onion	½	teaspoon salt
2	cloves garlic, chopped	½	teaspoon black pepper
1	tablespoon butter	3	eggs, beaten
1	tablespoon minced fresh parsley	⅓	cup shredded Cheddar cheese
1	cup chopped spinach, cooked		

Cut ends from zucchini and boil until tender, but not soft. Cut zucchini in half lengthwise and scoop out centers; reserving pulp. Arrange zucchini in a greased shallow baking dish. Sauté onion and garlic in butter. Add parsley, spinach, bread crumbs, salt, pepper and reserved zucchini pulp. Stir in eggs and spoon mixture into zucchini shells. Bake at 350 degrees for 15 minutes. Top with cheese and bake until cheese is hot and bubbly. Yield: 6 servings.

Swiss Onion Bake

2	tablespoons butter	¾	cup milk
2	cups sliced Vidalia onions	½	teaspoon prepared mustard
6	hard-cooked eggs, sliced	6	slices French bread, cut into ½-inch
6	ounces Swiss cheese, shredded		thick slices and buttered on top
1	(10¾-ounce) can condensed cream of chicken soup		

Melt butter in a skillet. Add onions and cook until tender. Spread onions in the bottom of a 10x6-inch baking dish. Arrange egg slices over onions and sprinkle with Swiss cheese. Mix soup with milk and mustard. Heat and stir until smooth. Pour soup mixture over casserole, being sure some of sauce mixture seeps to the bottom. Place slices of bread on top, overlapping them a little. Bake at 350 degrees for 35 minutes or until hot. Broil a few minutes to toast bread, if needed. Yield: 6 servings.

To quickly rid your hands of the smell of garlic, press them onto a stainless steel surface, such as a sink or a mixing bowl or run a knife blade over your fingers under running water. The metal will counteract the strong odor.

Vidalia Chrysanthemums

4	large Vidalia onions	1	cup shredded sharp Cheddar cheese
½	cup margarine, melted	2	tablespoons chopped pimento
1	(10¾-ounce) can condensed cream of chicken soup		

Cut onions into 6 wedges without cutting all the way through the bottom. Place onions in a greased 2-quart casserole dish. Pour margarine over onions. Spread soup over onions and sprinkle with cheese and pimento. Bake at 350 degrees for 40 to 45 minutes or until bubbly. Yield: 4 to 6 servings.

Vidalia Onions au Gratin

5	cups chopped onions	¼	teaspoon black pepper
2	cups shredded sharp Cheddar cheese, divided	½	teaspoon salt
½	cup self-rising flour	6	tablespoons margarine, melted

Mix onions with 1 cup cheese, flour, pepper, salt and margarine. Pour mixture into a 2-quart casserole or baking dish. Sprinkle with remaining 1 cup cheese. Bake at 350 degrees for 30 minutes or until bubbly at the sides. Yield: 10 to 12 servings.

Vidalia Soufflé

6	ounces stale or day-old French or Italian bread, cut into chunks	1	cup shredded Swiss cheese
½	cup butter	1	pint light cream
3	large sweet onions, cut into thin slices	3	eggs, beaten
1	tablespoon fresh thyme, or ½ teaspoon dried		Salt and pepper to taste

Place bread chunks in a 1½-quart soufflé dish. Melt butter in a large skillet. Add onions and cook until slightly limp and translucent. Pour butter and onions over bread. Scatter thyme and cheese over top. Blend cream and eggs until light and frothy. Add salt and pepper. Pour cream mixture over cheese in soufflé dish. Press down to be sure all bread is thoroughly soaked. Baked at 350 degrees for 45 minutes or until a knife inserted in the center comes out clean. Serve with a salad. Yield: 6 to 8 servings.

Add chopped ham or cooked bacon pieces for a different flavor, or add more onions, if you like.

Warm Asparagus with Eggs Mimosa

2	eggs	3	tablespoons extra virgin olive oil
1	tablespoon champagne vinegar		Salt and freshly ground black pepper
1	shallot, minced	2¼	pounds large asparagus spears

Have a bowl of ice water ready. Bring a small saucepan three-fourths full of water to a boil. Reduce heat to medium and add eggs, being careful not to crack them. Simmer 10 minutes or until hard-cooked. Using a slotted spoon, transfer eggs to ice water and cool 30 minutes. In a small bowl, whisk together vinegar, shallot, olive oil and salt and pepper; set vinaigrette aside.

Remove eggs from water and peel. Press through a coarse-mesh sieve into a bowl; set aside. Cut or snap off the tough stem ends from the asparagus spears and discard. Using a vegetable peeler, peel the bottom 3 inches of each spear to remove the tough outer skin. (If the ends have been snapped off, this will not be necessary.) Bring a large skillet of salted water to a boil. Add asparagus spears and reduce to medium heat. Cook 4 to 6 minutes or until just tender. Using tongs, transfer asparagus to double-thickness paper towels to drain briefly. Arrange spears on a warmed platter or individual plates. Drizzle vinaigrette evenly over warm asparagus. Sprinkle eggs over the center of the asparagus and serve immediately. Yield: 6 servings.

Zucchini Flats

¾	cup grated Parmesan cheese, plus extra for sprinkling	¾	teaspoon salt
2	eggs	¼	teaspoon black pepper
2	tablespoons all-purpose flour, plus extra for dusting	2	cloves garlic, minced
2	tablespoons finely chopped fresh parsley	¼	cup milk
		2	large zucchini (about 7-inches long each)
		¼	cup salad oil

Combine ¾ cup cheese, eggs, 2 tablespoons flour, parsley, salt, pepper, garlic and milk in a shallow bowl. Beat with a wire whisk until smooth. Cover and refrigerate 15 minutes.

Cut zucchini in half crosswise (if you use smaller zucchini, you may not cut), then lengthwise into ¼-inch thick slices. Lightly dust each piece with flour. Heat oil in a wide skillet over medium heat. Dip each zucchini slice into cheese mixture using a fork, thickly coating both sides. Place in hot oil, a few pieces at a time. Cook, turning once, until golden brown on both sides. Drain briefly on paper towels. Transfer to a serving plate and keep warm until all are cooked. Sprinkle with extra cheese to taste. Yield: 4 to 6 servings.

Main Dishes & Meats

Beef Bourguignonne

½	pound salt pork, cut into ¼-inch dice	¼	cup cognac
	Olive oil	2	cups Beef Stock (page 120)
8	shallots, finely diced	2	sprigs fresh thyme
2	yellow onions, diced	3	cups dry red wine
2	carrots, diced	1	bay leaf
2	cloves garlic, minced	5	tablespoons unsalted butter
2	cups flour	18-24	pearl onions, peeled
	Salt and freshly ground black pepper	2	tablespoons sugar
	Ground nutmeg	1	pound fresh mushrooms, stems removed
3	pounds well-marbled stewing beef, cut into 2-inch cubes		Chopped fresh parsley

Cook salt pork in a skillet over medium heat for 8 to 10 minutes or until fat is rendered. Using a slotted spoon, transfer pork bits to paper towels to drain; set aside. Add enough olive oil to fat in skillet to measure ¼ cup. Add shallots, diced onion, carrot and garlic and sauté 10 minutes or until vegetables are slightly softened. Transfer vegetables to a large heavy pot using a slotted spoon, reserving fat in skillet.

Mix flour, salt and pepper and nutmeg on a plate. Coat beef cubes with flour mixture. Over high heat, add oil, as needed, to fat in skillet. Add beef, in batches, to hot oil and cook 15 minutes or until well browned. Use a slotted spoon to transfer beef to pot with vegetables. Add cognac and a little stock to skillet and deglaze over high heat, stirring to dislodge any brown bits. Add to beef along with all but ½ cup of remaining stock, thyme, wine and bay leaf. Bring to a boil. Reduce heat, cover and simmer on stove or bake at 325 degrees, for 3 hours or until beef is tender.

Warm 2 tablespoons butter in a sauté pan over medium heat. Add pearl onions an a single layer and sprinkle with sugar. Cook and stir 8 to 10 minutes or until tender and golden. Add only enough of remaining ½ cup stock to prevent scorching. Transfer to a bowl; set aside. Warm remaining 3 tablespoons butter in same sauté pan over medium heat. Add mushrooms and brown on both sides for a few minutes; set aside.

During last 30 minutes of cooking beef, add mushrooms and pearl onions to beef. Adjust seasonings. To serve, sprinkle with salt pork bits and parsley. Yield: 6 servings.

When making individual Beef Wellingtons, place tenderloin in freezer until "stiff", but not frozen. The meat will be easier to handle and cut.

Beef Stew

4	pounds stew beef		Worcestershire sauce (about 8 shakes)
	Salt and pepper to taste	2	(14-ounce) cans chicken or beef broth
2	tablespoons flour, plus extra for dredging	6	medium Idaho potatoes, cut into chunks
3	tablespoons olive or vegetable oil	1	(1-pound) bag carrots, cut into chunks
2-3	cloves garlic, crushed	2-3	onions, quartered

Lightly season beef with salt and pepper and dredge generously in flour. Heat oil in a large heavy pot. Add dredged beef and garlic and brown, adding Worcestershire sauce while browning. When brown, sprinkle about 2 tablespoons more flour into pot and allow to brown. Add 2 cans of broth plus one can full of water. Add potatoes, carrots and onions. Cover and simmer 2 hours. Yield: 6 to 8 servings.

Add half a head of cabbage to the stew after other vegetables are cooked and cook until cabbage is tender.

Add an 8-ounce can tomato sauce to the stew when the vegetables are added. Serve over rice (if desired) with cornbread.

Beef Stir-Fry with Rice

6	tablespoons vegetable oil	¾	cup dry sherry
3	pounds top round or sirloin steak, thinly sliced diagonally across the grain	¾	cup soy sauce
		3	tablespoons cornstarch
6	cups thinly sliced onion	1½	tablespoons five spice powder
3	cups thinly sliced mushrooms	12	cups torn well washed fresh spinach leaves, or one 10-ounce package frozen
3	cups diagonally sliced carrots		
3	cups canned beef broth	6	cups hot cooked long-grain rice

Heat oil in a skillet. Add beef and cook just until done; remove from skillet and keep warm. Add onion, mushrooms and carrots to skillet and cook, stirring quickly and frequently, until carrots are tender. In a bowl, combine broth, sherry, soy sauce, cornstarch and five spice powder and stir until cornstarch is dissolved. Pour mixture over vegetables and bring to a boil, stirring constantly. Reduce heat and stir in beef and spinach. Simmer, stirring occasionally, until heated. Serve over hot rice. Yield: 6 to 8 servings.

Beef Stock

2½	pounds meaty beef or veal bones		6	stems parsley
½	yellow onion, coarsely chopped			Pinch of dried or fresh thyme
1	small carrot, coarsely chopped		½	bay leaf

Place bones in a roasting pan, spacing them well apart. Bake on center rack of oven at 400 degrees for 1 to 2 hours or until bones are russet brown. Transfer bones to a stockpot or large saucepan. Add onion and carrot. Place parsley, thyme and bay leaf on a small square of cheesecloth and gather the corners together. Tie with a kitchen string to form a bouquet garni bag. Add bag to pot with bones. Add water to cover bones by 2 to 3 inches.

Place roasting pan with pan drippings on stovetop. Add about ½ cup water and bring to a boil. Deglaze pan, scraping up any browned bits stuck to the bottom, and add to pot with bones.

Bring pot to a boil. Immediately reduce heat to a simmer. Simmer, uncovered, for 4 to 5 hours or until stock has a good flavor and meat has fallen from the bones. Skim surface of stock occasionally while simmering to remove any froth that forms. Add water as needed to maintain the original liquid level.

Strain stock through a fine-mesh sieve into a bowl. Use immediately, or refrigerate and allow to cool completely. Remove and discard hardened fat and from the surface. To store, transfer stock to a container with a tight fitting lid and refrigerate up to 3 days, or freeze up to 2 months. Yield: About 6 cups.

Beef Tenderloin

1	beef tenderloin		Garlic
	Salt		Wine

Have a butcher tie beef tenderloin with twine, wrapping the smaller tail end into the loin. Rub beef with salt, garlic and wine. Place tenderloin in a large, shallow pan. Roast at 500 degrees for 30 minutes. Turn oven off and leave roast in oven 30 minutes longer. Do not open the oven door. Remove beef from oven and cover loosely with foil. The thick end will be medium to medium-rare, the smaller end will be well done. Slice and serve.

Bourbon Filets

2	cloves garlic, minced	8	ounces mushrooms, sliced
3	tablespoons butter	1	cup beef broth
4	medium filets mignon	1	cup half-and-half
½	cup bourbon		Salt and pepper to taste

Sauté garlic in butter in a skillet until softened. Add filets and cook, turning to brown on both sides, until filets are medium-rare to medium. Add bourbon. If desired, ignite bourbon and let flame subside. (This is not necessary, but is impressive.) Remove filets to a hot platter, reserving pan drippings. Place filets in a preheated 350 degree oven and turn oven off.

Add mushrooms to pan drippings and cook until tender. Add broth and bring to a boil. Add cream gradually, whisking to mix well. Simmer 10 to 15 minutes or until thickened, stirring constantly. Season with salt and pepper. Place filets on a serving dish. Pour mushroom sauce over filets and serve immediately. Yield: 4 servings.

Chili

4	tablespoons vegetable oil, divided	1	tablespoon ground oregano
3	pounds ground beef chuck	2	teaspoons ground coriander
3	onions, chopped	1½	cups lager-style beer
8	cloves garlic, minced	2½	cups beef broth
1	jalapeño pepper, seeded and minced	1	(28-ounce) can crushed tomatoes
½	cup chili powder	1	(15-ounce) can pinto beans
2	tablespoons ground cumin		Salt to taste

Heat 1 tablespoon oil in a stockpot over medium-high heat. Add half the beef and cook and stir 5 to 7 minutes or until browned. Transfer to a colander and repeat with 1 tablespoon oil and remaining beef, transferring to colander when browned. Add remaining 2 tablespoons oil to pot. Add onion and sauté 5 to 7 minutes or until softened. Stir in garlic, jalapeño, chili powder, cumin, oregano and coriander and cook 1 minute longer. Add beef, beer, broth and tomatoes. Simmer 40 to 50 minutes, stirring occasionally. Add beans and cook 5 to 7 minutes or until chili is thickened. Season with salt. Yield: 8 to 10 servings.

Corned Beef and Cabbage

6	pounds corned brisket of beef	3	onions, quartered
6	peppercorns, or packaged pickling spices (these often come packaged with the corned beef)	2	potatoes, quartered
		1	medium head green cabbage, quartered or cut into wedges
3	carrots, quartered		Melted butter (about 4 tablespoons)

Place beef in a large pot and cover with water. Add peppercorns and cover pot. Bring to a boil. Reduce heat and simmer 5 hours or until tender, skimming top of liquid occasionally. During last hour of cooking, add carrots, onions and potatoes and cover pot again. During final 15 minutes, add cabbage. Transfer meat and vegetables to a platter. Brush vegetables with melted butter. Yield: 6 servings with meat leftover for sandwiches.

French Market Meatloaf

1	(8-ounce) package Cajun sausage links, diced	½	teaspoon dried thyme
1	medium onion, diced	½	teaspoon dried oregano
1	small green bell pepper, diced	2	pounds ground beef
2	cloves garlic, minced	½	cup beef broth
2	teaspoons salt	½	cup tomato sauce
1	teaspoon black pepper	¼	cup soft bread crumbs
		1	egg, lightly beaten

Tomato Gravy

2	tablespoons butter	1	(8-ounce) can tomato sauce
2	tablespoons all-purpose flour	¼	teaspoon salt
⅓	cup beef broth	¼	teaspoon black pepper

Cook sausage, onion, bell pepper, garlic, salt, pepper, thyme and oregano in a large nonstick skillet over medium-high heat, stirring often, for 10 minutes or until vegetables are tender. Drain on paper towels and cool.

Stir together beef, broth, tomato sauce, bread crumbs and egg in a large bowl. Stir in sausage mixture. Shape meat mixture into an 11x4-inch loaf and place in a lightly greased, foil-lined 15x10-inch jelly roll pan. Bake at 375 degrees for 50 minutes or until no longer pink in the center. Drain meat loaf and let stand 10 minutes. Serve with tomato gravy.

To make gravy, melt butter in a small saucepan. Whisk in flour and cook 1 minute, whisking constantly. Gradually whisk in broth and tomato sauce. Reduce heat and simmer until thickened. Season with salt and pepper. Cook 5 minutes longer. Yield: 8 to 10 servings.

Country Fried Steak

2	pounds round steak		Oil for frying
	Salt and pepper to taste	1	(14½-ounce) can beef broth
2	tablespoons flour, plus extra for dredging		

Tenderize round steak by pounding, or use cubed steak. Season steak with salt and pepper and dredge in flour. Fry steak in a skillet in hot oil until browned; transfer to a plate. Pour all but about 2 tablespoons of oil from skillet. Add 2 tablespoons flour to hot oil and cook and stir until flour is brown. Add broth and cook until slightly thickened, adding a little water if needed. Return steak to skillet. Cover and simmer for a few minutes. Serve with rice or mashed potatoes. Yield: 6 servings.

Add a can of French onion soup to the skillet with the broth for gravy.

Add a can of condensed cream of mushroom soup to the skillet with the broth for gravy.

Fillet of Beef with Port Butter

3	cups beef broth	2	tablespoons minced shallots or onion
1	cup plus 2 tablespoons tawny port, divided	2	tablespoons red wine vinegar
		½	cup unsalted butter, melted
1	(6-pound) beef fillet, at room temperature, trimmed and tied	½	teaspoon salt
		¼	teaspoon coarsely ground black pepper

Combine broth and 1 cup port in a saucepan. Bring to a boil and cook until reduced to about ¾ cup; set aside.

Place beef in a 450 degree oven and immediately reduce heat to 375 degrees. Roast meat 35 to 40 minutes or to 125 degrees on a meat thermometer. If you like your meat cooked more, leave it in a little longer. Set aside. Drain all but 1 tablespoon fat from roasting pan. Add shallots, remaining 2 tablespoons port and vinegar. Bring to a boil, scraping sides and bottom of pan. Boil over medium heat for 1 minute. Add reduced port liquid and boil another 2 minutes. Remove from heat and mix in butter, 2 tablespoons at a time, with a wire whisk. Season with salt and pepper. Slice fillet and arrange on a serving platter. Spoon sauce over slices, serving remaining sauce on the side in a sauceboat. Yield: 12 to 14 servings.

Beef

Herb and Spice Roasted Beef Tenderloin with Red Wine Shallot Sauce

Tenderloin

2	tablespoons fresh rosemary leaves	1	teaspoon black pepper
2	tablespoons fresh thyme leaves	½	teaspoon ground nutmeg
4	large cloves garlic, peeled	¼	teaspoon ground cloves
2	bay leaves	2	tablespoons olive oil
1	large shallot, peeled and quartered	2	(2-pound) beef tenderloin pieces
1	tablespoon orange zest		(large end), trimmed
1	tablespoon coarse salt		

Sauce

2	tablespoons olive oil	1	teaspoon orange zest
2½	cups sliced shallots (about 12 ounces)		Pinch of ground nutmeg
2	tablespoons minced garlic		Pinch of ground cloves
1	teaspoon sugar	3¼	cups canned beef broth
1	tablespoon all-purpose flour	1½	cups dry red wine
1	tablespoon fresh thyme	¼	cup brandy
2	teaspoons minced fresh rosemary	4	tablespoons unsalted butter, softened
1	bay leaf		Salt and pepper to taste

To prepare tenderloin, grind rosemary, thyme, garlic, bay leaves, shallot, orange zest, salt, pepper, nutmeg and cloves in a food processor. With machine running, add oil and blend. Spread mixture evenly over all sides of tenderloins. Place tenderloins in a large glass baking dish. Cover with foil and refrigerate at least 6 hours.

Transfer beef to a rack in a large roasting pan. Roast at 400 degrees for 35 minutes or until a meat thermometer inserted in the center of beef registers 125 degrees for rare, or cook to desired degree of doneness. Remove from oven and cover with foil. Let stand 10 minutes. Transfer beef to a cutting board and slice.

Meanwhile, prepare sauce. Heat oil in a large saucepan over medium-low heat. Add shallots and garlic and sauté 10 minutes or until tender. Stir in sugar and sauté 15 minutes or until shallots are golden. Add flour, thyme, rosemary, bay leaf, orange zest, nutmeg and cloves and stir 1 minute. Pour in broth, wine and brandy. Boil sauce 20 minutes or until reduced to 1¾ cups. Discard bay leaf. Pour any accumulated juice from roasted beef into sauce. Bring sauce to a boil. Remove from heat and whisk in unsalted butter. Season with salt and pepper. Serve sauce with sliced beef. Yield: 8 servings.

Meatball Stroganoff

1	pound ground beef chuck	8	ounces shiitake mushrooms, thinly sliced
2	cloves garlic, minced	½	cup dry sherry
1	teaspoon salt	2	cups chicken broth
1	teaspoon freshly ground black pepper	2	tablespoons unsalted butter, softened
½	cup soft bread crumbs	2	tablespoons all-purpose flour
2	egg yolks	2	tablespoons chopped fresh dill
½	cup water	½	cup sour cream
1	medium onion, finely chopped, divided		Salt and freshly ground black pepper
2	tablespoons extra virgin olive oil		to taste

Combine beef, garlic, salt, pepper, bread crumbs, egg yolk, water and half the onion in a large bowl. Mix well and form into 1-inch diameter meatballs. Heat olive oil in a large nonstick skillet over medium-high heat. Add meatballs and cook, shaking pan and turning meatballs, for 5 minutes or until well browned. Do not crowd pan; work in batches if necessary. Transfer to paper towels to drain.

Pour off excess fat from the skillet, leaving 3 tablespoons in the pan. Add remaining onion and cook, stirring often, for 5 minutes or until softened. Add mushrooms and cook and stir 7 to 10 minutes until any liquid released from mushrooms evaporates. Pour in sherry and broth and bring to a boil.

Rub the butter with the flour in a small bowl until a smooth paste forms. Pinch off pea-size pieces and add little by little into boiling sauce, whisking constantly for 3 minutes. Add meatballs, dill and sour cream. Season with salt and pepper and cook over low heat until meatballs are just heated through. Serve hot. Yield: 4 to 6 servings.

Overnight Brisket

1	(4- to 5-pound) beef brisket	Salt and pepper to taste
	Fresh garlic cloves, halved	Barbeque sauce of choice

Rub brisket with garlic and sprinkle with salt and pepper. Wrap brisket in foil and place, fat-side up, in a roasting pan. Bake overnight at 225 degrees. The next morning, open the foil and scrape off the fat on top with a knife. Rewrap brisket in fresh foil and refrigerate until cool. Slice and place in a casserole dish. Pour barbeque sauce over meat. Cover dish with foil and heat in oven at 350 degrees until hot. Use for sandwiches or barbeque plates. This is very good and easy when you have a large crowd. Yield: 15 to 20 servings.

Rib Roast

1	(6½-pound, 3-rib) standing rib roast of beef, or with ribs removed
3-4	cloves garlic, crushed

Coarse salt and freshly ground black pepper
Horseradish Sauce (page 251) or Epicurean Sauce (page 250)

With the tip of a paring knife, make small slits all over the roast. Insert garlic into slits. Rub the roast with salt and pepper and place on a rack in a shallow pan. Roast at 450 degrees for 25 minutes. Reduce oven temperature to 350 degrees. Roast about 1¾ hours longer or until and instant-read thermometer registers 135 to 140 degrees for medium-rare. Let meat rest before carving. Serve with Horseradish Cream or Epicurean Cream. Yield: 8 servings.

Roast Peppered Rib Eye of Beef

1	(5- to 6-pound) boneless rib eye of beef
½	cup coarsely cracked black pepper
1	tablespoon ground cardamom seed
1	tablespoon tomato paste
½	teaspoon garlic powder

1	teaspoon paprika
1	cup soy sauce
¾	cup vinegar
1	cup water, or more

Trim fat from beef and discard. Combine pepper and cardamom. Rub mixture all over beef and press into meat with the heel of your hand. Place beef in a shallow baking dish. Mix together tomato paste, garlic powder and paprika. Gradually stir in soy sauce, then vinegar. Pour soy mixture over meat and refrigerate overnight, spooning marinade over meat occasionally. Remove meat from marinade and let stand at room temperature for 1 hour. Wrap beef in foil and place in a shallow pan. Roast at 300 degrees for 2 hours for medium-rare. Open foil and ladle drippings into a saucepan. Return to oven and brown roast, uncovered, at 350 degrees while making gravy.

To make gravy, strain drippings and skim off excess fat. To every cup of meat juices, add 1 cup water and bring to a boil. If desired, add a little marinade. Serve au jus, or thicken by stirring in a mixture of 1½ tablespoons cornstarch and ¼ cup cold water and cooking until thickened. Yield: 8 to 10 servings.

Roast Beef Tenderloin with Morel Cream Sauce

2	ounces dried morels (2 cups)	3	tablespoons unsalted butter, divided
1½	cups boiling water	1	tablespoon vegetable oil
1	(3¼-pound) beef tenderloin roast, trimmed and tied	2	large shallots, minced
	Salt and freshly ground black pepper	1¼	cups heavy cream

In a large heatproof bowl, soak morels in boiling water for 20 minutes or until softened. Drain, reserving the soaking liquid. Rub morels under running water to remove any grit. Coarsely chop large mushrooms.

Season beef roast with salt and pepper. Melt 2 tablespoons butter with oil in a very large ovenproof skillet. Brown roast in fat over medium-high heat on 3 sides, cooking about 4 minutes per side. Turn roast on fourth side and roast at 375 degrees for 35 minutes or until an instant-read thermometer inserted in the center of the roast registers 125 degrees for rare. Transfer roast to a carving board and cover loosely with foil. Let rest 10 minutes before carving into ½-inch thick slices.

Meanwhile, discard fat from skillet and set over high heat. Slowly pour in reserved mushroom liquid, stopping before allowing grit from bottom of liquid into skillet. Boil liquid, scraping up the browned bits from the bottom of the skillet, for 3 minutes or until reduced to ½ cup. Strain liquid through a fine sieve set over a bowl. Wipe out skillet and add remaining 1 tablespoon butter. Add shallots and cook over medium heat for 4 minutes or until softened. Stir in morels. Add cream and reduced mushroom liquid. Simmer over medium heat for 7 minutes or until sauce is thickened. Season with salt and pepper. Serve sliced roast with sauce.

Savory Oven Stew

½	cup flour	½	teaspoon dried thyme
2	teaspoons salt	1	teaspoon brown sugar
1½	pounds lean beef, cut into 2-inch cubes	2	cups beef broth
¼	cup cooking oil	¼	cup red wine
¾	cup sliced onion	4	carrots, cut into chunks
3	cloves garlic, mashed	4	potatoes, cut into chunks
½	cup chopped fresh parsley	12	mushrooms, sliced (optional)
1	bay leaf		

Sift flour with salt. Dredge beef in seasoned flour and brown beef in cooking oil a few pieces at a time. Add onion and cook about 2 minutes. Add garlic. Transfer mixture to a casserole dish and add parsley, bay leaf, thyme, brown sugar, broth and wine. Cover and bake at 325 degrees for about 3 hours. During final hour of cooking, add carrots, potatoes and mushrooms. Yield: 4 to 6 servings.

Skillet Beef Supreme

8	ounces lean beef (sirloin is good), cut into strips	4	teaspoons cornstarch
2	tablespoons vegetable oil	1	tablespoon soy sauce
1	onion, sliced	¾	cup water
1	green bell pepper, sliced	4	ounces fresh mushrooms, sliced
1	cup sliced celery		Salt to taste
1	cup sliced green beans		Pimento for garnish

Brown beef in vegetable oil in a skillet. Add onion and bell pepper and cook until softened. Add celery and green beans and cook 3 to 5 minutes. Combine cornstarch with soy sauce and water and add to skillet. Stir in mushrooms. Cook and stir 10 minutes or until liquid is clean and shiny and beans are tender. Season with salt and garnish with pimento. Serve with rice. Yield: 4 servings.

Steak with Shallots and Lyonnaise Potatoes

3	tablespoons extra virgin olive oil, divided	2	tablespoons red wine vinegar, divided
3	large Yukon Gold potatoes, peeled and sliced ¼-inch thick	4	(7-ounce, 1-inch thick) sirloin steaks
		2	tablespoons unsalted butter, divided
1	large sweet onion, halved lengthwise and very thinly sliced crosswise	4	very large shallots, very thinly sliced
	Salt and freshly ground black pepper	½	cup dry red wine
		2	tablespoons finely chopped parsley

Heat 2 tablespoons olive oil in a nonstick skillet. Add potatoes, slightly overlapping, and cook over medium-high heat, stirring, for 8 minutes or until golden. Add onion and season with salt and pepper. Cook and stir 5 minutes or until tender. Add ½ tablespoon vinegar and toss. Cover loosely and keep warm.

In a separate large skillet, heat remaining 1 tablespoon olive oil. Season steaks with salt and pepper. Cook steaks in hot oil over medium-high heat for 8 to 10 minutes (for medium-rare) or until crusty on both sides. Transfer steaks to a serving platter and keep warm.

Add 1 tablespoon butter to skillet used for cooking beef. Add shallots and cook over medium heat for 5 minutes or until softened. Add remaining 1½ tablespoons vinegar and cook about 30 seconds or until evaporated. Add wine and cook 2 minutes or until reduced by two-thirds. Remove from heat and swirl in remaining 1 tablespoon butter. Add parsley and any accumulated juices from serving platter. Season with salt and pepper and spoon over steaks. Serve steaks immediately with potatoes. Yield: 4 servings.

Shepherd's Pie

White Sauce

1	tablespoon butter	½	cup milk
1	tablespoon flour		

Meat Sauce

1½   pounds ground beef round
1   small onion, chopped
1   (10¾-ounce) can cream of chicken
     soup
½   cup White Sauce

½   tablespoon dried parsley
½   tablespoon chopped chives
    Salt and pepper to taste
    Seasoned salt to taste

Mashed Potatoes

2   large baking potatoes
4   tablespoons butter
½   cup sour cream

Splash of milk
Salt and pepper to taste

Topping

1   cup shredded Cheddar cheese
    Paprika

To make white sauce, melt butter in a heavy saucepan. As soon as butter starts to bubble, blend in flour. Stir in milk and whisk briskly until sauce thickens; set aside.

For meat sauce, brown beef in a Dutch oven. Add onion and cook until softened; drain. Add soup, reserved white sauce, parsley and chives. Season with salt and pepper and seasoned salt. Mix well and simmer 20 minutes.

To prepare potatoes, peel and cook in boiling water for 20 minutes. Drain potatoes and place in a bowl. Whip potatoes with an electric mixer. Add butter, sour cream and milk. Season with salt and pepper and mix well.

Line bottom of a 1-quart baking dish with half the meat sauce. Add ½ cup cheese and half the potatoes. Repeat meat sauce and potatoes layers. Sprinkle remaining ½ cup cheese and paprika on top. Bake at 350 degrees for 30 minutes. Yield: 4 to 6 servings.

Spaghetti Sauce

1	medium onion, chopped	1	tablespoon brown sugar
1	pound ground beef or Italian sausage	4	cloves garlic, minced
2	(14-ounce) cans diced tomatoes, undrained	1-2	teaspoons dried basil
1	(8-ounce) can tomato sauce	1-2	teaspoons dried oregano
1	(6-ounce) can tomato paste	1	teaspoon salt
1	bay leaf	1	teaspoon dried thyme

Cook onion and meat in a skillet over medium heat until meat is no longer pink. Drain and transfer to a crockpot. Add tomatoes, tomato sauce, tomato paste, bay leaf, sugar, garlic, basil, oregano, salt and thyme. Cover and cook on low heat for 7 to 8 hours. Discard bay leaf. Serve over hot cooked spaghetti.

Swiss Steak with Vegetables

3½	pounds round steak, ¼-inch thick	1½	(10¾-ounce) cans condensed tomato soup
½	cup flour	1	soup can water
1½	teaspoons salt	8	whole new potatoes, or more, unpeeled
½	teaspoon black pepper		
¼	cup salad oil	6	carrots, quartered
2	cups sliced onion	1	(10-ounce) package frozen peas

Cut steak into 8 pieces and pound with the edge of a meat mallet. Mix flour with salt and pepper. Dredge steak in seasoned flour. Heat oil in a Dutch oven. Brown steak in hot oil on both sides. Add onion and cook until starting to brown. Add soup and water and cover pot. Simmer 30 minutes or until meat is tender. Add potatoes and carrots and simmer, covered, for about 25 minutes. Taste and adjust seasonings as needed. Break block of peas in half. Place half on each side of pot, pushing peas slightly down into hot juices. Cover and cook 10 minutes longer or until all are tender. Yield: 8 servings.

Stuffed Flank Steak

2-2½	pounds flank steak	2	bay leaves
	Stuffing (recipe below)	1	teaspoon chopped thyme leaves
1	tablespoon oil	1	cup beef broth or water
1	tablespoon butter	1	cup dry red wine
¾	cup diced carrot	2	tablespoons arrowroot or cornstarch
¾	cup finely chopped onion	¼	cup water
1	tomato, coarsely chopped		Salt and pepper to taste

Stuffing

5	slices bread, cut into ¼-inch cubes (2½ cups)	½	cup finely chopped celery
		2	tablespoons finely chopped fresh parsley
¼	cup vegetable oil		
3	tablespoons unsalted butter	2	cloves garlic, minced
1	pound ground round	1½	teaspoons salt
2	eggs	½	teaspoon black pepper
¾	cup finely chopped onion	¼	teaspoon dried thyme, crumbled

Take the steak and, keeping it flat on a cutting board with one hand, cut into steak lengthwise with a small sharp paring knife to make a pocket for the stuffing. Lift the upper "lip" and cut deeper into the steak, keeping your blade horizontal. Be careful not to come out at either end or the opposite side, thus losing the "pocket" effect. If you do cut through the steak by accident, slice a thin piece of an end where it won't affect the pocket and use as a patch to plug the hole; the stuffing will keep it in place. Set steak aside while preparing stuffing.

To make stuffing, brown bread cubes in vegetable oil and butter in a large skillet; turn into a large bowl. Add ground round, eggs, onion, celery, parsley, garlic, salt, pepper and thyme to bread and mix lightly until just combined. Push stuffing into the center of prepared steak, making sure pocket is filled to the corners. Bring lower "lip" of steak against the stuffing, then bring upper "lip" down on top to form a nice loaf. Tie securely with string every 2 inches, then bring string around lengthwise to secure ends.

Heat oil and butter in a Dutch oven. Brown rolled steak in fat slowly and evenly on all sides. Add carrot, onion, tomato, bay leaves and thyme to pot. Cook, uncovered, for 5 minutes, stirring occasionally. Add broth and wine and bring to a boil. Reduce heat and cover. Cook over medium heat, or bake in 350 degree oven, for 1½ hours, turning steak occasionally. Lift meat out of Dutch oven onto a serving platter. Remove strings and keep warm while making sauce. Skim off fat from surface of cooking liquid. Mix arrowroot with water and stir into cooking liquid. Bring to a boil; cook and stir until sauce thickens. Season with salt and pepper. Yield: 4 to 6 servings.

Baked Country Ham

1	(14-pound) bone-in fully cooked ham	1	teaspoon peppercorns
1	cup sliced carrot	¾	(750 ml) bottle vermouth or port wine
1	cup sliced onion		Chicken broth
1	cup sliced celery		

Scrub ham with a vegetable brush under warm water to clean. Remove the skin and score the fat into diamond shapes. Place the ham on a rack in a roasting pan. Scatter carrot, onion, celery and peppercorns around ham. Pour wine over the ham and vegetables. Add enough broth to make about 1 inch of liquid in the bottom of the pan. Bake at 400 degrees on lower shelf of the oven for 20 minutes. Reduce temperature to 325 degrees and cook until ham reaches 140 degrees on a meat thermometer. Transfer ham to a cutting board. Strain pan juices, using the back of a spoon to press extra juice from the vegetables. Slice and serve the ham with pan juices on the side. Yield: 14 to 16 servings.

Barbeque Ribs

1	rack baby back ribs	3	tablespoons Worcestershire sauce
1	cup ketchup	1	teaspoon liquid smoke
¼	cup cider vinegar	½	teaspoon salt
3	tablespoons dark brown sugar		

Cook ribs in boiling water for 1 hour. Combine ketchup, vinegar, sugar, Worcestershire sauce, liquid smoke and salt in a saucepan and boil 30 minutes. Drain ribs and place in a pan or ovenproof dish. Pour sauce over ribs and broil 6 to 7 minutes. Yield: 2 servings.

Back Bones and Rice

2-3	pounds fresh pork back bones	1¾	cups dry rice
1	large onion, quartered		Salt and pepper to taste
1	(14-ounce) can chicken broth, if needed		

Place back bones and onion in a large pot with enough water to cover. Boil 30 to 40 minutes or until tender. Remove bones to a bowl. When cool enough to handle, remove meat and discard bones. Strain liquid from pot and measure. Add enough chicken broth to equal 4 cups liquid. Pour liquid back into pot and bring to a boil. Add pork meat, rice and salt and pepper. Cover and cook until rice is tender and liquid is absorbed. Yield: 6 to 8 servings.

Baked Stuffed Ham

1 (10- to 12-pound) cooked ham, deboned with joint end removed	½ cup coarse grain mustard
Savory Stuffing (recipe below)	¼ cup medium dry white wine
	½ cup dark brown sugar

Have the butcher debone the ham. Cut the rind from the ham and remove excess fat. Score remaining fat. Spoon stuffing lightly into ham, being careful not to pack stuffing in. Truss ham and place in oven. Bake at 350 degrees for 20 minutes or until fat begins to brown. Meanwhile, combine mustard, wine and sugar to make a paste. Smear paste over browned ham and bake 25 minutes longer, basting several times with pan juices. Yield: 12 servings.

Savory Stuffing

4 tablespoons butter	Generous ¼ cup coarsely chopped walnuts
1 cup coarsely chopped onion	
½ cup chopped green bell pepper	2 cups coarse fresh bread crumbs, toasted
4 cups coarsely chopped mushrooms	
½ teaspoon dried sage	½ teaspoon freshly ground black pepper
½ teaspoon dried thyme	½ teaspoon salt
½ cup chopped fresh parsley	3-4 tablespoons medium-dry white wine

Melt butter in a large skillet. Add onion and bell pepper and sauté about 5 minutes. Add mushrooms and sauté over low heat 15 minutes longer. Stir in sage, thyme, parsley, walnuts, bread crumbs, black pepper and salt. Remove from heat and toss. Mix in wine and toss again.

If any stuffing is left over, place in a greased shallow baking dish and bake, covered, along with the ham. Uncover for final 15 minutes, allowing time to lightly brown. Yield: About 4 cups stuffing.

Crockpot Pork Roast

1 large onion, sliced	1 tablespoon ketchup
2½ pounds boneless pork loin	½ teaspoon black pepper
1 cup hot water	½ teaspoon salt
¼ cup sugar	¼ teaspoon garlic powder
3 tablespoons red wine vinegar	Dash of hot pepper sauce (optional)
2 tablespoons soy sauce	

Place onion in the bottom of a crockpot. Place pork on top of onion. In a medium bowl, combine hot water, sugar, vinegar, soy sauce, ketchup, pepper, salt, garlic powder and hot sauce. Pour mixture over pork. Cook on low for 6 to 7 hours or until internal pork temperature reaches 160 to 170 degrees on a meat thermometer. Yield: 4 to 6 servings.

Crown Roast of Fresh Pork with Wild Rice, Fennel and Sausage Stuffing

2	teaspoons salt	Vegetable oil for rubbing on pork
1	teaspoon freshly ground black pepper	Wild Rice, Fennel and Sausage Stuffing
1½	teaspoons dried thyme, crumbled	(recipe below)
1½	teaspoons dried sage, crumbled	Leafy fennel tops or dill sprigs for
1	(16-rib) crown roast of fresh pork	garnish
	(about 8 pounds)	

Combine salt, pepper, thyme and sage in a small bowl. Rub seasoning mixture all over pork, cover and refrigerate overnight. Pat pork dry with paper towels and rub it all over with oil. In the middle of a lightly oiled shallow roasting pan, arrange pork on an oiled round of heavy-duty foil slightly larger than the bottom of the pork. Mound the stuffing in the center of the crown. Cover the stuffing with another oiled round of foil. Roast at 450 degrees for 20 minutes. Reduce heat to 325 degrees and roast 2 hours or until a meat thermometer registers 170 degrees. Transfer pork with the foil underneath to a platter and let stand 15 minutes. Discard foil from the top of stuffing and decorate the rib tips with metallic papillotes, if desired. Yield: 8 to 12 servings with plenty of leftovers.

Wild Rice, Fennel and Sausage Stuffing

1½	cups dry wild rice, rinsed well and	2	cups chopped onion
	drained	4	tablespoons unsalted butter
2	teaspoons fennel seeds	2	small fennel bulbs, finely chopped
3	cups chicken broth		(about 2 cups)
1½	cups water		Salt and pepper to taste
1	pound sweet Italian sausage, casings		
	discarded, or ground pork sausage		

Combine rice, fennel seeds, broth and water in a saucepan and bring to a boil. Reduce heat and simmer, partially covered, for 45 to 55 minutes or until rice is tender. Drain rice in a sieve and transfer to a bowl.

In a heavy skillet over medium heat, cook sausage, stirring and breaking up lumps, until no longer pink. Pour off the fat and add sausage to bowl with rice. Add onion and butter to skillet and cook over medium-low heat, stirring occasionally, until softened. Add chopped fennel, cover and cook, stirring occasionally, for 5 to 7 minutes or until fennel is crisp-tender. Add onion and fennel mixture to rice. Season with salt and pepper and toss stuffing well. The stuffing may be made 2 days in advance. Cool, cover and refrigerate; bring to room temperature before using. You will have more stuffing than needed for the crown roast. Place extra in an ovenproof dish, cover with foil and bake at 350 degrees for 25 minutes. Yield: About 12 cups stuffing.

Family Reunion Ham Loaf

3	pounds ground smoked ham	1	(10¾-ounce) can condensed tomato
3	pounds ground pork		soup
3	eggs	1	cup cracker crumbs
1	(12-ounce) can evaporated milk		

Combine all ingredients and mix thoroughly. Pack into two 5x9-inch loaf pans. Bake at 350 degrees for 2 hours. Serve hot or cold with Epicurean Sauce (recipe follows). Yield: 25 to 30 servings.

Epicurian Sauce

1	pint heavy cream	4	teaspoons prepared mustard
¼	cup mayonnaise	2	teaspoons salt
½	cup prepared horseradish	½	cup chopped fresh parsley

Whip cream until stiff. Fold in mayonnaise, horseradish, mustard, salt and parsley until well blended. Serve chilled.

Fresh Pork Ham Roast

Order a boned 7- to 8-pound fresh pork ham from your butcher. If you prefer, you may cook this with the bone in, but it is easier with the bone removed.

Salt and Spice Marinade

¼	cup salt	¼	teaspoon paprika
1	teaspoon freshly ground black pepper	¼	teaspoon ground sage
¼	teaspoon ground allspice	¼	teaspoon dried thyme
1	whole bay leaf		

Mix marinade in a bowl. Rub over inside and outside of pork. Place meat in a large zip-lock bag and refrigerate overnight.

Remove all the skin and most of the fat from the ham. Lightly score remaining fat. Tie ham with twine and place in a roasting pan. Bake at 425 degrees on center rack of oven for 15 minutes. Reduce temperature to 350 degrees. Roast 3½ hours or until a meat thermometer reaches 160 degrees. Remove from oven and discard twine.

Pan may be deglazed with ½ cup port wine mixed with ½ cup water. Yield: 12 servings.

Medallions of Pork with Red Wine Sauce

8	(3-ounce) slices boneless loin of pork, trimmed of excess fat	1	whole clove
	Salt and freshly ground black pepper to taste	½	cup dry red wine
		1	teaspoon balsamic vinegar
1	tablespoon grated fresh ginger	2	teaspoons honey
2	sprigs fresh thyme, or ½ teaspoon dried	1	tablespoon olive oil
		2	tablespoons finely chopped shallots
1	bay leaf	2	tablespoons butter

Place pork slices on a flat surface and pound lightly with a mallet or meat pounder. Sprinkle with salt and pepper and place in a dish. Combine ginger, thyme, bay leaf, clove, wine, vinegar and honey in a bowl and blend well. Pour mixture over pork and marinate 10 minutes. Drain pork and pat dry, reserving marinade.

Heat oil in a nonstick skillet large enough to hold pork slices in a single layer. When oil is hot, add pork and cook over medium-high heat for 5 minutes or until browned. Turn slices and cook about 5 minutes. Reduce heat and cook about 2 minutes longer. Transfer pork medallions to a warm serving platter and keep warm.

In the same skillet, cook and stir shallots until wilted. Add reserved marinade and cook, stirring and scraping the bottom. Add any pork juices that have accumulated on the platter. Scrape the bottom with a wooden spatula and cook until the marinade reduces to three-fourths of its original volume. Swirl in butter and pour sauce over pork medallions. Remove bay leaf, thyme sprig and clove before serving. Yield: 4 servings.

Pork Chop and Rice Casserole

4	(¾-inch thick) pork loin chops	1	teaspoon salt
	Seasoned salt		Dash of black pepper
½	cup dry regular or quick-cooking white rice	4	medium onions, sliced
		2	large carrots, cut on diagonal into 1-inch slices
1	(12-ounce) can beef gravy (1¼ cups)		
¼	cup water		

Trim some of fat from chops and heat fat in a skillet. Sprinkle chops well with seasoned salt. Brown chops well on both sides in hot skillet; transfer to a 2-quart casserole dish. Add rice to skillet drippings and cook, stirring, until browned. Stir in gravy, water, salt and pepper. Arrange onions and carrots on top of chops. Pour gravy mixture over vegetables and cover dish. Bake at 350 degrees for 1 hour or until chops and vegetables are tender. Yield: 4 servings.

Pork St. Tammany

1 (6-ounce) package long-grain and wild rice mix	1 tablespoon chopped fresh parsley
½ cup boiling water	⅛ teaspoon salt
⅓ cup chopped dried apricots	⅛ teaspoon black pepper
2 green onions, finely chopped	Dash of cayenne pepper
½ cup chopped fresh mushrooms	Dash of garlic powder
¼ cup chopped green bell pepper	5-6 pounds pork loin
2 tablespoons butter	4 slices bacon
3 tablespoons chopped pecans	Canned apricot halves and fresh parsley sprigs for garnish

Cook rice according to package directions; set aside. Pour boiling water over dried apricots and let stand 20 minutes to soften; drain. Sauté onions, mushrooms and bell pepper in butter until tender. Add rice, drained apricots, pecans, parsley, salt, pepper, cayenne and garlic powder and stir until combined. Cut a lengthwise slit on top of the pork being careful not to cut through the bottom and sides. Spoon rice stuffing into the slit. Tie slit together securely with string at 1-inch intervals and place on a rack in a roasting pan. Top with bacon slices and tent foil over pan. Bake at 325 degrees for 1½ to 2 hours or until a meat thermometer registers 170 degrees. Remove foil during last 30 to 40 minutes of baking. Remove from oven and let stand 5 minutes. Remove string and slice. Garnish with apricot halves and parsley sprigs. Yield: 10 to 12 servings.

Pork Scaloppine

1 tablespoon unsalted butter	3 teaspoons kosher salt, divided
1 tablespoon olive oil	1 cup chicken broth
2 (1-pound) pork loins, each cut into 5 cutlets	1 teaspoon lemon juice
¼ teaspoon freshly ground black pepper	1 teaspoon lemon zest

Heat butter and oil in a large nonstick skillet over medium heat. Pound cutlets to ⅛-inch thick and season with pepper and 2 teaspoons salt. Add cutlets to skillet and cook 1 minute per side or until lightly browned, tender and cooked through. Remove from skillet. Set aside 4 cutlets on a platter and keep warm; freeze 6 cutlets for another day.

Add broth to skillet and simmer, scraping up the brown bits with a wooden spoon, for 5 minutes or until slightly thickened. Remove from heat and stir in lemon juice and remaining 1 teaspoon salt. Drizzle skillet juices over meat on platter and sprinkle with zest. Yield: 4 servings.

Roast Pork Loin Florentine

1	(3- to 4-pound) center cut pork loin, bones removed	1	tablespoon vinegar
1½	tablespoons salt	1	pound fresh spinach, washed and stems trimmed
1	teaspoon freshly ground black pepper	1	medium onion, coarsely chopped
2	teaspoons dried oregano or tarragon, crushed (optional)	2	cloves garlic, coarsely chopped
1	quart water, with ⅓ teaspoon salt added	1	stalk celery, coarsely chopped
		1	small carrot, coarsely chopped
		2-4	cups light broth or water

Ask butcher to cut pork loin along its length, as you would unroll a jelly roll, so it turns out into a large flat piece about ½-inch thick. Sprinkle inside of pork with some of salt, pepper and oregano.

Bring 1 quart salted water to a boil. Add vinegar and spinach and bring to a vigorous boil. Boil and stir 1 minute. Drain and immediately place spinach in cold water to cool. Remove and pat dry with paper towels. Cover almost entire inside surface of pork with spinach. Roll pork back to its original shape and tie with twine. Rub outside surface with remaining salt, pepper and oregano. Scatter onion, garlic, celery and carrot in a roasting pan. Add broth, using just enough to almost cover vegetables. Place pork on vegetables and cover pan. Roast at 350 degrees, basting every 15 to 20 minutes, for 2 hours or until a meat thermometer inserted in thickest part of pork registers 170 degrees. Remove roast from oven and place on a serving platter. Let stand in a warm place for at least 30 minutes.

Meanwhile, strain pan liquid from vegetables, pressing juice from vegetables and discarding vegetables. Skim fat from top of liquid. Boil liquid rapidly until reduced by one-half to a light gravy.

To serve, carve roast into ½-inch thick slices. Arrange slices on a platter and serve with gravy in a sauceboat on the side. Yield: 8 servings.

If you're cooking on an outdoor grill and need to bake part of your meal, put the food in an aluminum pan covered with foil and place it on the side of the grill where the fewest coals are burning.

Pork Tenderloin in Wine Sauce

1	(1-pound) whole pork tenderloin	¼	cup water
	Freshly ground black pepper	¼	cup red wine
1	tablespoon butter	⅛	teaspoon dried basil, crushed
1	tablespoon cooking oil		

Sauce

1	tablespoon cornstarch	3	tablespoons water
⅓	cup dry red wine		

Rub pork with pepper. Melt butter in a large skillet with cooking oil. Add tenderloin and quickly brown on all sides. Remove from heat and carefully add water, wine and basil. Cover and cook over low heat for 30 to 45 minutes or until pork is done. Remove tenderloin and keep warm. Drain pan drippings, reserving ⅓ cup.

For sauce, combine cornstarch with dry wine and water and mix with a wire whisk until cornstarch is dissolved. Stir in reserved pan drippings. Cook over medium heat, stirring constantly, until thickened and bubbly. Slice tenderloin and serve with sauce. Yield: 4 servings.

Baked Chicken or Cornish Hens

2	broiler chickens or 4 Cornish hens	½	cup seedless grapes, halved
1	(6-ounce) package long-grain and wild rice, prepared according to package directions	½	cup slivered almonds, toasted
		½	teaspoon salt
		½	teaspoon dried thyme
1	small onion, chopped	4	tablespoons butter, melted
1	stalk celery, chopped		

Wash and pat dry hens. Combine prepared rice, onion, celery, grapes, almonds, salt and thyme and mix thoroughly. Lightly fill neck and body cavities with rice stuffing; skewer opening shut. Place hens in a large shallow roasting pan and brush with butter. Roast at 400 degrees for 1 hour or until well browned and drumsticks twist easily out of thigh joint. Baste several times with butter while roasting. Yield: 4 servings.

Breasts of Chicken Florentine

4 large boneless chicken breast halves	Salt and freshly ground black pepper to taste
1 pound fresh spinach, or 1 (10-ounce) package frozen	½ cup finely chopped Gruyère cheese
1 tablespoon butter	Mushroom Sauce (recipe below)
¾ cup finely chopped onion	2 tablespoons chopped fresh basil
⅛ teaspoon freshly grated nutmeg	

With breast halves skin-side down, make slight incisions, left and right, starting at the center; do not cut through. Open up cut portions and flatten. Pound lightly with a smooth mallet without breaking the skin.

If using fresh spinach, pick over to remove tough stems or blemished leaves. Rinse thoroughly and drain well.

Heat butter in a skillet. Add onion and sauté until wilted. Add spinach and cook until wilted. Continue to cook and stir until liquid evaporates. Add nutmeg and salt and pepper. Transfer to plate to cool.

Divide spinach mixture evenly among center of each breast half. Spoon equal amounts of chopped cheese in center of each mound of spinach. Fold over edges of chicken to enclose spinach. Arrange pieces, skin-side up, in the rack of a steamer and smooth out the skin. Partially fill steamer with water. Cover and bring to a boil. Place rack over boiling water and cover loosely. Steam 10 minutes. Or, bake at 350 degrees for 20 minutes. Transfer chicken to a warm serving dish and spoon mushroom sauce over the top. Sprinkle with fresh basil. Yield: 4 servings.

Mushroom Sauce

1 tablespoon butter	Salt and freshly ground black pepper to taste
2 tablespoons finely chopped shallots	¼ cup dry white wine
8 ounces mushrooms, thinly sliced	1 cup chicken broth
Juice of ⅓ lemon	1 cup heavy cream

Heat butter in a saucepan. Add shallots and cook briefly until wilted. Add mushrooms and lemon juice and cook, stirring, until mushrooms release liquid. Season with salt and pepper and cook until most of liquid has evaporated. Add wine and broth and cook over high heat until most of liquid is evaporated. Add cream and cook 5 minutes. Yield: 1¾ cups sauce.

Chicken and Dumplings

1	(2- to 3-pound) fryer, cut into parts, or 1 hen (the hen will take longer to cook tender, but makes better chicken and dumplings)	1	tablespoon salt
		½	teaspoon black pepper
		¼	teaspoon garlic powder
3	quarts water	4	tablespoons butter (only if using a fryer)
1	carrot	1	(14-ounce) can chicken broth (only if using a fryer)
1	onion		Dumplings (recipes below)
2	stalks celery or celery tops		

Combine chicken, water, carrot, onion, celery, salt and pepper in a large kettle. Cover and boil 50 minutes or until chicken is tender (1½ to 2 hours for a hen). Remove chicken and strain broth, discarding vegetables. Debone chicken, discarding skin and bones, and chop meat into bite-size pieces; set aside.

Return broth to kettle and bring to a boil. Add garlic powder. Add butter and canned chicken broth if using a fryer chicken. Season with extra salt and pepper if needed. Lower heat to maintain a gentle boil. Gradually add dumplings. Simmer, covered, for 15 minutes. Stir in reserved chicken. Cover and let stand 5 minutes. Ladle into bowls to serve. Yield: 4 to 6 servings.

After chicken has been cooked and the broth is back on the stove, you may add 1½ cups rice instead of the dumplings and cook until rice is tender, adding chicken back to pot just before the rice is done.

Drop Dumplings

½	cup shortening	1⅓	cups milk
3	cups self-rising flour		

Cut shortening into flour until crumbly. Stir in just enough milk to make a soft dough. Drop by rounded teaspoonfuls into boiling broth, spacing as evenly as possible.

Rolled Dumplings

½	cup shortening	1	cup buttermilk
4	cups self-rising flour, divided		

Cut shortening into 3 cups flour until crumbly. Stir in buttermilk until a stiff dough forms, gradually adding remaining flour, if needed. Turn dough onto a well-floured surface and knead until smooth. Divide dough into thirds. Roll each third on a floured surface until very thin. Cut into 1x3-inch strips. Drop strips, a few at a time, into boiling broth. Stir gently once or twice. (Broth needs to boil slightly harder for these dumplings.)

For a chewier dumpling, use plain flour with ½ teaspoon salt.

Chicken Breasts in Wine

1	cup dry rice	1	soup can water
6	chicken breasts	1	cup sherry
1	(10¾-ounce) can condensed cream of mushroom soup	1	envelope onion soup mix
			Slivered almonds

Spread dry rice evenly over the bottom of a greased 9x13-inch pan. Arrange chicken on top of rice. Mix mushroom soup and water and pour over chicken. Drizzle sherry over the top and sprinkle with soup mix and almonds. Cover pan with foil. Bake at 350 degrees for 1½ hours. Yield: 4 to 6 servings.

Chicken Breasts with Artichokes

3	tablespoons butter, divided	1	(9-ounce) package frozen artichoke hearts, thawed and cut into halves
8	boneless, skinless chicken breast halves	¾	cup chicken broth
½	cup dry white wine	½	teaspoon dried thyme
1	large sweet onion, cut in half and then into ½-inch thick slices		Salt and freshly ground pepper to taste
		1	lemon, thinly sliced

Melt 2 tablespoons butter in a 4-quart heavy pot over medium heat. Working in batches if necessary, add chicken breasts and brown on all sides, cooking 8 to 10 minutes or until a rich golden color. Using a slotted spoon, transfer chicken to a dish. Pour wine into pot and deglaze over medium-high heat, stirring with a large spoon to dislodge any browned bits from the bottom. Pour liquid over chicken and wipe pot clean.

In same pot over medium heat, melt remaining 1 tablespoon butter. Add onion and sauté 5 minutes or until translucent. Return chicken and juices to the pot and add artichokes, broth and thyme. Stir well and bring to a simmer over medium-low heat. Cover and gently simmer 20 to 25 minutes or until the chicken is tender and cooked through. To test for doneness, cut into chicken with a sharp knife; the meat should be opaque throughout. Season with salt and pepper. Spoon into warmed shallow bowls and garnish with lemon slices. Yield: 6 servings.

Chicken Piccata

8	boneless, skinless chicken breast halves	⅓	cup olive oil
2	tablespoons lemon juice	2	tablespoons butter
1	cup plus 2 tablespoons water, divided	½	cup dry white wine
1½	teaspoons salt, divided	1	chicken bouillon cube
¼	teaspoon black pepper	2	lemons
⅓	cup flour		Parsley sprigs for garnish

Marinate chicken in lemon juice and 2 tablespoons water for 30 minutes. Place chicken between layers of wax paper and pound with a meat mallet to ⅛-inch thickness. Sprinkle with 1 teaspoon salt and pepper, then dredge in flour. Heat oil and butter in a 12-inch skillet over medium heat. Add chicken breasts to skillet and sauté, in batches, until lightly browned on both sides, adding more oil if needed. Remove chicken from skillet and reduce heat to low. Stir remaining 1 cup water, remaining ½ teaspoon salt, wine and bouillon cube into drippings in skillet. Deglaze and stir to loosen browned bits. Return chicken to skillet. Cover and simmer 15 minutes or until tender. Remove chicken to a warm platter. Squeeze juice of 1 lemon into liquid in skillet. Stir and heat to a boil. Pour liquid over chicken. Thinly slice remaining lemon and arrange with parsley over chicken. Serve over cooked fettuccine. Yield: 8 servings.

Chicken Wild Rice

1	cup dry wild rice	3	cups diced cooked chicken
½	cup chopped onion	¾	cup diced pimento
½	cup butter	2	tablespoons snipped fresh parsley
¼	cup flour	1½	teaspoons salt
1	(6-ounce) can sliced mushrooms	¼	teaspoon black pepper
1	cup chicken broth	½	cup blanched slivered almonds
1½	cups light cream		

Prepare rice according to package directions. Cook onion in butter until just tender but not brown. Remove from heat and stir in flour. Drain mushrooms, reserving liquid. Combine reserved liquid with chicken broth and gradually stir into flour mixture. Add cream. Cook and stir until mixture thickens. Stir in cooked rice, mushrooms, chicken, pimento, parsley, salt and pepper. Transfer mixture to a 2-quart casserole dish and sprinkle with almonds. Bake at 350 degrees for 25 to 30 minutes. Yield: 6 servings.

Chicken Pie with Crust

Chicken

1	hen		Carrots
	Celery		Onions

Filling

6	tablespoons butter	1	large onion, cubed
¼	cup flour		Coarsely chopped cooked chicken
4-6	cups broth (from cooking chicken)		(from cooking chicken)
2	baking potatoes, peeled and cubed		Salt and pepper to taste
2	large or 3 small carrots, sliced		

Crust

2	cups flour	¾	cup milk
4	teaspoons baking powder	4	tablespoons butter, melted
¼	teaspoon salt	1	egg

Combine hen, celery, carrots and onions in a large pot or pressure cooker. Add enough water to cover. Cook about 1½ hours on stove top, or 30 minutes in a pressure cooker. Remove chicken from broth. When cool enough to handle, remove chicken meat from bones, discarding bones and skin. Coarsely chop meat and strain broth; reserve both for filling.

To prepare filling, melt butter in a large 2-inch deep pan. Blend in flour. Cook and stir until bubbly. Mix in broth and bring to a boil. Add potatoes, carrots and onion and cook 20 minutes. Add chicken. Season with salt and pepper. Leave on low heat to stay hot.

For crust, mix flour, baking powder and salt. Blend in milk, butter and egg.

To assemble, spoon filling into a large baking dish. Roll out crust and place on top of filling. Cut slits into crust for vents. Bake at 400 degrees until crust is brown. Yield: 6 to 8 servings.

Unbaked refrigerated pie crust may be used for the top.

Easy Chicken and Rice

5	boneless, skinless chicken breasts, cooked and shredded	1	cup chopped onion
1	(6-ounce) box wild rice mix, cooked according to directions on package	½	cup chopped green bell pepper
		½	cup chopped red bell pepper
1	cup shredded Cheddar cheese	½	cup chopped celery
1	cup shredded Swiss cheese	6	tablespoons butter
1	(10¾-ounce) can condensed cream of mushroom soup		Salt and freshly ground black pepper to taste
		4	lemons, thinly sliced

Mix chicken, prepared rice, cheeses and soup in a bowl. Sauté onion, bell peppers, and celery in butter until softened. Add sautéed vegetables to chicken mixture and season with salt and pepper. Transfer to a 9x13-inch casserole dish. Arrange lemon slices on top. Sprinkle with extra black pepper and cover with foil. Bake at 375 degrees for 20 minutes or until heated through. Yield: 4 to 6 servings.

You may substitute 2 to 3 pounds shrimp for the chicken.

Creamed Chicken and Biscuits

1½	teaspoons butter	½	cup milk
½	large onion, chopped	½	cup chopped pimento
4	cups chopped cooked chicken	1	cup shredded mild Cheddar cheese, divided
1	(10¾-ounce) can condensed cream of chicken soup	6	frozen biscuits, thawed, or homemade
1	cup sour cream		

Melt butter in a small skillet over medium-high heat. Stir in onion and sauté until tender. Combine sautéed onion with chicken, soup, sour cream, milk and pimento in a medium bowl. Mix well and spoon mixture into a greased 11x7-inch baking dish. Bake at 350 degrees for 15 minutes. Remove from oven and sprinkle with ¾ cup cheese. Arrange biscuits in a single layer on top and sprinkle with remaining ¼ cup cheese. Bake 20 minutes longer or until biscuits are golden brown and sauce is bubbly. Serve immediately. Yield: 4 to 6 servings.

Helen's Chicken Pie with Self-Crust

1	(3-pound) frying chicken	2	tablespoons butter
2	hard-cooked eggs, chopped	1	cup self-rising flour
1¼	cups chicken broth	½	cup mayonnaise
1	(10¾-ounce) can condensed cream of	1	cup milk
	celery soup	¼	teaspoon black pepper

Place chicken in a pot and cover with water. Cook until done. Debone chicken and cut meat into bite-size pieces. Spread meat in the bottom of a 9x13-inch baking dish. Sprinkle with chopped eggs. Blend broth and soup and pour over chicken and eggs.

Make a crust by mixing butter, flour, mayonnaise, milk and pepper with a fork. Pour crust over chicken mixture. Bake at 425 degrees for 30 minutes. Yield: 4 to 6 servings.

Herb Roasted Turkey

1	(about 16-pound) fresh turkey	1	bay leaf
	Salt and freshly ground black pepper to taste	8	tablespoons unsalted butter, softened, divided
4	tablespoons poultry herb blend, divided	¾	cup unsalted turkey or chicken broth
		½	cup Madeira wine

Remove neck, heart and gizzard from turkey and reserve for making giblet gravy. Let turkey stand at room temperature for up to 2 hours. Rinse inside and out and pat dry with paper towels. Trim off and discard excess fat. Season turkey inside and out with salt and pepper and place 2 tablespoons herb blend and bay leaf inside body cavity. Truss turkey, if desired, and spread 2 tablespoons butter over turkey breast. Evenly coat outside of turkey with remaining 2 tablespoons herb blend. Place turkey on a rack in a large roasting pan. Fold a 3-foot square piece of cheesecloth into quarters, dampen with water and drape over turkey breast, leaving drumsticks exposed. Place on lower rack in a preheated 325 degree oven.

In a saucepan over medium heat, melt remaining 6 tablespoons butter with broth and wine. After roasting 30 minutes, baste turkey with butter mixture through cheesecloth. Continue roasting, basting every 20 minutes, for 1½ hours longer. Then baste every 30 minutes with butter mixture and pan juices for another 1½ hours or until an instant read thermometer inserted into the thickest part of the thigh away from the bone registers 175 degrees. Total roasting time for turkey will be about 3½ hours. Transfer turkey to a cutting board. Cover loosely with foil and let stand 20 minutes before carving. Yield: 12 servings.

How to Roast a Duck

Cut duck along both sides of backbone using either a boning knife or kitchen sheers. Remove excess fat deposits. This cutting will remove the backbone and allow the duck to be flattened for roasting. (The flattened duck may be placed directly in a roasting pan.) If desired, the duck may be seasoned with salt and pepper or brushed with soy sauce before roasting. Roast at 400 degrees for 45 minutes or until duck is pink next to the bone, or broil on top level of oven until duck meat is pink at the bone and skin is brown and crisp. During roasting or broiling, drain fat as it accumulates in the pan.

Remove duck, cool, split into halves or quarters and remove breast and rib bones with your hands.

When ready to serve, return to roasting pan and place under broiler. Broil until meat is warm and skin is crisp.

Alternately, the duck may be left whole and roasted as described above. Duck may be halved or quartered and the bones removed as above.

Duck is best served by precooking, cooling and removing bone early in the day. Then reheated just before serving.

Amaretto Apricot Sauce for Duck

½	cup unsalted butter		Salt and freshly ground pepper to taste
⅓	cup thinly sliced shallots or green onions	1	cup amaretto liquor
¾	cup fresh orange juice, strained	½	cup slivered almonds, toasted
¼	cup fresh lemon juice	1	(16-ounce) can whole apricots, drained and seeded
2	tablespoons Dijon mustard		

Melt butter in a saucepan. Add shallots, orange and lemon juices, mustard and salt and pepper. Cook briefly to soften shallots and combine ingredients. Add amaretto and simmer, stirring occasionally, for 35 minutes or until sauce coats a spoon. Stir in almonds and apricots before serving.

Hot Chicken Salad

4	cups diced cooked chicken	¾	cup chicken broth
2	(10¾-ounce) cans condensed cream of chicken soup	1	teaspoon salt
2	cups diced celery	1	teaspoon black pepper
¼	cup minced onion	¼	cup freshly squeezed lemon juice
2	cups slivered almonds	6	hard-cooked eggs, finely chopped
1	cup mayonnaise	1	cup cracker crumbs

Combine all ingredients except cracker crumbs. Transfer mixture to a greased 3- or 4-quart casserole dish. Sprinkle cracker crumbs on top. Bake at 350 degrees for 40 minutes. Yield: 12 servings.

Lemon Chicken with Noodles

Sauce

1	(10½-ounce) can chicken broth	¼	teaspoon dried basil
1½	tablespoons lemon juice	¼	teaspoon dried coriander
⅓	cup butter	¼	teaspoon dried parsley
⅓	cup Madeira wine	⅛	teaspoon black pepper
¼	teaspoon salt		

Chicken and Noodles

4	chicken breasts	2	tablespoons fresh lemon juice
	Flour for dusting	8	ounces dry spaghetti, cooked and
	Salt and white pepper to taste		drained
2	tablespoons butter		

Combine all sauce ingredients in a saucepan and simmer 15 minutes.

Meanwhile, pound chicken breasts until thin. Season flour with salt and pepper and use to lightly dust chicken. Brown chicken in butter and remove from pan. Pour lemon juice into pan to loosen brown bits from sides and bottom. Pour juice over chicken. Pour simmered sauce over cooked noodles and serve with chicken. Yield: 4 servings.

Mabel's Chicken Enchiladas

2	boneless, skinless chicken breast halves	1	tablespoon vegetable oil, plus extra for cooking tortillas
6	tomatoes		
1	clove garlic	18	corn or flour tortillas
1	onion, coarsely chopped	1	cup shredded Cheddar cheese
1	canned chipotle chili pepper	1	poblano chile, roasted and julienned for garnish

Place chicken in a saucepan and cover with water. Bring to a boil. Reduce heat, cover pan and simmer 25 minutes or until tender. Drain and cool. Shred chicken and set aside.

In a heavy skillet, sauté tomatoes, garlic, onion and chipotle chile, stirring often, for 3 to 4 minutes or until charred. Remove from heat. Transfer vegetables to a blender or food processor and purée. Warm 1 tablespoon oil in a skillet. Add purée and cook 5 minutes or until thickened; set aside.

In a separate skillet, fry tortillas in hot oil for 5 seconds on each side or until softened; drain. Dip each tortilla in puréed sauce. Top with chicken and roll tortilla into a cylinder. Place, seam-side down, in a baking dish. Pour remaining puréed sauce over top and sprinkle with cheese and julienned poblano chile. Bake at 350 degrees for 10 minutes or until cheese melts. Yield: 6 to 8 servings.

Oven-Fried Chicken

½ cup butter or margarine
4 skinless chicken breast halves, or
  assorted chicken pieces
  Flour

Paprika
Lemon pepper
Garlic salt

Melt butter in a shallow baking dish. Dredge chicken in flour, then place, skin-side down, in butter. Sprinkle liberally with paprika, lemon pepper and garlic salt. Bake, uncovered, at 425 degrees for 30 minutes. Turn chicken pieces and sprinkle again with seasonings. Bake 20 minutes longer. Yield: 4 servings.

Pan Roasted Turkey Breast

2 (about 2½ pound) boneless turkey
  breast halves
  Salt and freshly ground pepper to taste
2 tablespoons chopped fresh flat-leaf
  parsley
1 tablespoon chopped fresh thyme

1 tablespoon unsalted butter
2 tablespoons vegetable oil
1 cup turkey or chicken broth
½ cup turkey gravy base
½ cup milk
2 tablespoons dry sherry

Let turkey breasts stand at room temperature for up to 2 hours. Season turkey breasts with salt and pepper. Lay one breast half, skin-side down, on a clean work surface. Lay the other breast, skin-side up, on the first with the thickest parts of each breast at opposite ends. Using kitchen twine, tie halves together at 2-inch intervals. Coat the turkey with parsley and thyme. Melt butter with oil in an oval roasting pan over medium-high heat. When hot, sear turkey roast for 3 to 4 minutes on each side or until browned. Transfer pan to center rack in oven. Roast at 350 degrees, turning turkey occasionally, for 2 hours or until an instant-read thermometer inserted into the center registers 165 degrees. Transfer turkey roast to a carving board, cover loosely with foil and let stand 20 minutes before carving.

Meanwhile, set roasting pan over medium heat and skim fat. Add broth and bring to a simmer, stirring to scrape up any browned bits. Cook 2 to 3 minutes. Mix gravy base with milk and add to roasting pan with sherry. Bring to a simmer and cook 3 to 5 minutes or until thick enough to coat the back of a spoon. Season with salt and pepper.

Carve turkey and transfer to a platter. Serve gravy on the side. Yield: 6 to 8 servings.

If not using prepared gravy base, brown ½ cup plain flour in the turkey juices after removing from the oven. Add 3 to 4 cups chicken broth and sherry and cook until thickened.

Peppered Lemon Chicken Pasta

8	ounces dry spaghetti or linguine, broken in half	3	tablespoons fresh lemon juice
4	tablespoons butter	½	teaspoon salt
1	pound chicken stir-fry meat, or boneless, skinless chicken breasts, chopped	¼	teaspoon cayenne pepper
		¾	cup sliced green onions

Cook spaghetti as directed on package in a 4-quart saucepan; drain, remove from pan and keep warm. Melt butter in same pan until sizzling. Add chicken and cook over medium-high heat, stirring often, for 6 to 8 minutes or until chicken is golden brown. Stir in lemon juice, salt and cayenne pepper. Return cooked spaghetti to pan and toss to coat. Stir in green onions. Yield: 4 servings.

Fresh, uncooked and peeled shrimp can be substituted for the chicken.

Quail

10-12	quail	1	cup finely chopped celery
	Salt to taste (no pepper)	1	cup finely chopped carrot
	Flour for dusting	1	cup sliced fresh mushrooms
1	cup buttery-flavored Wesson oil, or ½ cup butter and ½ cup cooking oil	1½	tablespoons flour (approximate)
		3	cups chicken broth
1	cup finely chopped onion	1	cup white wine

Rub quail with salt and dust lightly with flour. Tie ends of legs together or "tuck in" and hold with a toothpick. In a heavy pan, sauté quail in oil to a light golden brown. Remove to a heated casserole dish, arranging in rows with breasts up.

Heat 3 tablespoons of fat used to sauté quail in a saucepan. Add onion, celery, carrot and mushrooms and sauté 5 minutes or only until onion is clear.

Remove all but two tablespoons of the fat from the pan quail were browned in. Blend in flour. Stir in enough broth to make a thin gravy. Stir in sautéed vegetables and wine. Pour entire mixture over quail and cover dish tightly with foil. Bake at 325 degrees for 25 to 30 minutes. Remove foil to allow birds to brown and bake 30 minutes longer, basting at least 3 times to prevent quail from drying out. Serve with Cabin Bluff Rice (page 93). Yield: 10 to 12 servings.

Rolled Turkey Breast

4-6	pounds turkey breast		2	fresh sage leaves, minced, or a dash of
	Vegetables for making broth			powdered dried
6	ounces prosciutto ham			White pepper
4	cloves garlic		½	cup cream
	Salt		½	cup butter, cut into pieces
1½	tablespoons minced fresh rosemary, or			
	2 teaspoons dried			

Bone turkey breasts, reserving bones. Place bones in a stock pot with vegetables such as carrot, onion and celery and enough water to cover. Bring to a boil. Reduce heat and simmer, covered, for about 1 hour. Strain broth, discarding vegetables and bones.

Pound raw turkey breasts to an even thickness. Lay ham strips over turkey. Purée garlic with salt and mix in minced rosemary and sage. Spread garlic mixture evenly over ham. Sprinkle with salt and white pepper. Roll turkey breasts and tie with a string. Sprinkle with more rosemary and cover with foil. Bake at 400 degrees for 45 to 55 minutes. Slice into servings.

Meanwhile, cook about 2 cups strained broth in a saucepan over medium heat until reduced to ½ cup. Add cream and reduce over medium heat by half. Beat butter into reduced sauce. Ladle sauce over sliced turkey roll and serve. Yield: 6 to 8 servings.

Southern Fried Chicken

1	frying chicken, cut into pieces for frying	¾	cup flour
	(with a pulley bone)		Salt and pepper to taste
1	cup buttermilk		Vegetable oil for frying

Soak chicken in buttermilk for 30 minutes; drain. Season flour with salt and pepper. Dredge chicken in seasoned flour. Heat oil 2½ inches deep in a heavy iron skillet to about 350 degrees. Place chicken in hot oil, cover with a lid and fry about 10 minutes on one side or until golden brown. Turn chicken over to brown on other side. Cover and fry 5 minutes longer. Remove the lid to watch chicken while cooking until chicken is brown and done. Yield: 3 to 4 servings.

Baked Flounder with Parmesan Crumbs

4	(8-ounce) flounder fillets	½	cup coarse fresh bread crumbs
	Salt and freshly ground pepper to taste	4	tablespoons unsalted butter, melted
¾	cup freshly grated Parmesan cheese	2	tablespoons extra virgin olive oil

Season fish with salt and pepper in a baking dish. Mix cheese, bread crumbs, butter and olive oil and sprinkle over fish. Bake at 425 degrees for 15 minutes or until fish is cooked and the topping is golden. Let stand 5 minutes before serving. Yield: 4 servings.

Baked Salmon with Chinese Mustard Glaze

2	tablespoons orange juice	1	teaspoon sesame oil
2	tablespoons Dijon mustard	1	teaspoon soy sauce
1	tablespoon grated fresh ginger		Freshly ground black pepper to taste
1	tablespoon rice vinegar	1	(3-pound) salmon, head and tail
2	teaspoons honey		removed, butterflied open

Stir together orange juice, mustard, ginger, vinegar, honey, sesame oil, soy sauce and several grinds of black pepper. Line a large baking pan, such as the bottom of a broiling pan, with foil. Lightly oil foil and place fish, spread open, in pan. Spread with half the mustard glaze. Bake at 450 degrees for 5 minutes. Spread with remaining glaze and bake 5 minutes longer. Run under a hot broiler for 2 minutes or until glaze is lightly browned. Yield: 8 servings.

Beer Batter for Shrimp

1	pound unpeeled large raw shrimp	¼	cup beer
¼	cup all-purpose flour	2	tablespoons butter, melted
¼	cup cornstarch	1	egg yolk
⅛	teaspoon salt		Vegetable oil for frying

Peel shrimp, leaving tails intact. Devein, if desired. Combine flour, cornstarch and salt. Add beer, butter and egg yolk and stir until smooth. Pour oil 2 inches deep into a Dutch oven and heat to 375 degrees. Dip shrimp in beer batter, then fry in hot oil, a few at a time, until golden. Drain on paper towels. Yield: 2 to 4 servings.

Cloris LeBlanc's Cajun Jambalaya

1	pound ground beef	1	(10¾-ounce) can condensed cream of chicken soup
½	pound smoked Cajun sausage, cut into bite-size pieces	1	(10¾-ounce) can condensed cream of mushroom soup
1	onion, chopped		
1	green bell pepper, chopped	1	(10-ounce) can tomatoes and chiles
1	pound shrimp, peeled and deveined	1½	cups dry rice
			Cayenne pepper to taste

Brown beef and sausage in a 2-quart ovenproof dish with a lid. Add onion and bell pepper and sauté 10 minutes. Mix in shrimp, soups, tomatoes and chiles, rice and cayenne. Bake, covered, at 350 degrees for 1½ hours or until done, checking for doneness after 1¼ hours. Yield: 6 to 8 servings.

Crab Cakes

1	pound lump crabmeat (Dungeness preferred)	1	large green onion, finely chopped
½	cup mayonnaise	¼	teaspoon dry mustard
⅔	cup French bread crumbs, made in food processor		Freshly ground black pepper to taste
		1	egg, lightly beaten
⅓	cup minced fresh parsley	2	tablespoons olive oil

Combine crab, mayonnaise, bread crumbs, parsley, onion, mustard, pepper and egg in a large mixing bowl. Heat olive oil in a large skillet. Shape crab mixture into 2½-inch patties. Cook in hot oil until golden brown on one side. Flip and cook until golden brown on other side. Serve with Garlic Rémoulade Sauce (recipe below). Yield: 6 crab cakes.

Garlic Rémoulade Sauce

2	cups mayonnaise	4	cornichons, minced
½	cup chopped fresh parsley	1	teaspoon strong Dijon mustard
2	green onions, minced	2	cloves garlic, minced

Combine all sauce ingredients. Refrigerate until serving. The longer the sauce is stored, the stronger it becomes. To tone down the flavor, add mayonnaise to taste.

The garlic gives the sauce a strong flavor. For a milder sauce, use ½ clove of garlic.

Crabmeat Rémoulade

2	cups mayonnaise	2	tablespoons Creole mustard
¼	cup grated onion	1	tablespoon paprika
¼	cup minced celery	1	tablespoon minced garlic
1	tablespoon horseradish	1	pound lump crabmeat

Combine mayonnaise, onion, celery, horseradish, mustard, paprika and garlic in a large bowl. Fold in crabmeat. Serve on a bed of lettuce. Yield: 4 to 6 servings.

This also makes a great dip for boiled shrimp. Make a day ahead for flavors to blend, adding crabmeat just before serving.

Deviled Crab

1	cup diced celery	3	dashes hot pepper sauce
1	cup diced onion	1	tablespoon lemon juice
2	cloves garlic, mashed	6	eggs, well beaten
1	green bell pepper, chopped	1	(10¾-ounce) can condensed cream of
½	cup butter		mushroom soup
1	quart crabmeat	½	cup evaporated milk
1	tablespoon salt	2	cups bread crumbs, plus extra for
1	teaspoon black pepper		topping
¼	cup Worcestershire sauce		

Simmer celery, onion, garlic and bell pepper in butter in a covered skillet until tender. In a bowl, combine crabmeat, salt, pepper, Worcestershire sauce, hot sauce, lemon juice, eggs, soup, milk and 2 cups bread crumbs. Mix in cooked vegetables. Fill mixture into crab shells or custard cups. Sprinkle top with extra bread crumbs. Bake at 350 degrees for 35 minutes. Yield: 6 servings.

Heavenly Broiled Fish

¼	cup grated Parmesan cheese	½	teaspoon salt
½	cup butter, softened		Dash of hot pepper sauce
3	tablespoons mayonnaise	2	pounds fish fillets, skinned
3	tablespoons chopped green onion	2	tablespoons lemon juice

Combine cheese, butter, mayonnaise, green onions, salt and hot sauce in a small bowl; set aside. Place fillets in a single layer on a well-greased broiler pan. Brush fish with lemon juice. Broil fillets 4 inches from the heat source for 4 to 6 minutes. Spread cheese mixture over fillets. Broil 2 minutes longer or until lightly browned. Yield: 6 servings.

Grilled Salmon with Orange Glaze

½ cup orange marmalade
2 teaspoons sesame oil
2 teaspoons soy sauce
¼ teaspoon grated fresh ginger
1 clove garlic, crushed
3 tablespoons white rice vinegar, or
    other white vinegar

1 pound boneless, skinless salmon fillet,
    cut into 4 pieces
6 green onions, thinly sliced, green only
    (optional)
¼ cup toasted sesame seeds (optional)

Combine marmalade, oil, soy sauce, ginger, garlic and vinegar. Heat grill. Brush glaze mixture on each side of salmon pieces. Grill about 5 minutes on each side. Top with green onions and sesame seeds. Yield: 4 servings.

Hot Crab Newburg

½ cup butter
½ cup all-purpose flour
1 quart heavy cream
4 egg yolks, lightly beaten
    Salt and pepper to taste
½ teaspoon lemon juice

1 teaspoon sugar
½ teaspoon dry mustard
¼ cup sherry
    Dash of Worcestershire sauce
2 pounds crabmeat

Melt butter in a 4-quart saucepan. Add flour and stir well. Mix in cream, egg yolks and salt and pepper and cook and stir until thickened. Add lemon juice, sugar, mustard, sherry and Worcestershire sauce. Fold in crabmeat and heat through. Serve with toast points. Yield: About 12 servings.

Hollandaise Sauce

½ cup butter, softened
¼ cup hot water
¼ teaspoon salt

    Dash of black pepper
4 egg yolks, lightly beaten
2 tablespoons lemon juice

Combine butter with hot water, salt and pepper. Blend a small amount of hot mixture into egg yolks. Gradually beat in remainder of hot mixture. Transfer to a double boiler over hot, not boiling, water. Beat until thick and smooth. Blend in lemon juice. If sauce curdles, add 1 teaspoon hot water. Blend well. Yield: 1 cup.

Jambalaya

4	tablespoons butter	1	bay leaf
1	pound andouille sausage, sliced	½	teaspoon dried thyme
½	pound smoked ham, diced	¼	teaspoon cayenne pepper
¼	cup flour		Black pepper to taste
2	medium-size white onions, finely chopped	3	cups chicken broth
		2	pounds shrimp, shelled and deveined
6	green onions, chopped	1	cup diced cooked chicken
1	small green bell pepper, chopped	2	cups dry long-grain rice
4	cloves garlic, minced	1	teaspoon salt
4	ripe tomatoes, peeled and chopped		

Melt butter in a large heavy saucepan. Add sausage and ham and sauté until lightly browned. Stir in flour. Add onions, green onions, bell pepper and garlic and sauté until vegetables are softened. Stir in tomatoes with any accumulated juices, bay leaf, thyme, cayenne, black pepper, broth, shrimp, chicken, rice and salt. The liquid in the pan should just cover the contents. Bring to a boil. Reduce heat to a simmer and cover saucepan. Cook until liquid is absorbed and rice is tender. Remove bay leaf. Yield: 8 to 10 servings.

Marinated Grilled Tuna

½	cup soy sauce	¼	cup vegetable oil
½	cup dry sherry	1	clove garlic, minced
1	tablespoon lemon juice	8	(½-inch thick) tuna fillets

Combine soy sauce, sherry, lemon juice, oil and garlic in a shallow bowl. Add tuna fillets, turning to coat both sides. Cover bowl and marinate in refrigerator for 1 to 2 hours; drain. Do not marinate longer than 2 hours or the flavor will be too strong. Grill or broil for 5 to 6 minutes on each side or until tuna flakes easily. Yield: 8 servings.

Lake Trout Amandine

½	cup slivered blanched almonds		Milk
4	tablespoons butter		All-purpose flour
12	large bass or trout fillets	½	cup vegetable oil
	Salt and pepper to taste	2	teaspoons chopped parsley
	Dried thyme to taste		Lemon wedges

Sauté almonds in butter until golden brown; set aside. Sprinkle fillets with salt and pepper and thyme. Dip fillets in milk, then dredge in flour. Fry fillets in hot vegetable oil over medium heat until golden brown on both sides. Drain on paper towels. Remove to a serving dish. Sprinkle with almonds and parsley. Garnish with lemon wedges. Yield: 6 to 8 servings.

Lemon Stuffed Baked Fish

⅓	cup chopped celery	1	teaspoon lemon zest
⅓	cup chopped onion		Dash of black pepper
5	tablespoons butter	½	teaspoon salt
3	cups dry bread crumbs	2	tablespoons lemon juice
1	tablespoon chopped fresh parsley	2	pounds fresh or frozen fish fillets

Sauté celery and onion in butter. Add bread crumbs, parsley, lemon zest, pepper, salt and lemon juice and mix well. Partially thaw fillets, if frozen. Place half the fillets flat in a greased baking dish. Spoon stuffing mixture over fillets. Place remaining fillets over stuffing. Cover dish with foil. Bake at 350 degrees for 20 minutes or until fish flakes easily with a fork. Yield: 6 servings.

Salmon Puffs

4	slices fresh white bread, trimmed	1	(7-ounce) can salmon, drained
1	cup milk	¼	teaspoon salt
1	thin slice onion	½	teaspoon dry mustard
4	eggs		

Tear bread into small pieces and place in a blender or food processor. Add milk, onion, eggs, salmon, salt and mustard. Blend on high speed for about 20 seconds. Pour mixture into 4 individual 10-ounce greased casserole dishes. Bake at 325 degrees for 30 minutes. Yield: 4 servings.

Salmon Thermidor

4	salmon steaks (about 1¼ pounds total)	2	tablespoons cooking sherry
½	cup milk	2	hard-cooked eggs, sliced
¼	teaspoon salt	½	cup shredded Swiss cheese
⅛	teaspoon black pepper		Paprika
1	(10¾-ounce) can condensed cream of mushroom soup		

Place salmon in a shallow baking dish. Pour milk over salmon and sprinkle with salt and pepper. Bake at 350 degrees for 30 minutes or until salmon flakes when tested with a fork. Meanwhile, heat and stir undiluted soup in a saucepan until smooth. Add sherry and heat to a boil. When salmon is done, arrange egg slices around salmon and pour soup mixture over the top. Sprinkle with cheese and paprika. Broil on a low setting for 5 minutes or until bubbling hot. Yield: 4 servings.

Salmon Croquettes

1	(16-ounce) can red or pink salmon	1	egg, lightly beaten
	Milk	¼	teaspoon salt
¼	cup minced onion		Dash of black pepper
3	tablespoons butter	⅔	cup soft bread crumbs
¼	cup flour		Shortening or oil for frying

Breading

1	egg	1	tablespoon water
1	tablespoon undiluted evaporated milk	1½-2	cups fine, very dry bread crumbs

Drain salmon, reserving juice. Add milk to juice to measure ⅔ cup. Remove skin and bones from salmon. Sauté onion in butter until tender. Stir in flour until well blended. Add salmon juice mixture and egg and cook until thickened. Mix in salmon, salt, pepper and soft bread crumbs. Chill. Divide mixture and shape into 8 balls.

For breading, beat egg, milk and water together. Roll each ball in egg mixture until completely covered; then roll in dry bread crumbs. Chill again. Fry in hot fat until brown. Serve with Green Olive, Mustard, or Hollandaise Sauce (recipes below). Yield: 4 servings.

Green Olive Sauce

6	tablespoons butter		Dash of black pepper
6	tablespoons flour	½	cup sliced stuffed green olives
2	cups chicken broth		

Melt butter. Stir in flour until blended and slightly browned. Add broth and cook, stirring constantly, until thickened. Add pepper and olives.

Mustard Sauce

2	tablespoons butter	½	teaspoon salt
2	tablespoons flour	1	teaspoon prepared mustard
1	cup half-and-half		

Melt butter in a heavy saucepan. Stir in flour; do not brown. Add half-and-half and salt. Stir constantly until thickened. Add mustard.

Salmon with Curried Spinach

6	pounds fresh spinach, stemmed and washed but not dried, or four 10-ounce packages frozen leaf spinach, thawed	1	cup chicken broth, regular or low sodium
2	tablespoons vegetable oil	2	tablespoons Pernod or other anise liqueur
1	large Vidalia onion, chopped	4	teaspoons fresh lemon juice, divided
3	large cloves garlic, minced		Salt and freshly ground pepper to taste
2½	tablespoons curry powder	2	boneless sides of salmon, skinned (4½ to 5 pounds total)
2	cups heavy cream	2	tablespoons unsalted butter, melted
		1	large lemon, thinly sliced

If using fresh spinach, wilt in batches in a large Dutch oven over high heat, stirring with tongs. As each batch is done, transfer to a colander set over a plate. When the spinach is cool enough to handle, gently squeeze it to remove some of the water but leave the spinach moist. Coarsely chop fresh or thawed spinach. Heat oil in the Dutch oven. Add onion and cook over medium-low heat, stirring occasionally, for 10 minutes or until softened but not browned. Add garlic and curry powder and cook and stir 5 minutes or until fragrant. Stir in spinach, cream, broth and Pernod and simmer over low heat for 10 minutes. Add 2 teaspoons lemon juice and season with salt and pepper. Divide spinach mixture between 2 generously greased large shallow baking dishes. Place one side of salmon, skinned-side down, in each dish on top of spinach, tucking the thin tail ends under the fillets, if needed. Rub each fillet with 1 teaspoon lemon juice and brush with melted butter. Season with salt and pepper. Bake at 500 degrees for 20 minutes or until salmon is just cooked through and the spinach is bubbling. Remove from oven and let stand 5 minutes. Using a spatula, cut each fillet into 6 pieces. Spoon spinach onto warmed individual plates and top each with a salmon fillet. Garnish with lemon slices. Yield: 12 servings.

Scalloped Oysters

3	quarts extra-select oysters		Seasoned salt and pepper to taste
4	cups butter cracker crumbs, divided	1	cup heavy cream
1½	cups butter, melted, divided		Paprika

Drain oysters well in a colander. Layer a third of the cracker crumbs in a greased casserole dish. Pour ½ cup butter over crumbs. Layer half of the oysters over the crumbs. Sprinkle with seasoned salt and pepper. Drizzle with half the cream. Repeat layers once. Top layers with remaining cracker crumbs and butter. Dust with paprika. Bake at 325 degrees for 30 to 40 minutes or until casserole bubbles and top is lightly browned. Yield: 10 to 12 servings.

Use less cream if oysters are very juicy.

Seafood Gumbo

1 pound fish fillets	1 tablespoon dried parsley
6-8 strips bacon	1 tablespoon minced garlic
1 cup chopped onion	1 teaspoon paprika
1 cup chopped celery	½ teaspoon chili powder
1 cup sliced fresh mushrooms	⅛ teaspoon cayenne pepper
¾ cup chopped green bell pepper	1 (10-ounce) package frozen cut okra, thawed
1 tablespoon flour	
1 (16-ounce) can tomato wedges, undrained	8 ounces shelled fresh or frozen shrimp
1 (8-ounce) can tomato sauce	1 cup oysters (optional)
½ cup water	Tabasco sauce
1½ tablespoons Worcestershire sauce	Hot cooked rice

Poach fillets in a small amount of water just until done. Drain, cube and set aside. In a large soup pot with a cover, cook bacon until crisp. Remove bacon, crumble and set aside, reserving bacon drippings in pot. Add onion, celery, mushrooms and bell pepper to bacon drippings and sauté. Stir in flour. Add tomatoes, tomato sauce, water, Worcestershire sauce, parsley, garlic, paprika, chili powder and cayenne pepper. Bring to a boil. Reduce heat and add okra, shrimp, oysters and cooked fish. Cook until shrimp are done. Remove from heat and let stand 30 minutes to allow flavors to blend. Reheat to serving temperature. Season with Tabasco sauce. Serve over hot rice in bowls. Sprinkle bacon on top. Yield: 6 to 8 servings.

Shrimp Creole

1 green bell pepper, chopped	1 large bay leaf
3 stalks celery, chopped	Dash of ground cloves
1 large onion, chopped	1 teaspoon sugar
2 cloves garlic, chopped	Salt and pepper to taste
2 tablespoons cooking oil	2 pounds raw shrimp, peeled and deveined
1 (14½-ounce) can tomatoes	
Few sprigs fresh parsley	Flour
½ teaspoon dried thyme	½ cup sherry wine

Sauté bell pepper, celery, onion and garlic in oil until vegetables are glazed. Add tomatoes, parsley, thyme, bay leaf, cloves, sugar and salt and pepper. Simmer slowly for 1 hour. Dredge shrimp heavily in flour and add to simmering sauce. Cook, stirring constantly, for 15 to 18 minutes longer, depending on the size of the shrimp. Stir in sherry. Serve over rice. Yield: 4 to 6 servings.

Seafood Casserole

1	green pepper, chopped	1	small jar chopped pimento
2	stalks celery, chopped	3	pounds shrimp, boiled and peeled
1	medium onion, chopped	1	pound fresh crabmeat
2	tablespoons butter	5	boiled eggs, sliced

Sauté pepper, celery and onion in butter. Add pimento, shrimp, crabmeat and eggs.

Cream Sauce

4	tablespoons butter	3	cups half-and-half
4-5	tablespoons flour	1	cup shredded Cheddar cheese

Cook butter and flour until smooth. Add half-and-half and cook until thick. Add cheese and conrinue to cook until melted.

Combine all of the above into a greased 3-quart casserole dish. Top with Ritz cracker crumbs and dot with butter.

May be served over toast points.

Shrimp Étouffée

1	pound raw shrimp	1	teaspoon dried parsley
	Salt and pepper to taste	1	teaspoon Italian seasoning
½	cup butter	2	hard-cooked eggs
2	onions, chopped	1	(12-ounce) can V-8 or tomato juice
1	bell pepper, chopped		Lemon
1	stalk celery, chopped		

Cook shrimp in boiling water seasoned with salt and pepper for 15 minutes. Drain, peel and devein. Melt butter in a large skillet. Add onions, bell pepper and celery and sauté. Add parsley and Italian seasoning and cook 10 minutes or until vegetables are tender. Remove yolks from the eggs. Mash yolks with enough water to make a thick paste. Add yolk paste to vegetable mixture. (The yolks make the gravy thicker.) Stir in V-8 juice. Add shrimp and cook about 7 minutes. If there is not enough gravy, add a little more V-8 juice. Season with salt and pepper. Squeeze a little lemon juice over mixture. Serve over rice. Yield: 4 servings.

Southern Fried Shrimp

2	cups flour	1	pound pink shrimp, peeled and
2	cups cracker meal		deveined
	Salt and pepper to taste	1½	cups milk
			Vegetable oil for frying

Combine flour, cracker meal and salt and pepper in a paper bag. Dip shrimp in milk, then toss in breading mixture in bag. Place shrimp on a pan and let stand about 10 minutes. (This will help the breading to adhere.) Fry shrimp in 350 degree oil until just light golden; do not overcook. Yield: 4 to 6 servings.

Shrimp Mull

1	cup uncooked diced bacon	16	drops hot pepper sauce
1½	cups diced onion	1	(14-ounce) bottle ketchup
1	cup chopped celery	3	tablespoons Worcestershire sauce
2	quarts water	¼	teaspoon allspice
2	(14½-ounce) cans peeled tomatoes	¼	teaspoon curry powder
1	(10¾-ounce) can condensed tomato soup	¾	cup butter, divided
2	cloves garlic, minced	5	pounds raw shrimp, peeled and deveined
	Juice of 1 lemon	1	cup sherry
1	teaspoon celery seed	2	cups dry rice

Sauté bacon, onion and celery in a skillet until limp. Transfer to a 5-quart Dutch oven. Add water, tomatoes, soup, garlic, lemon juice, celery seed, hot sauce, ketchup, Worcestershire sauce, allspice, curry and ½ cup butter. Boil gently for 2 hours. Add shrimp and sherry and simmer 45 minutes. Cook rice, according to package directions, with remaining ¼ cup butter. Serve shrimp mixture over rice. Yield: 10 servings.

Shrimp Portau Lindsey

4	tablespoons butter	¼	teaspoon paprika
3	tablespoons flour	3	cups cooked, peeled and deveined shrimp
2	cups half-and-half	3	(10-ounce) packages frozen chopped spinach
	Salt and white pepper to taste		Freshly grated Parmesan cheese
1	clove garlic, grated		
½	teaspoon Worcestershire sauce		
2-3	drops Tabasco sauce		

To make a béchamel sauce, melt butter in a heavy saucepan. Sprinkle flour over butter and gently cook, stirring constantly, for about 5 minutes; do not allow flour and butter to brown. Meanwhile, bring half-and-half to a boil in a separate saucepan. Remove butter mixture from heat and pour in hot half-and-half all at once. Stir vigorously with a wire whisk. Return pan to medium heat and bring to a boil, stirring constantly, for 5 minutes. Season with salt and pepper, garlic, Worcestershire sauce, Tabasco and paprika. Mix in shrimp.

Prepare spinach according to package directions. Drain until all moisture is removed. Pour shrimp sauce into a greased casserole dish. Scatter spinach on top. Bake at 350 degrees until hot and bubbly. Remove from oven and sprinkle with Parmesan cheese. Yield: 6 servings.

This is a good dish for a ladies luncheon. Can be baked in individual scallop shells.

Deer Steak Marinade

½ cup dry red wine
½ teaspoon ground cumin
1 clove garlic, crushed

½ cup olive oil
3 tablespoons soy sauce
2 large or 4 small deer steaks

Combine all ingredients except deer. Pour marinade over deer and marinate at room temperature for 2 to 3 hours, turning occasionally. Drain steaks, reserving marinade. Grill over charcoal to desired doneness. Brush deer with marinade while cooking. Yield: 4 servings.

Fried Venison

1 venison roast, cut into chunks
Salt and pepper to taste
Milk

2 cups dry pancake mix
Flour

Season venison with salt and pepper. Soak venison in milk in refrigerator for 2 hours. Remove from milk and dip in pancake mix. Add flour to a paper bag and season with salt and pepper. Place dipped venison in bag and shake to coat. Deep fry in 350 degree fat, maintaining temperature while cooking. Serve as an appetizer or entrée.

Kielbasa Hot Pot

1½ pounds smoked kielbasa sausage,
   sliced on the diagonal
3 potatoes, peeled and cut into chunks
3 carrots, peeled and cut into chunks

3 onions, peeled and cut into chunks
1 medium head cabbage, cut into large
   slices
Salt and pepper to taste

Combine sausage, potatoes, carrots and onions in a large pot. Add enough water to barely cover. Place cabbage on top and season with salt and pepper. Cover pot and cook 30 to 40 minutes or until vegetables are tender. Serve with cornbread. Yield: 4 to 6 servings.

Veal Piccata

Sauce

1¼	cups chicken broth	1	tablespoon fresh lemon juice
⅓	cup dry white wine		Salt and pepper to taste
1	tablespoon all-purpose flour	2	tablespoons chopped fresh flat-leaf
2	tablespoons water		parsley
1	tablespoon unsalted butter		

Veal

2	pounds veal cutlets, sliced ¼-inch thick		Flour (optional)
¾	teaspoon salt	1	lemon, thinly sliced
½	teaspoon black pepper		

Boil broth and wine in a 2- to 3-quart heavy saucepan for 3 minutes or until reduced by half (about ¾ cup). Whisk together flour and water in a cup, then blend into broth. Boil, stirring constantly, for 1 minute. Remove from heat and stir in butter and lemon juice. Season with salt and pepper. Keep sauce warm.

To prepare veal, cut cutlets into 3-inch pieces and pat dry with paper towels. Lightly oil a grill and preheat. Sprinkle veal with salt and pepper, and if desired, lightly dredge in flour to help veal to brown. Grill veal, in batches, for 30 seconds on each side or until browned. Transfer to a platter with tongs and keep warm. Grill lemon slices, in batches if necessary, until lightly browned and transfer to platter with veal.

Stir parsley into warm sauce and pour over veal. Serve with buttered noodles and chives. Yield: 8 servings.

Veal may be browned in a lightly oiled hot skillet if a grill is not available. Capers may also be added.

Venison Cutlets

2	pounds venison cutlets	1	cup milk
1½	tablespoons dried dill	1½	cups bread crumbs
	Salt and pepper to taste	8	ounces salt pork, sliced
2	eggs		

Pound venison to ¼-inch thickness. Sprinkle cutlets on both sides with dill and salt and pepper. Beat eggs and milk together in a shallow dish. Dip venison in egg mixture, then dredge in bread crumbs. Render fat from salt pork in a skillet. Fry venison in hot rendered fat. Yield: 4 servings.

Venison Pepper Steak

2	tablespoons oil	1	cup chopped tomatoes
1	pound venison, cut into thin strips	1½	tablespoons cornstarch
1	small to medium onion, cut into rings	2	teaspoons soy sauce
1	clove garlic, minced	¼	cup water
2	green bell peppers, cut into strips		Salt and pepper to taste
1	cup beef broth		

Heat oil in a skillet. Add venison, onion and garlic and sauté. Add bell peppers and broth. Cover and cook about 30 minutes. Add tomatoes and cook 5 minutes longer. Combine cornstarch, soy sauce and water and stir into skillet. Cook 5 minutes, stirring constantly. Season with salt and pepper. Serve over rice. Yield: 4 servings.

Venison Roast

1	(6- to 8-pound) venison roast	4	slices lemon
3-6	slices bacon	1	large carrot, sliced
1	cup burgundy	1	tablespoon salt
8	tablespoons oil, divided	10	whole black peppercorns
½	cup cider vinegar	2	bay leaves
1	cup water	1	clove garlic, crushed
2	celery tops	¼	cup unsifted all-purpose flour
1	medium onion, sliced		

Wipe roast with a damp towel. Arrange bacon slices over inside surface of meat. Roll up roast; tie or secure with toothpicks and place in a large pot. Combine burgundy, 6 tablespoons oil, vinegar, water, celery, onion, lemon slices, carrot, salt, peppercorns, bay leaves and garlic and pour over roast. Cover pot and refrigerate 12 to 24 hours, turning roast occasionally. Remove roast from marinade, reserving 2 cups marinade. Dredge roast in flour to coat. Brown roast on all sides in remaining 2 tablespoons hot oil. Add 1 cup reserved marinade and bring to a boil. Reduce heat and cover. Simmer 4 hours or until roast is tender, basting occasionally with pan liquid and adding remaining cup of marinade as needed. Pan juices may be thickened to a gravy consistency with flour or cornstarch. Yield: 12 servings.

Wiener Schnitzel

1	pound veal scaloppine, each slice about 2 ounces		2	eggs, beaten with a pinch of salt
	Salt and freshly ground black pepper to taste		1	cup bread crumbs
¾	cup flour		6	tablespoons clarified butter
			8	lemon wedges for garnish

Season scaloppine on both sides with salt and pepper. Place flour, beaten eggs and bread crumbs each in separate shallow bowls. Dip each slice of veal in flour, shaking off excess, then in egg and finally in bread crumbs. Place the slices of veal on a clean, dry plate until ready to cook. The scaloppine can be prepared up to 3 hours ahead to this stage, but will taste better if breaded at the last minute.

Heat clarified butter in a large skillet over medium-high heat; butter should be hot but not smoking. To test temperature, dip in a piece of veal - if bubbles dance around, butter is ready. Fry veal pieces for 30 seconds on each side. Do not crowd pan or the veal will stew rather than fry crisp; use 2 pans if necessary. Serve immediately, garnished with lemon wedges for squeezing. Yield: 4 servings.

When serving foie gras, ask the clerk in the store for the domestic variety; it is equally delicious and about half the price of the kind made in France.

Desserts

Boston Cream Pie

Cake

¾	cup unsalted butter, softened	2	cups cake flour
1¼	cups sugar	2½	teaspoons baking powder
1	teaspoon vanilla	½	teaspoon salt
2	eggs	¾	cup milk

Custard

3	tablespoons cornstarch	½	cup heavy cream
⅓	cup sugar	¼	teaspoon salt
1	cup milk	1	vanilla bean
3	eggs	3	tablespoons unsalted butter

Glaze

6	ounces fine quality bittersweet chocolate, chopped	2	tablespoons unsalted butter
3	tablespoons water	1½	tablespoons light corn syrup
		¼	teaspoon salt

Beat together butter, sugar and vanilla in a bowl with an electric mixer until light and fluffy. Beat in eggs, one at a time, beating well after each addition. In a separate bowl, sift together flour, baking powder and salt. Beat dry ingredients into butter mixture in 3 additions alternately with milk, beginning and ending with dry ingredients. Pour batter into a greased and floured 9½-inch springform pan. Bake in center of oven at 350 degrees for 50 to 55 minutes or until a tester comes out clean. Cool cake in pan on a rack.

To make custard, whisk together cornstarch, sugar and milk in a saucepan. Add eggs, cream and salt and whisk until smooth. Split vanilla bean lengthwise and scrape seeds into cream mixture, reserving pod for another use. Bring custard to a boil over medium heat, whisking constantly. Boil 2 minutes. Remove from heat and whisk in butter. Cool completely, whisking occasionally.

Melt chocolate with water, butter, syrup and salt in the top of a double boiler over simmering water, stirring until smooth. Remove from heat.

To assemble, remove side of springform pan and halve cake horizontally with a long, serrated knife. Arrange bottom half, cut-side up, on a plate and top with custard, spreading it to the edges. Place top half of cake, cut-side down, over custard. Pour glaze over top, spreading glaze to the edge and letting it drip down the sides. This pie may be made up to 1 day ahead, covered loosely and chilled. Yield: 8 servings.

Brenda's Texas Sheet Cake

1 cup brewed coffee	2 eggs
2 tablespoons Kahlúa liqueur	2 cups plain flour
1 cup butter	1 teaspoon baking soda
¼ cup unsweetened cocoa powder	½ teaspoon salt
2 cups sugar	½ cup sour cream

Frosting

½ cup butter	1 teaspoon vanilla
6 tablespoons milk	1 (16-ounce) package powdered sugar
¼ cup unsweetened cocoa powder	1 cup chopped pecans

Cook coffee until reduced by 2 tablespoons. Add Kahlúa to coffee. Stir in butter and cocoa powder and bring to a boil. Cool. Mix in sugar, eggs, flour, baking soda, salt and sour cream. Pour batter into a greased 8½x11-inch baking pan. Bake at 350 degrees for 30 minutes.

Combine all frosting ingredients except pecans in a saucepan. Cook and stir over medium-high heat until thoroughly mixed. Simmer a few minutes. Stir in pecans. Pour frosting over hot cake. Yield: 8 to 10 servings.

Candied White Fruitcake

2½ cups cake flour	1 cup walnuts, coarsely chopped (about 5 ounces)
1 teaspoon baking powder	
½ teaspoon salt	1 cup butter, softened
2½ cups golden raisins	1 cup sugar
1 cup candied cherries	5 eggs
1 cup canned pineapple chunks, drained and quartered	2 teaspoons lemon zest
	2 teaspoons orange zest
1 cup blanched almonds, coarsely chopped (about 5 ounces)	2 teaspoons vanilla extract
	1 teaspoon almond extract

Line three 5x9-inch loaf pans with parchment paper and generously grease paper. Sift flour, baking powder and salt into a large bowl and stir with a fork to blend. Add raisins, cherries, pineapple, almonds and walnuts and toss gently to coat. Cream butter with sugar in a separate bowl until light and smooth. Gradually add fruit mixture to creamed mixture alternately with eggs, one at a time, beating well after each addition. Blend in lemon zest, orange zest, vanilla and almond extract. Divide batter evenly among prepared pans. Bake at 275 degrees for 2 hours or until a tester inserted in the center of each cake comes out clean. Cool 30 minutes. Turn out onto a rack and peel off paper. Cool completely. Yield: 3 loaves.

Caramel Frosting

3   cups sugar, divided   ⅔   cup milk
10 tablespoons butter

Brown ½ cup sugar in a skillet until caramel colored. Stir in butter until melted. In a saucepan, heat remaining 2½ cups sugar and milk to boiling point. Mix a little of hot milk mixture into skillet with the browned sugar. When blended, pour all of skillet contents back into saucepan and boil hard for about 2 minutes. Beat until creamy. Spread between layers and on top of cake. This recipe will ice a three-layered cake.

Creamy Cheesecake

Graham Cracker Crust
1½ cups graham cracker crumbs   5   tablespoons unsalted butter, melted
2   tablespoons sugar

Filling
2   (8-ounce) packages cream cheese,   3   tablespoons fresh lemon juice
      softened   1½ teaspoons vanilla
1   cup sugar   ½   teaspoon salt
6   egg yolks   3   cups sour cream

Combine crumbs and sugar. Mix in melted butter. Press mixture into the base and partway up the sides of an 8-inch springform pan. Be sure to press the bottom thoroughly so that the crumbs are evenly distributed. You can lay plastic wrap over the crumbs to keep them from sticking to your fingers. Wrap the outside of the pan with a double layer of heavy foil to prevent leaking. Cover crust with plastic wrap and refrigerate until needed.

To prepare filling, beat together cream cheese and sugar with an electric mixer for 3 minutes or until very smooth, scraping the bowl and beaters as needed. Beat in egg yolks until batter is smooth, scraping sides of bowl as needed. Add lemon juice, vanilla and salt and beat until incorporated. Beat in sour cream just until blended.

Pour batter over crust in springform pan. Set pan in a larger pan and add very hot water to larger pan to 1 inch depth. Bake at 350 degrees for 45 minutes. Turn oven off without opening the door and let cake cool in oven for 1 hour. Transfer cheesecake to a rack (the center will still jiggle) and cool 1 hour or until room temperature. Cover pan with plastic wrap and refrigerate at least 6 hours or overnight. Yield: 10 to 12 servings.

This cake is not as dense as a regular cheesecake. It has a light texture due to the amount of sour cream used.

Chocolate Pound Cake

1	cup butter, softened	½	teaspoon salt
½	cup vegetable shortening	½	teaspoon baking soda
3	cups granulated sugar	5	tablespoons unsweetened cocoa
1	teaspoon vanilla		powder
5	eggs	1	cup milk
3	cups plain flour		

Cream butter and shortening until thoroughly mixed. Add sugar and vanilla and beat until fluffy. Add eggs, one at a time, beating well after each addition. Sift together flour, salt, baking soda and cocoa in a separate bowl. Add dry ingredients to creamed mixture alternately with milk, beginning and ending with dry ingredients. Pour batter into a tube pan. Bake at 350 degrees for 1½ hours or until done.

Creamy Cheesecake Tarts

Crust

2	cups cinnamon crisp graham cracker crumbs	1	teaspoon cinnamon
2½	tablespoons sugar	¼	teaspoon nutmeg
		½	cup butter, melted

Filling

3	(8-ounce) packages cream cheese, softened	5	eggs, separated
1¼	cups sugar, divided	1	egg
2	tablespoons all-purpose flour	1½	cups sour cream
⅛	teaspoon salt	¼	cup lemon juice

Line mini muffin or regular muffin pans with paper baking cups. Combine all crust ingredients and mix well. Firmly press mixture into bottom of baking cups and chill.

For filling, beat cream cheese with an electric mixer until light and fluffy. Gradually beat in 1 cup sugar. Add flour and salt. Add 5 egg yolks plus 1 whole egg, one at a time, beating well after each addition. Stir in sour cream and lemon juice and mix well. Beat 5 egg whites, that have been allowed to come to room temperature, until foamy. Gradually add remaining ¼ cup sugar, beating until stiff peaks form. Fold egg whites into cream cheese mixture. Spoon filling over crust in baking cups, filling three-fourths full. Bake at 300 degrees for 20 minutes for small tarts or 30 minutes for large tarts. Chill. Top each tart with a strawberry half.

To convert this recipe into a cheesecake, prepare crust and firmly press into a 9-inch springform pan. Prepare filling and pour over crust. Bake at 300 degrees for 1½ hours. Turn oven off and allow to cool in oven for 2 hours. Chill at least 4 hours before removing sides of pan and serving. Yield: 12 servings.

Carrot Cake

2	cups flour	1½	cups salad oil
2	teaspoons baking powder	4	eggs
1½	teaspoons baking soda	2	cups grated carrot
2	teaspoons cinnamon	1	(8½-ounce) can crushed pineapple
1½	teaspoons salt	½	cup chopped nuts
2	cups sugar	1	(3½-ounce) can flaked coconut

Cream Cheese Frosting

½	cup butter, softened	1	teaspoon vanilla
1	(8-ounce) package cream cheese, softened	1	(1-pound) package XXX powdered sugar
		½	cup chopped nuts

Combine flour, baking powder, baking soda, cinnamon and salt in a bowl. Add sugar, oil and eggs and beat well with an electric mixer. Add carrot, pineapple, nuts and coconut. Stir thoroughly. Pour batter into three 9-inch greased and floured cake pans. Bake 35 to 40 minutes. Cool.

To make frosting, cream together butter, cream cheese and vanilla. Beat in sugar until creamy. Stir in nuts. Spread frosting over cooled cake.

Fresh Apple Nut Cake

Batter

1½	cups cooking oil	1	teaspoon salt
2	cups sugar	2	teaspoons vanilla
4	eggs	3	cups diced apple
3	cups self-rising or plain flour	1	cup pecans, toasted and chopped
1	teaspoon baking soda		

Glaze

¾	cup margarine	¼	cup milk
1	cup brown sugar	1	teaspoon vanilla

Mix oil, sugar and eggs until creamy. Sift flour, baking soda and salt together and add to creamed mixture. Beat well. Mix in vanilla, apple and pecans. Pour batter into a well-greased and floured tube pan. Bake at 325 degrees for 1½ hours.

To make glaze, mix margarine, sugar and milk in a saucepan. Boil slowly for 10 minutes. Add vanilla. Cool and pour over cake.

Decadent Fudge Cake

1	cup butter, softened	2	(4-ounce) bars sweet baking chocolate, melted and cooled
1½	cups sugar		
4	eggs	⅓	cup chocolate syrup
½	teaspoon baking soda	2	teaspoons vanilla
1	cup buttermilk	4	ounces white chocolate, chopped
2½	cups all-purpose flour	2	tablespoons plus 2 teaspoons vegetable shortening, divided
1½	cups mini semisweet chocolate chips, divided		Chocolate and white chocolate leaves (optional)

Cream butter in a large mixing bowl with an electric mixer. Gradually beat in sugar. Add eggs, one at a time, beating well after each addition. Dissolve baking soda in buttermilk, stirring well. Add to creamed mixture alternately with flour, beginning and ending with flour. Add 1 cup mini chips, melted chocolate, chocolate syrup and vanilla. Stir just until blended; do not overbeat.

Spoon batter into a heavily greased or sprayed and floured 10-inch Bundt pan. Bake at 300 degrees for 1 hour and 25 to 35 minutes or until cake springs back when touched. Invert cake immediately onto a serving plate and cool completely.

Combine white chocolate and 2 tablespoons shortening in the top of a double boiler over boiling water. Reduce heat to low and cook until mixture is melted and smooth. Remove from heat and drizzle over cooled cake. Melt remaining ½ cup chocolate chips with remaining 2 teaspoons shortening in a small saucepan over low heat. Cool and drizzle over white chocolate. Garnish with chocolate leaves. Yield: 10-inch cake.

Elise's Pistachio Pound Cake

1½	cups butter, chilled	1	(3-ounce) box instant pistachio pudding mix
3	cups sugar		
5	eggs	½	teaspoon baking soda
3	cups all-purpose flour	1	cup sour cream
		1½	teaspoons almond extract

Cream butter until light and fluffy. Add sugar gradually. Beat in eggs. Add flour and pudding mix and blend until moistened. Stir baking soda into sour cream and add to batter along with almond extract. Beat well and pour into a greased and lightly floured tube pan. Bake at 350 degrees for 1 hour, 15 minutes.

Fresh Banana Layer Cake

Batter

2¼	cups sifted cake flour (not self-rising)
¾	teaspoon baking soda
½	teaspoon baking powder
½	teaspoon salt
1	cup mashed very ripe banana (about 2 large)
¼	cup plain yogurt or well-shaken buttermilk
1	teaspoon vanilla
½	cup unsalted butter, softened
1	cup sugar
2	eggs, separated

Frosting

1	(1-pound) package powdered sugar
1	(8-ounce) package cream cheese, softened
½	cup unsalted butter, softened
2	teaspoons vanilla
	Pinch of salt
2-3	large firm ripe bananas for assembly

Sift together flour, baking soda, baking powder and salt. In a small bowl, whisk together banana, yogurt and vanilla. In a large bowl, beat together butter and sugar until light and fluffy. Beat in egg yolks, one at a time, beating well after each addition. Stir in dry ingredients and banana mixture alternately, beginning and ending with dry ingredients and stirring after each addition until just combined. Beat egg whites until stiff. Fold whites into batter. Grease and flour three 8-inch round cake pans. Divide batter evenly among prepared pans, smoothing tops. Bake in upper and lower thirds of oven, switching position of pans halfway through baking, at 350 degrees for 18 minutes or until layers are springy to the touch and a tester inserted in the center comes out clean. Cool in pans on wire racks for 10 minutes. Run a thin knife around the edges of the pans and invert onto racks to cool completely.

For frosting, sift powdered sugar into a large bowl. In a separate large bowl, beat together cream cheese and butter with an electric mixer until light and fluffy. Beat in vanilla and salt. Beat in powdered sugar, a little at a time, until smooth.

To assemble, cut 2 bananas into thin slices. Place a cake layer on a serving plate and spread with a thin coating of frosting. Arrange a layer of banana slices, overlapping them slightly, over frosting. Top with second cake layer and spread with another thin coating of frosting. Arrange another layer of banana slices in same manner over frosting, using third banana if needed. Top with remaining cake layer and spread remaining frosting over top and sides of cake.

Fresh Coconut Cake

Batter

1	fresh coconut	4½	cups sifted cake flour
	Milk	5	teaspoons baking powder
1	cup vegetable shortening	1½	teaspoons salt
½	cup butter, softened	1	tablespoon vanilla
3	cups sugar	8	egg whites, stiffly beaten

Divinity Icing

4	cups sugar	4	egg whites
1	cup water	1	tablespoon vanilla
¼	cup light corn syrup		

Drain milk from coconut. Add milk to coconut milk to equal 2 cups; set aside. Place coconut on a baking sheet or small pan. Bake at 350 degrees until coconut cracks. Remove from oven and remove shell. Using a potato peeler, peel off brown covering. Grate white coconut pulp and set aside.

Cream together shortening, butter and sugar. In a separate bowl, sift together flour, baking powder and salt. Add vanilla to coconut milk mixture. Add dry ingredients to creamed mixture alternately with coconut milk mixture, beginning and ending with dry ingredients. Fold egg whites carefully into batter; do not overmix.

Spray three 9-inch cake pans with cooking spray. Line bottom of pans with parchment or wax paper and spray paper with cooking spray. Divide batter evenly among pans. Bake at 350 degrees for 25 to 30 minutes or until a toothpick inserted in the center comes out clean.

To make icing, mix sugar, water and corn syrup together in a heavy saucepan. Cook until a candy thermometer registers at soft-ball stage. Meanwhile, beat egg whites until stiff. Pour hot syrup into egg whites, beating constantly until reaching a spreading consistency. Stir in vanilla.

Spread icing between layers and on top of cake. Sprinkle freshly grated coconut over icing between the layers and on top of cake.

Fresh Orange Cake

Batter

1	large orange	5	tablespoons butter, softened
	Milk	1⅛	cups sugar
2	cups all-purpose flour	2	eggs
1	tablespoon baking powder	1	teaspoon vanilla
¼	teaspoon salt		

Glaze

1½	cups sifted powdered sugar	½	teaspoon vanilla
1½-3	tablespoons orange juice		

Grate zest from orange; set aside. Juice orange and combine with enough milk to equal 1 cup liquid; set aside.

In a small bowl, combine flour, baking powder and salt. In a large mixing bowl, cream butter and sugar with an electric mixer on medium-high speed until light and fluffy. Add eggs, one at a time, beating well on medium speed after each addition. Mix in vanilla. Add dry ingredients alternately with orange liquid, beating on low speed after each addition just until combined. Stir in reserved orange zest. Pour batter into a greased and floured 9x13-inch baking pan and smooth evenly on top. Tap pan on counter to remove air bubbles. Bake at 350 degrees for 30 to 35 minutes or until a toothpick inserted near center comes out clean. Cool on a wire rack for 10 minutes.

While cake cools, prepare glaze. Combine powdered sugar with enough orange juice to reach a drizzling consistency. Add vanilla and beat until smooth. Drizzle glaze evenly over warm cake. Let stand 2 hours before cutting. Yield: 12 servings.

You may omit glaze and frost the cake with the following frosting:

Orange Frosting

1	(3-ounce) package cream cheese, softened	2	tablespoons orange juice
		½	teaspoon orange extract
5	tablespoons butter, softened	½	teaspoon vanilla extract
1	(1-pound) package powdered sugar, sifted, divided		

Combine cream cheese and butter in a mixing bowl. Beat with and electric mixer on medium speed until combined. Gradually add 2 cups powdered sugar and beat until combined. Add remaining powdered sugar, orange juice and extracts. Beat until smooth. Spread over cake.

Fresh Pineapple Upside-Down Cake

For the caramel:

4	tablespoons water	1	cup sugar

In a heavy saucepan with a tight fitting lid, stir the water and sugar together. Bring to a boil over medium high heat, swirling occasionally. Cover the pan for about 4 minutes so the steam washes down the sugar crystals from the sides of the pan. Uncover and boil for about 12 minutes or until the caramel turns light amber. Remove from the heat and immediately pour the syrup into a buttered cake pan or a buttered iron skillet.

Cut off the top of a fresh pineapple and cut a slice from the bottom so it will stand upright. Cut the pineapple into quarters. Cut away the peel and core and then cut each wedge crosswise into ¼ inch slices. Arrange the slices in rings on the hardened caramel, overlapping them evenly, with flat edges up.

For the cake:

1½	cups all-purpose flour	⅔	cup granulated sugar
1½	teaspoons double-acting baking powder	2	large eggs
½	teaspoon salt	1	teaspoon vanilla
1	stick unsalted butter, softened	¾	cup milk

With an electric mixer, cream the butter. Gradually add the sugar, beating until mixture is light. Add the eggs one at a time, beating for about 15 seconds to incorporate each. Add vanilla. Sift together the flour, baking powder and salt. With the mixer on low speed, add half of the dry ingredients to the butter mixture and mix just until the flour disappears. Add the milk and mix again. Add the remaining dry ingredients, mixing just until the flour disappears. Spoon large dollops of the batter over the sliced fruit, taking care not to disturb the arranged fruit slices. Smooth out the batter.

Bake the cake in a preheated 350 degree oven about 50 minutes, or until done. Remove the cake from the oven and run a knife between the cake and the pan. Set a serving platter upside down on top of the cake pan. Invert the platter and the pan, and let them rest for 4 to 5 minutes to allow the caramelized fruit to settle onto the cake. Gently lift the pan from the cake and serve alone or with ice cream or whipped cream. Yield: 7 servings.

Note: I cook this cake in a cast iron skillet with very good results.

German Chocolate Roulage

Batter

6	eggs, separated
¼	cup sugar
¼	cup plus 1 to 2 tablespoons unsweetened cocoa powder, divided

1	teaspoon vanilla
½	teaspoon cream of tartar
⅛	teaspoon salt
½	cup sifted cake flour

Coconut Filling

1	(14-ounce) can sweetened condensed milk
1½	cups flaked coconut, toasted

1	cup chopped pecans, toasted
2	teaspoons vanilla
5	tablespoons half-and-half

Chocolate Topping

⅔	cup heavy cream
2	tablespoons light corn syrup
2	(4-ounce) bars sweet baker's chocolate, finely chopped

Toasted flaked coconut, chocolate autumn leaves and meringue mushrooms for garnish

Spray the bottom and sides of a 10x15-inch jelly roll pan with cooking spray; line bottom of pan with wax paper or parchment and spray paper with cooking spray.

Beat egg yolks on high speed with an electric mixer until foamy. Gradually add sugar, beating 2 minutes or until thick and pale. Gradually add ¼ cup cocoa, beating well. Stir in vanilla.

Beat egg whites on high speed until foamy. Add cream of tartar and salt and beat until stiff peaks form. Fold about one-fourth of beaten egg white into yolk mixture. Gradually fold in remaining egg white. Sift flour over batter and gently fold in until combined. Spread batter evenly in prepared pan. Bake at 325 degrees for 16 to 17 minutes or until top springs back when lightly touched. Meanwhile, sift 1 to 2 tablespoons cocoa in a 15x10-inch rectangle on a cloth towel. When cake is done, immediately loosen cake from sides of pan and turn out onto towel. Peel off wax paper. Starting at narrow end, roll up cake and towel together. Cool rolled cake, seam-side down, on a wire rack.

Pour milk into a heavy medium saucepan. Cook over medium-low to medium heat, stirring constantly, for 20 minutes or until milk turns a light caramel color. Remove from heat and stir in coconut, pecans, vanilla and half-and-half. Unroll cake and remove towel. Spread coconut filling over cake. Carefully re-roll cake without towel. Place cake, seam-side down, on a wire rack over wax paper.

For topping, combine cream and corn syrup in a saucepan. Bring to a boil over medium heat. Remove from heat and add chocolate, stirring until smooth. Pour about three-fourths of chocolate mixture over cake, letting excess drip onto wax paper. Let remaining chocolate sit at room temperature for 45 minutes or until the consistency of frosting. Spread remaining chocolate mixture onto ends of cake roll. Garnish with toasted coconut. Let cake stand until chocolate is firm. Place on a serving platter. Yield: 8 to 10 servings.

Jo's Lane Cake

Batter

3¼	cups sifted flour	1	cup milk
2	teaspoons baking powder	8	egg whites
1	cup butter, softened	1	teaspoon vanilla
2	cups sifted granulated sugar		

Filling

8	egg yolks	1	cup finely chopped raisins
1	cup sugar	4	ounces whiskey or brandy
½	cup butter, softened	1	teaspoon vanilla

Icing

2	egg whites	¼	teaspoon cream of tartar
1½	cups sugar	1	teaspoon vanilla
5	tablespoons cold water		

Line bottom of four 8-inch cake pans with ungreased parchment paper. Sift flour and baking powder together 3 times. Cream butter with sugar until perfectly light. Add dry ingredients and milk, alternately, to creamed batter, adding a little at a time until all are used, beginning and ending with flour. Beat egg whites until well whipped. Add whipped egg whites and vanilla to batter. Divide batter among prepared pans. Bake at 375 degrees for 30 minutes.

For filling, beat egg yolks with sugar and butter. Transfer mixture to the top of a double boiler and cook, stirring constantly, until very thick. While still hot, mix in raisins, whiskey and vanilla. Spread thickly between cake layers.

To make icing, combine egg whites, sugar, cold water and cream of tartar in the top of a double boiler over rapidly boiling water. Beat constantly with a beater for 7 minutes. Remove from stove and add vanilla. Keep beating until thick enough to spread on cake. Spread over top and sides of cake.

Here is another icing for this cake:

1½	(3-ounce) packages cream cheese, softened	3	tablespoons bourbon
¾	cup powdered sugar, divided	1½	teaspoons vanilla
		1½	cups heavy cream, chilled

Beat cream cheese and ¼ cup powdered sugar in a medium bowl until smooth. Beat in bourbon and vanilla. Beat cream with remaining ½ cup powdered sugar in a large bowl until soft peaks form. Add cream cheese mixture to whipped cream and beat until stiff enough to spread.

For garnish, place pecan halves around edge of cake. Using a rolling pin, roll apricot halves between sheets of plastic wrap. Cut out leaf shapes and arrange on cake.

Italian Cream Cake

Batter

½	cup butter, softened	1	teaspoon baking soda
½	cup vegetable shortening	1	cup buttermilk
2	cups sugar	1	teaspoon vanilla
5	eggs, separated	1	(3½-ounce) can coconut
2	cups cake flour	1	cup chopped pecans

Frosting

½	cup butter	1	teaspoon vanilla
1	(8-ounce) package cream cheese	½	cup chopped pecans, toasted
1	(16-ounce) package powdered sugar		

Cream butter and shortening together. Add sugar and beat well. Add egg yolks, one at a time, beating well. Sift together four and baking soda. Add dry ingredients and buttermilk alternately to creamed mixture. Stir in vanilla, coconut and pecans. Beat egg whites until stiff and fold into batter. Divide batter among 3 greased and floured cake pans. Bake at 350 degrees for about 25 minutes. Cool thoroughly before applying frosting.

To make frosting, cream butter and cream cheese together. Add sugar and vanilla. Stir in pecans. Spread on top of layers and over top and sides of cake.

Lemon Cheese Cake

1	cup butter, softened	1	cup buttermilk
2	cups sugar	1	teaspoon vanilla extract
3	cups cake flour	1	teaspoon lemon extract
½	teaspoon salt	6	egg whites, stiffly beaten
1	tablespoon baking powder		

Lemon Cheese Frosting

1	cup butter	6	egg yolks
2	cups sugar		Zest and juice of 2 lemons

Cream butter and sugar until light and fluffy. Sift together flour, salt and baking powder. Combine buttermilk and both extracts. Add dry ingredients and buttermilk mixture alternately to creamed mixture, beginning and ending with dry ingredients. Fold in egg whites. Pour into 3 greased and paper-lined layer pans. Bake at 350 degrees for 25 to 30 minutes.

For frosting, combine all ingredients in the top of a double boiler. Cook and stir until thickened. Spread frosting between layers and on top of cooled cake.

This is a very old recipe from my aunt. There is no cheese in this cake, however, it is called Lemon Cheese.

Lemon Chiffon Cake

2	cups cake flour (I use Swan's Down)	⅔	cup cold water
1⅓	cups sugar	1	tablespoon lemon juice
1	tablespoon baking powder	1	teaspoon lemon zest
1	teaspoon salt	1	cup egg whites (about 7)
½	cup less 1 tablespoon salad oil	½	teaspoon cream of tartar
5	egg yolks		

Lemon Confectioners' Icing

1-1½	(16-ounce) boxes powdered sugar, sifted	1	tablespoon lemon juice
1½	tablespoons water	1	teaspoon lemon zest
1	tablespoon butter, softened	1	teaspoon corn syrup

Have ready a 10-inch tube pan; do not grease. Place rack on lower shelf of oven. Preheat oven to 325 degrees 10 minutes before baking.

Sift flour, measure and resift 3 times with sugar, baking powder and salt, sifting last time into a 3-quart mixing bowl. Make a well in the center of dry ingredients and pour in salad oil. Add egg yolks, cold water, lemon juice and zest. Place egg whites and cream of tartar in a 4-quart mixing bowl. Let whites stand while beating yolk mixture with a wooden spoon for 75 to 80 strokes or until smooth and well blended. Clean off spoon and sides of bowl with a rubber scraper, leaving scraper in the bowl. Beat egg whites with an electric mixer until stiff peaks form; whites should be stiffer than for angel food or meringue, but not stiff enough to look dry. Quickly shake whites from beater and immediately pour egg yolk mixture in a steady stream over egg whites, cutting and folding in with rubber scraper as you pour. When almost all yolk mixture is added, quickly scrape excess from sides of bowl into whites, continuing to cut and fold in until just well blended and no longer. (Never stir and never overmix as this toughens cake.) Carefully flow batter at once into pan, quickly and lightly scraping out batter adhering to bowl. Place immediately in oven. Bake at 325 degrees for 55 minutes or until cake springs back when lightly touched with finger. When done, immediately invert over a large funnel or bottle heavy enough to support cake. Cool at least 1 hour before removing pan. Loosen sides with a thin bladed spatula and turn onto a serving plate. Frost with Lemon Confectioners' Icing. Cut with a saw-tooth cake knife.

To make icing, combine all ingredients and mix to a spreading consistency. Spread over cooled cake. You may add more liquid or more sugar, as needed, to reach a good spreading consistency. I sometimes wet my spatula to make the icing spread more smoothly.

This is a very good light cake to serve at a ladies luncheon or as a dessert after a seafood or heavy dinner. It is my granddaughter's favorite cake so I make it for her birthday. I sugar pansies in the spring to decorate it.

Lemon Coconut Cake

3¾ cups sifted cake flour
4½ teaspoons baking powder
1½ teaspoons salt
6 egg whites
2¼ cups granulated sugar, divided
1½ cups plus 1 tablespoon milk

1½ teaspoons vanilla extract
½ teaspoon almond extract
¾ cup vegetable shortening, softened
Lemon Filling (recipe below)
Divinity Icing (page 175)
1 cup flaked coconut

Lemon Filling

1 cup granulated sugar
¼ cup cornstarch
½ cup butter
8 egg yolks

3 tablespoons lemon zest
½ cup lemon juice
¾ cup boiling water

Sift flour, baking powder and salt together 3 times. In a large bowl of an electric mixer, beat egg whites until foamy on high speed. Gradually beat in ¾ cup sugar, beating only until mixture holds soft peaks. Turn into another large bowl and set aside. Combine milk and both extracts; set aside.

In the large bowl of the mixer, mix shortening with remaining 1½ cups sugar on medium speed until very light and fluffy. Reduce speed to low and beat in flour mixture in fourths alternately with milk mixture in thirds just until smooth. Add beaten egg whites and mix thoroughly. Pour batter into 3 greased and wax paper-lined 9-inch layer pans. Bake at 375 degrees for 25 minutes or until a cake tester inserted in the center comes out clean. Cool on a wire rack for 15 minutes. Loosen around edges of cooled cake with a spatula. Place a wire rack over top of one cake layer and invert onto rack. Lift off pan and peel off paper. Place a second rack over cake and invert again so layer is right side up. Repeat with remaining cake layers. Cool layers completely on racks.

To make lemon filling, combine sugar and cornstarch in the top of a double boiler. Add butter, egg yolks, lemon zest and juice. Add boiling water. Cook and stir until mixture mounds when dropped from a spoon. Cover with wax paper and cool slightly. Spread filling between layers of cake. Spread a 5-inch circle of filling in the center of top layer of cake.

Spread divinity icing on sides and about 3 inches on the top sides of cake around the lemon filling, leaving filling showing in the center. Press coconut to sides and on top of icing.

You can leave the coconut off and just have a lemon cake. Candied pansies or candies violets make a good decoration for this cake. Candied lemon peel tied in bows are also good decorations.

Mrs. Middleton's Caramel Cake

4	eggs, chilled	1	tablespoon baking powder
½	cup butter	½	teaspoon salt
½	cup vegetable shortening	1	cup milk
2	cups sugar	1	teaspoon vanilla extract
3	cups sifted cake flour (Swans Down)	½	teaspoon almond extract

Caramel Filling and Frosting

3	cups sugar	1	teaspoon vanilla
1	cup milk	1	(16-ounce) can crushed pineapple,
1	(12-ounce) can evaporated milk		drained
6	tablespoons butter		

Remove eggs from refrigerator and separate while they are cold. Beat egg whites until stiff; set aside. Cream butter and shortening together. Gradually add sugar and beat until light and fluffy. Add egg yolks one at a time, beating well after each addition. Sift flour with baking powder and salt in a separate bowl. Combine milk and both extracts in a cup. Add dry ingredients alternately with milk mixture to creamed mixture, beating after each addition until smooth, beginning and ending with dry ingredients. Beat in stiff egg whites. Pour batter into 3 greased and floured 9-inch layer pans. Bake at 350 degrees for about 25 minutes. Remove from pans and cool.

To make frosting, combine sugar, milk, evaporated milk, butter and vanilla in a saucepan. Cook over very low heat, stirring mixture until it starts to boil. Cook as you would fudge candy to soft ball stage. Beat until cool. Spread frosting over bottom cake layer and top with half of pineapple. Repeat with second cake layer. Add top cake layer and spread frosting over top and sides of entire cake.

No Fail Caramel Icing

½	cup butter	¼	cup milk
1	cup dark brown sugar	2	cups powdered sugar
¼	teaspoon salt		

Melt butter in a saucepan over low heat. Add brown sugar and salt and bring to a boil over medium heat. Boil hard for 2 minutes, stirring constantly. Remove from heat and stir in milk. Cool to lukewarm. Stir in powdered sugar and beat until smooth. If icing is too thick, beat in a little extra milk. Recipe will frost 2 layers or a sheet cake.

Sixteen Layer Chocolate Fudge Cake

1	pound unsalted butter, softened	½	teaspoon baking powder
⅓	cup vegetable shortening		Pinch of coarse salt
3	cup sugar	1	cup evaporated milk
6	eggs, room temperature	1	tablespoon pure vanilla extract
3	cups all-purpose flour, plus extra for dusting		

Chocolate Glaze

6	tablespoons cocoa	¼	cup light corn syrup
3	cups sugar	¾	cup butter, softened
¼	cup water	1	tablespoon vanilla
1	(12-ounce) can evaporated milk		

Cut sixteen 8-inch rounds of parchment paper, slightly smaller that bottom of an 8-inch cake pan. Coat three 8-inch cake pans with cooking spray. Line each pan with a parchment circle. Coat parchment with cooking spray and dust with flour, shaking out the excess. Set pans aside.

In the bowl of an electric mixer fitted with a paddle attachment, cream butter and shortening on medium-high speed for about 1 minute. Add sugar and beat 3 minutes or until fluffy. Use a rubber spatula to scrape down the sides as needed. Add egg, one at a time, beating after each addition. Scrape down the sides of the bowl after last egg and beat 1 minute longer. Sift together flour, baking powder and salt. Combine milk and vanilla. Reduce mixer speed to low and add dry ingredients alternately with milk mixture, beginning and ending with dry ingredients. Beat after each addition until fully incorporated.

Spoon exactly ½ cup of batter into each of the prepared pans using on offset spatula to spread evenly. Bake at 325 degrees for 8 to 10 minutes or until barely golden along the edges; do not overbake or the cake will be dry. Rotate pans halfway through baking. Remove cakes from the oven and cool in pan on wire racks for 2 minutes. Use an offset spatula to loosen edges of cake and invert over a cardboard cake round with plastic wrap. (I invert to my hand and lay on cake round.) The baked layers should be about ¼-inch thick. Stack the warm layers with plastic wrap between each layer. It is not necessary to wash the cake pans between baking the layers. Brush pans out with paper towel and prepare and bake as before.

Prepare the chocolate glaze after all layers are baked. Mix sugar and cocoa well in a saucepan. Add water to make a paste. Stir in milk and corn syrup. Add butter and bring to a boil, stirring constantly. When it comes to a boil, cook 3 minutes. Remove from heat. Beat 1 minute with a large whisk. Add vanilla. Assemble cake while glaze is hot.

To assemble, place one cake layer on a cardboard cake round slightly smaller than the layer. Place on a wire rack with wax paper underneath. Ladle a scant 2 tablespoons of glaze over cake layer. Place second cake layer on top, pressing down gently to secure and create a level cake. Repeat until all layers are used making sure the cake remains level by adjusting the layers as needed. Pour the remaining glaze over the top of the cake and let it drip down the sides. Use a spatula to smooth the sides so they are completely covered. With 2 heavy spatulas, move the cake to the serving dish. Let stand 30 minutes before serving. The cake is best when eaten shortly after it is assembled and should not be refrigerated. It will keep at room temperature for 1 to 2 days. It never lasts that long.

I move the cake before I discard any leftover glaze so I can repair any accidental touches.

Pound Cake

1	pound butter, softened	1	scant teaspoon mace
3⅓	cups sugar, plus extra for topping		Pinch of salt
10	eggs		Zest and juice of 1 lemon
4	cups plain flour		

Cream butter with sugar. Add eggs, one at a time, beating well after each addition. Sift together flour, mace and salt and add slowly to creamed mixture, beating until smooth. Add lemon zest and juice. Line the bottom of a tube pan with wax or parchment paper and spray sides with cooking spray. Pour batter into pan. Bake at 325 degrees for 1½ hours or until done; the top may crack while baking.

While still warm, rub sugar over top and sides of cake.

Seven Minute Icing

2	egg whites, unbeaten		Pinch of salt
1⅔	cups sugar	1	teaspoon vanilla
5	tablespoons light corn syrup		

Combine all ingredients except vanilla in the top of a double boiler. Cook, beating constantly with an electric mixer at high speed, until stiff peaks form. Stir in vanilla. Recipe will frost a 3 layer cake.

White Chocolate Layer Cake with Raspberry Filling

2	(6-ounce) packages white chocolate baking bars, chopped	
¼	cup milk	
2	cups all-purpose flour	
¾	teaspoon baking soda	
½	teaspoon salt	

¼	teaspoon baking powder
½	cup butter, softened
¾	cup sugar
1	teaspoon vanilla
4	eggs
¾	cup sour cream

Raspberry Filling

¼	cup fresh or frozen (and thawed) raspberries	½	cup heavy cream
		1	tablespoon sugar

Buttercream Frosting

1	(6-ounce) package white chocolate baking bar	1	cup butter, chilled and cut into pieces
¼	cup heavy cream	1	cup powdered sugar

Combine chocolate and milk in the top of a double boiler over hot, but not boiling, water. Stir until melted and smooth. In a small bowl, combine flour, baking soda, salt and baking powder; set aside.

In a large bowl, beat butter and sugar until light and fluffy. Gradually stir in chocolate mixture and vanilla. Add eggs, one at a time. Beat in dry ingredients alternately with sour cream. Pour batter into 3 greased 8-inch round baking pans lined with wax paper. Bake at 350 degrees for 35 minutes or until a cake tester inserted in the center comes out clean. Cool on wire racks 15 minutes before removing pans. Cool completely.

For filling, combine raspberries, cream and sugar and beat until stiff peaks form. Refrigerate until ready to use.

To make frosting, melt chocolate with cream in the top of a double boiler over hot, but not boiling, water. Stir until smooth. Transfer to a large bowl and cool to room temperature. Gradually beat in butter and sugar until light and fluffy.

To assemble cake, spread 1 cup buttercream frosting over one cake layer. Top with second layer. Spread raspberry filling over second layer and top with third cake layer. Frost top and sides of entire cake with remaining buttercream frosting. Refrigerate until ready to serve.

Daiquiri Balls

1	cup semisweet chocolate pieces	1	tablespoon lemon zest
½	cup sour cream	1	tablespoon orange zest
8	ounces vanilla wafers	2½	tablespoons lemon juice
1	cup powdered sugar, plus extra for rolling	1½	tablespoons maple syrup
¼	teaspoon salt	¼	cup rum
3	tablespoons unsweetened cocoa	1	cup finely chopped pecans

Melt chocolate pieces over hot water; cool. Mix in sour cream and refrigerate overnight. Form chilled mixture into balls, using ½ tablespoon of mixture for each ball. (These will be used as centers.)

Crush vanilla wafers. Add 1 cup powdered sugar, salt, cocoa and fruit zests. Blend in lemon juice, syrup, rum and pecans. Press mixture around chocolate centers to form balls the size of walnuts. Roll in powdered sugar. Store in airtight containers, or freeze until needed. Yield: 54 balls.

Easy Chocolate Fudge

4½	cups sugar	12	ounces German sweet chocolate
4	tablespoons butter	2	cups marshmallow cream
	Pinch of salt	2	cups chopped pecans
1	(14-ounce) can evaporated milk		
12	ounces semisweet chocolate		

Combine sugar, butter, salt and milk in a saucepan and bring to a boil. Once mixture comes to a boil, boil 6 minutes. Remove from heat and beat in both chocolates, marshmallow cream and pecans until melted. Pour batter onto wax paper and allow to stand 3 hours. This recipe makes quite a lot so have a large place to pour it out. Yield: About 3 pounds.

This is excellent; it never dries out but remains moist for a week or more.

I butter the wax paper and lay it on the cool counter or a glass table top. A marble cutting board would work well.

Divinity

3	cups sugar	¼	teaspoon salt
¾	cup corn syrup	1	teaspoon vanilla
¾	cup water	¾	cup coarsely broken pecans or walnuts
⅓	cup fresh egg whites (from large 2 eggs or 3 small)		

Combine sugar, corn syrup and water in a saucepan. Heat to 262 degrees. Meanwhile, combine egg whites and salt in a bowl. When temperature reaches 262 degrees, remove saucepan from heat and let stand a minute or so while beating egg whites in bowl. Beat egg whites until they cling to the bowl, then, while beating constantly, pour hot syrup slowly over beaten whites. Beat 12 to 15 minutes or until candy will not flow from spoon in a continuous ribbon, but rather in broken pieces. The candy will begin to lose its shine. Quickly add vanilla and nuts. Drop from spoon onto greased wax paper.

Lori's Peanut Brittle

1½	cups shelled raw peanuts, skin on	1	teaspoon butter
1	cup sugar	1	teaspoon vanilla
½	cup light corn syrup	1	teaspoon baking soda
⅛	teaspoon salt		

Stir together peanuts, sugar, corn syrup and salt in a 1½-quart microwave-safe container. Microwave on high 4 minutes; stir. Microwave 4 minutes longer on high. Stir in butter and vanilla. Microwave 2 minutes longer on high. Stir in baking soda and quickly stir until light and foamy. Pour onto a lightly greased baking sheet, spread and pull. When cool, break into pieces and store in an airtight container.

Old Time Penuche

2	pounds (4½ cups) light brown sugar	¼	teaspoon salt
1	cup evaporated milk	1	teaspoon vanilla
½	cup butter	2	cups chopped walnuts or pecans

Mix sugar, milk, butter and salt in a saucepan. Cook and stir until sugar is dissolved. Continue to cook until mixture reaches 238 degrees on a candy thermometer. Remove from heat and let stand until lukewarm. Add vanilla and nuts. Pour into a greased 9-inch square pan. When firm, cut into squares.

Old Fashioned Fudge

1⅓	cups milk	4	tablespoons butter
4	ounces baking chocolate	2	teaspoons vanilla
4	cups sugar	1½	cups chopped pecans
¼	cup corn syrup		

Place milk in a saucepan and heat until it just starts to boil. Remove from heat and add chocolate. As soon as chocolate is melted, add sugar and corn syrup. Return to heat and bring to a boil, stirring until the sugar is dissolved. Cover pan with a lid and boil mixture for about 2 to 3 minutes. Remove lid and cook, stirring frequently, to 236 degrees on a candy thermometer. Remove from heat and add butter. Stir in vanilla. Allow fudge to stand at room temperature until candy reaches 110 degrees. Add pecans and stir continuously until the candy is very thick. Spread quickly into a greased pan to a thickness of about ¾-inch deep. Allow to cool completely. Cut into squares and place upside down on a tray to dry.

Maple Sugar Fudge

1½	cups pure maple syrup	1	tablespoon butter
2	cups sugar	1	cup chopped walnuts
⅔	cup milk		

Combine syrup, sugar and milk in a large saucepan. Cook, stirring constantly, over medium heat until sugar is dissolved. Reduce heat to medium-low and cook 15 minutes or until a soft ball forms when a drop of the mixture is put into cold water, or until mixture reaches 234 degrees on a candy thermometer. Remove from heat when soft-ball stage is reached and add butter. Cool fudge in saucepan until the bottom of the pan feels comfortably warm. Stir in walnuts. Beat fudge by hand until thick. The fudge will stiffen and lose its gloss. Spoon fudge into a greased 8-inch square pan. Cool and cut into squares. Yield: Thirty-six 1-inch pieces.

Vanilla Fudge

3	cups sugar	½	cup water
2½	tablespoons corn syrup	⅛	teaspoon salt
½	cup heavy cream	1	teaspoon vanilla

Mix sugar, corn syrup, cream, water and salt in a saucepan. Bring to a boil. Continue to boil moderately until mixture reaches 236 degrees on a candy thermometer. Stir in vanilla and cool slightly. Pour mixture into a greased pan and cool completely.

You may add 1½ cups chopped pecans or walnuts to the fudge when you add the vanilla.

Tips for Baking and Keeping Cookies

Most cookies freeze well. Meringues do not. Meringues, however, keep well wrapped and stored in a plastic container.

All Cookies

- Preheat oven at least 15 minutes before baking.

- Do not overbake.

- Use shiny, heavy-gauge aluminum sheet pans, not darkened ones, so cookies brown evenly but not excessively.

Drop Cookies

- To keep cookies from spreading too much, let baking sheet cool before reusing.

- Bake on only one oven rack at a time. You might get uneven browning if you use more than one rack. If you have a convection oven, you may bake on all the racks.

- For even baking, rearrange and rotate baking sheets in the oven, unless you have a convection oven.

- Store crisp and soft cookies separately in plastic bags or tightly covered containers. Most cookies can be stored successfully for up to three days at room temperature.

- To freeze, package tightly in freezer bags or airtight containers for up to a year. Thaw at room temperature for 15 minutes.

Bar Cookies

- Bake bars only in the size pan called for in the recipe. Using a larger or smaller pan may alter baking time and texture.

- To make bars for freezing, line the baking pan with foil, extending the foil over the edges. If the recipe directs, grease the foil instead of the pan. Follow the recipe for baking and cooling. Lift the bars out of the pan, foil and all. Place the uncut, unfrosted bars in freezer bags or overwrap in foil. Seal, label and freeze. Thaw at room temperature for 15 minutes, then frost and cut.

- To make even squares or rectangles, use a ruler to measure and toothpicks to mark cutting lines.

- Using a long knife, cut straight down into bars. For clean, straight edges, wipe the knife between cuts.

- For triangles, cut cookie bars into 2- to 2½-inch squares, then diagonally cut each square in half. For diamonds, first make straight parallel cuts 1- to 1½-inches apart, forming a diamond pattern.

Tips for Baking and Keeping Cookies *continued*

Sliced Cookies

- Coat a roll of cookie dough in finely chopped nuts, colored sugar or flaked coconut, pressing to make the coating stick. Chill as directed.

- For faster chilling, freeze the dough for one-third the refrigerator time. Do not freeze dough made with butter; it will become too firm to slice.

- To keep cookies round, rotate the roll frequently while slicing.

- To keep baked cookies from sticking together, do not stack or store until thoroughly cooked.

Cookies as Gifts

Package in the following attractive ways:

- In antique tins, on beds of colored tinsel.

- In old-fashioned cookie jars.

- In shoe boxes covered with decorative paper and lined with tissue.

- In a cookie tin tied with ribbons. Attach a favorite cookie cutter to the ribbon and perhaps the cookie recipe.

- In an old-fashioned mixing bowl, wrapped in clear cellophane and tied with plaid ribbons. Attach a wooden spoon to the gift tag and the cookie recipe.

- Make a hole in the center of each cookie and tie cookies together in bunches with a gold cord.

Almond Graham Cookies

1	cup butter		Graham crackers
¼	cup sugar	4	ounces sliced almonds

Melt butter in a saucepan. Add sugar. Boil hard for 2 minutes, stirring constantly. Line a jelly roll pan with foil, allowing extra foil at ends for removing from pan. Arrange graham crackers in a neat single layer on top of the foil. Carefully spoon butter mixture evenly over the crackers, spreading to cover all of the crackers. Sprinkle with almonds. Bake at 350 degrees for 8 minutes or until the butter mixture is bubbly. Watch carefully as it burns easily. Cool, then slice or break into cookies. This is easy and very good.

Apricot Cheese Pastry Hearts

1	cup sifted all-purpose flour		Apricot preserves
⅛	teaspoon salt	1	egg, beaten
½	cup butter, cut into small pieces		Sugar
½	(8-ounce) package cream cheese, cut into small pieces		

On the day before, if desired, make pastry. Sift flour and salt into a medium bowl. Cut in butter and cream cheese with a pastry blender or 2 knives until all is well blended. Shape dough into a ball and wrap in foil, wax paper or plastic wrap. Refrigerate.

Early in the day, or about 2 hours before serving, roll out dough to ⅛-inch thick. Cut with a 2¾x3-inch heart-shaped cookie cutter. Remove trimmings, reroll and cut out once or twice again. Drop a scant teaspoon of preserves in the center of half of the cookies. Top with remaining cookies. Brush edges with beaten egg and seal with the tines of a fork. Brush top with beaten egg and sprinkle lightly with sugar. Transfer to lightly greased baking sheets. Bake at 400 degrees until lightly browned. Yield: About 2 dozen.

Apricot Stars

½	recipe prepared Basic Butter Cookie Dough
⅔	cup apricot jam

Halve dough; cover and reserve one half in refrigerator. Roll out remaining dough between sheets of wax paper to about ⅛-inch thickness into about a 10-inch square. Freeze or chill on a baking sheet for 15 minutes or until firm. With a 1½- to 2-inch star-shaped cookie cutter, cut out dough and arrange stars about 1 inch apart on baking sheets. Gather scraps, reroll and cut for a total of 60 stars. If dough becomes too soft to work with, refreeze uncut dough until firm. Bake, in batches, at 350 degrees in center of oven for 8 minutes or until pale golden. Transfer carefully to racks to cool. Repeat with reserved dough, except use a smaller star or round cutter to cut and lift out center of these stars before baking.

In a small saucepan, simmer and stir jam for 2 minutes. Strain through a fine sieve into a bowl, pressing hard on solids.

On a work surface, arrange whole stars, bottom-sides up. Drop ¼ teaspoon of jam in the center of each cookie, spreading almost to the edges. Top with a cut-out star. Any remaining jam can be spooned into centers. Let cookies stand until set. Store between layers of wax paper in an airtight container. Cookies may be frozen up to 6 weeks. Yield: About 5 dozen.

Austria Twists

1	package dry yeast	1	(8-ounce) package cream cheese, softened
3	cups flour	1	cup sugar
1	cup butter, softened	1	cup finely chopped nuts
3	egg yolks	1	teaspoon cinnamon

Glaze

2	cups powdered sugar, sifted	1	teaspoon vanilla
2	tablespoons cream		

Combine yeast, flour and butter and mix well. Blend in egg yolks and cream cheese. Divide dough into 4 balls. Wrap each ball in wax paper and refrigerate overnight. Roll each ball into a ¼-inch thick circle. Mix together sugar, nuts and cinnamon. Sprinkle mixture over dough, dividing equally between circles. Cut each circle into 16 equal wedges. Roll each wedge from wide end to opposite point. Place each on a greased baking sheet, pointed-side down. Bake at 350 degrees for 18 to 20 minutes. Spoon glaze over twists while warm. Yield: 64 twists.

To make glaze, combine powdered sugar, cream and vanilla.

Basic Butter Cookie Dough

2	cups unsalted butter, softened	3	egg yolks
1⅓	cups sugar	2	teaspoons vanilla
¾	teaspoon salt	4⅔	cups all-purpose flour

In a large standing electric mixer, beat together butter, sugar and salt until light and fluffy. Beat in yolks, one at a time. Add vanilla and beat until smooth. Beat in flour gradually, beating dough until well combined. Chill. Roll out and cut into a variety of Christmas cookies. Yield: 3 pounds of dough.

Candy Cane Cookies

1¼	cups butter, softened	1	teaspoon salt
1	cup powdered sugar		Red food coloring
1	egg	4	candy canes
1	teaspoon vanilla	¼	cup granulated sugar
½	teaspoon almond extract	1	egg white, lightly beaten
3½	cups all-purpose flour		

Cream butter in a large mixing bowl. Add powdered sugar and mix well. Add egg, vanilla and almond extract. Mix flour and salt and add to butter mixture. Divide dough in half. Tint one-half light red with coloring. Keep dough chilled for easy handling.

For candy canes, roll 1½ teaspoon portions of both colors of dough into 4-inch long strips. Place strips side-by-side and twist together lightly. Carefully place on ungreased baking sheets and curve top down to form a handle.

Crush candy canes and mix with granulated sugar. Bush egg white over top of cookies and sprinkle with candy cane mixture. Bake at 350 degrees for 10 to 12 minutes. Yield: 4 to 5 dozen.

You can also make wreaths by forming circles with the twisted dough instead of canes. Use cinnamon red hot candies to garnish.

Chocolate Dipped Coconut Macaroons

4	egg whites	3½	cups lightly packed sweetened flaked dried coconut
⅔	cup sugar	4	ounces semisweet chocolate, chopped
1½	teaspoons vanilla	2	tablespoons butter
¼	cup all-purpose flour		

In a bowl, with an electric mixer on high speed, beat egg whites until frothy. Beat in sugar, vanilla and flour until well blended. Stir in coconut. Drop dough by 1 tablespoon portions, about 2 inches apart, onto greased and floured, or parchment paper-lined baking sheets. Bake at 325 degrees for 20 minutes or until macaroons are golden. If baking more than one pan at a time, switch pan positions halfway through baking. With a wide spatula, transfer macaroons to a rack to cool completely.

Melt chocolate in the top of a double boiler over simmering water. Add butter and whisk until smooth. Hold a macaroon on one edge and dip the other edge into chocolate to coat half the cookie. Shake off excess chocolate and place on a wax paper-lined baking sheet. Repeat with remaining cookies. Yield: About 24 cookies.

Cowboy Cookies

1	cup granulated sugar		½	teaspoon salt
1	cup brown sugar		½	teaspoon baking powder
½	cup butter		2	cups oatmeal (if using old-fashioned, put in a blender a few minutes)
½	cup shortening			
2	eggs		1	cup semisweet chocolate chips
1	teaspoon vanilla		1	cup milk chocolate chips
2	cups flour		1	cup butterscotch chips
1	teaspoon baking soda		1½	cups pecan pieces

Cream together both sugars, butter, shortening, eggs and vanilla in a large bowl of an electric mixer. In a separate bowl, sift together flour, baking soda, salt and baking powder. Blend dry ingredients into creamed mixture. With mixer on low speed, or by hand, mix in oatmeal, both chocolate and butterscotch chips and pecans. Dough will be very stiff. Drop by teaspoonfuls (walnut-sized) onto a greased baking sheet. Do not crowd as cookies will spread. Bake at 350 degrees for 10 to 12 minutes or until lightly browned. Yield: About 99 cookies.

Fruit Cake Cookies

1	pound candied pineapple, chopped		½	cup butter, softened
1	cup white raisins, chopped		4	eggs
1	pound candied cherries, chopped		1	scant teaspoon baking soda
3	cups sifted flour		3	tablespoons milk
1	teaspoon cinnamon		1	ounce vanilla-flavored brandy
1	teaspoon allspice		6	cups coarsely chopped pecans (I leave pecans in halves)
1	teaspoon nutmeg			
1	cup brown sugar			

Combine pineapple, raisins and cherries in a bowl. In a separate bowl, combine flour, cinnamon, allspice and nutmeg. Add dry ingredients to fruit mixture. In a separate bowl, beat together brown sugar, butter and eggs. Mix baking soda, milk and brandy and add to egg mixture. Add flour/fruit mixture to egg mixture. Stir in pecans. Drop by teaspoonfuls onto a lightly greased baking sheet. Bake at 300 degrees for 15 to 20 minutes. Yield: About 100 cookies.

Glazed Lemon Cookies

¾	cup sugar	¾	cup unsalted butter, cold, cut into
2	tablespoons lemon zest		½-inch cubes
3	cups all-purpose flour	2	tablespoons fresh lemon juice
¼	teaspoon baking powder	1	egg yolk
¼	teaspoon salt	½	teaspoon vanilla

Lemon Glaze

1	tablespoon cream cheese, softened	1½	cups powdered sugar
2	tablespoons fresh lemon juice		

In a food processor, process sugar and lemon zest for 30 seconds or until sugar looks damp and zest is thoroughly incorporated. Add flour, baking powder and salt. Pulse on and off about 10 times or until combined. Scatter butter pieces over top and pulse about 15 times or until mixture resembles fine cornmeal. In a measuring cup or small bowl, beat together lemon juice, egg yolk and vanilla with a fork to combine. With machine running, add juice mixture in a slow, steady stream. Continue processing 10 to 15 seconds longer or until the dough begins to form a ball.

Turn dough and any dry bits onto a clean work surface. Working quickly, gently knead together to ensure that no dry bits remain. Shape the dough into a log about 10 inches long and 2 inches in diameter. Wrap dough in parchment paper or plastic wrap and twist to seal. Chill until firm and cold, about 45 minutes in the freezer or 2 hours in the refrigerator.

Adjust the oven racks to the upper and lower middle positions. Remove dough log from wrapper and, using a sharp knife, slice dough into ⅜-inch thick rounds. Place the rounds on 2 parchment paper-lined or sprayed baking sheets, spacing them 1 inch apart. Bake at 375 degrees for 14 to 16 minutes or until centers of cookies just begin to color and the edges are golden brown, rotating the baking sheets front to back and top to bottom halfway through baking time. Cool on baking sheets about 5 minutes. Transfer to a wire rack with a wide metal spatula and cool to room temperature before glazing.

To make glaze, combine all ingredients. Working with one at a time, spoon a scant teaspoon of glaze onto each cooled cookie and spread evenly with the back of the spoon. Let cookies stand on wire rack for 1 hour or until glaze is set and dry. Yield: About 30 cookies.

Heavenly Bite Fingers

1½	cups butter, melted	½	cup powdered sugar, plus extra for
¼	cup vanilla		rolling
2	cups walnuts or pecans, chopped	4	cups plain flour
		2	tablespoons water

Combine all ingredients and mix well. Roll dough into small oblong fingers. Bake at 325 degrees for 30 minutes. Cool. Roll in extra powdered sugar.

Giant Chocolate Toffee Cookies

½	cup all-purpose flour	4	eggs
1	teaspoon baking powder	1	tablespoon vanilla
¼	teaspoon salt	5	(1.4-ounce) chocolate-covered English
1	pound bittersweet chocolate, chopped		toffee bars (such as Heath), coarsely
4	tablespoons unsalted butter		chopped
1¾	cups brown sugar	1	cup walnuts, toasted and chopped

Combine flour, baking powder and salt in a small bowl and whisk to blend. Stir chocolate and butter in the top of a double boiler over simmering water until melted and smooth. Cool to lukewarm. Using an electric mixer, beat sugar and eggs in a bowl for 5 minutes or until thick. Beat in chocolate mixture and vanilla. Stir in dry ingredients. Add toffee and walnuts. Chill dough 45 minutes or until firm.

Drop chilled dough by ¼-cupfuls onto 3 parchment paper-lined baking sheets, placing 2½ inches apart. Bake at 350 degrees for 15 minutes or until tops are dry and cracked but cookies are still soft to the touch. Cool on sheets. Yield: 18 cookies.

Lemon Cheese Cookies

1	cup butter, softened	½	teaspoon lemon extract
1	(3-ounce) package cream cheese, softened	1	teaspoon lemon zest
1	cup sugar	2½	cups sifted all-purpose flour
1	egg yolk	½	teaspoon salt

Cream together butter, cream cheese and sugar. Add egg yolk, lemon extract and lemon zest and beat until light. Add flour and salt and mix well. Force dough through a spritz gun or cookie press onto ungreased baking sheets. Bake at 350 degrees for about 13 minutes. Yield: 6 dozen cookies.

Roll dough into balls. Flatten with a fork and sprinkle with sugar before baking. You may also squeeze dough through a pastry bag with a star tube and with a handle of a wooden spoon, make an indentation in the center of the cookie. When the cookies are cool, fill with strawberry or apricot jam. I have also chilled this dough and rolled out to make cut-out cookies for Easter or Christmas.

I made these a lot when the children were small. I had a hard time keeping my sons and their friends from sneaking into the kitchen and eating the uncooked balls waiting for the oven.

Lemon Squares

1	cup butter	4	eggs
½	cup powdered sugar, plus extra for sprinkling	2	cups granulated sugar
		6	tablespoons lemon juice
2	cups plus 6 tablespoons all-purpose flour, divided	1	tablespoon lemon zest (be careful to not grate the white)
⅛	teaspoon salt		

Combine butter, ½ cup powdered sugar, 2 cups flour and salt. Mix with a pastry blender until mixture is well blended. (If mixing by hand, allow butter to come to room temperature first. If using a food processor to mix, use cold butter and do not overmix.) Pat dough evenly into a 15x10x1-inch jelly roll pan; wet hands, if needed, to pat dough into pan. Bake at 350 degrees for 20 minutes.

Beat eggs slightly with a wire whisk in a large mixing bowl. Stir in granulated sugar, remaining 6 tablespoons flour, lemon juice and zest. Mix well and spread over baked crust. Bake at 350 degrees for 25 minutes. Remove from oven and lightly sift powdered sugar over the top. Cool before cutting into squares. Yield: About 3 dozen bars.

Meringue Mushrooms

4	egg whites, room temperature	2	(1-ounce) squares semisweet chocolate, melted
¼	teaspoon cream of tartar		
¾	cup sugar		Unsweetened cocoa powder
½	teaspoon almond extract		

Using an electric mixer on high speed, beat egg whites and cream of tartar until soft peaks form. Sprinkle in sugar, 2 tablespoons at a time, beating well after each addition until sugar dissolves. Beat in almond extract. Whites should stand in stiff, glossy peaks.

Spoon meringue into a large decorating bag with a large writing tip. Onto 2 parchment paper-lined baking sheets, pipe meringue into 30 mounds, each about 1½ inches in diameter (to resemble mushroom caps). Pipe remaining meringue upright onto baking sheet into thirty 1¼-inch lengths (to resemble mushroom stems). Bake at 200 degrees for 1¾ hours. Turn oven off; let meringues stand in oven 30 minutes longer to dry. Cool completely on baking sheet on a wire rack.

With the tip of a small knife, cut a small hole in the center of the underside of the mushroom cap. Place a small amount of melted chocolate in the hole. Spread underside of cap with chocolate. Attach stem to mushroom cap by inserting pointed end of stem into hole in underside of cap. Repeat with remaining stems and caps. Let chocolate dry for about 1 hour. Store mushrooms in a tightly covered container. Just before serving, sprinkle tops of mushrooms lightly with cocoa. Yield: 30 mushrooms.

Melt Aways

1	cup butter, softened	2	tablespoons cornstarch
1¼	cups powdered sugar	¼	teaspoon salt
1	teaspoon vanilla	1	cup chopped walnuts or pecans
1	cup sifted flour	1	(9¾-ounce) bar milk chocolate, melted

Cream butter. Gradually beat in sugar and vanilla. In a separate bowl, combine flour, cornstarch and salt. Add dry ingredients to creamed mixture. Fold in nuts and chocolate. Shape dough into 120 balls, using 1 teaspoon dough for each cookie. Place balls on an ungreased baking sheet, allowing room for cookies to spread. Bake at 250 degrees for 40 minutes. Store in an airtight container. Cookies can be frozen. Yield: 120 cookies.

Old Fashioned Brownies

2	eggs	2	(1-ounce) squares unsweetened chocolate, melted
1	cup granulated sugar		
½	teaspoon salt	¾	cup all-purpose flour
1	teaspoon vanilla	1	cup chopped walnuts or pecans
⅓	cup shortening, melted		

Beat eggs lightly with a fork. Stir in sugar, salt and vanilla. Add shortening and chocolate. Stir in flour and nuts. Do not beat at any time. Spread mixture into a greased 8-inch square pan. Bake at 325 degrees for about 30 minutes. Brownies should still be soft. Cool in pan before cutting into bars. Yield: 18 bars.

Southern Gingerbread

4	tablespoons butter	¼	teaspoon salt
½	cup sugar	1	teaspoon ground ginger
2	eggs, beaten	½	cup buttermilk
2½	cups flour	½	cup maple syrup or black molasses
2	teaspoons baking soda		

Cream butter and sugar. Blend in eggs. In a separate bowl, sift together flour, baking soda, salt and ginger. Mix buttermilk and molasses in a measuring cup. Add dry ingredients and buttermilk mixture to creamed mixture alternately, beginning and ending with dry ingredients. Pour batter into a greased and floured 8-inch square pan. Bake at 325 degrees for 25 minutes or until done. Cut into serving pieces. Serve hot, topped with applesauce and whipped cream or ice cream. Yield: 6 to 8 servings.

Pecan Lace Cookies

1	cup pecan pieces	⅓	cup light corn syrup
½	cup unsalted butter	½	cup all-purpose flour
½	cup brown sugar	½	teaspoon salt

Coarsely grind pecans in a food processor. In a saucepan, heat butter, brown sugar and corn syrup, stirring occasionally, until sugar is dissolved. Remove from heat and stir in flour, salt and ground pecans until well combined. Drop heaping tablespoons of dough, about 4 inches apart, onto an ungreased baking sheet. Bake at 375 degrees in center of oven for 6 minutes or until golden.

Working quickly, remove cookies from baking sheet one at a time with a thin metal spatula. Immediately drape cookies over a rolling pin to create a curved shape. (If cookies become too brittle to drape on a rolling pin, return sheet to oven for a few seconds to allow them to soften.) Cool cookies completely on rolling pin. Store in an airtight container at room temperature for about 2 days. Yield: About 30 cookies.

Shortbread Cookies

1	cup butter	¾	cup cornstarch
⅓	cup powdered sugar	1	cup plain flour

Icing

1	cup powdered sugar	½	teaspoon vanilla
2	tablespoons butter, melted	1	teaspoon lemon juice

Cream butter. Blend in powdered sugar, cornstarch and flour. Refrigerate dough 30 minutes. Drop by teaspoons onto an ungreased baking sheet. Bake at 350 degrees for 10 to 12 minutes. Spread icing over cooled cookies.

To make icing, stir together all ingredients. If icing is too thin, add more powdered sugar. Yield: About 2 dozen cookies.

Whiskey Balls

1	(10-ounce) box vanilla wafers, ground	1	cup crushed nuts
1	cup XXXX powdered sugar, plus extra for rolling	2	tablespoons light corn syrup
		½	cup rye, brandy or sherry

Combine all ingredients and form into marble-size balls. Roll in extra powdered sugar. Prepare 2 weeks ahead.

For chocolate balls, add 2 tablespoons unsweetened cocoa powder and ¼ cup corn syrup.

Sugar Cookies

2	cups all-purpose flour, sifted	¾	cup sugar, plus more for topping
2	teaspoons baking powder	⅔	cup vegetable oil
½	teaspoon salt	2	teaspoons vanilla
2	eggs	1	teaspoon lemon zest

Sift flour, baking powder and salt into a medium bowl and mix well; set aside. Whisk eggs in a large bowl until blended. Add ⅔ cup sugar, oil, vanilla and lemon zest. Blend in dry ingredients. Cover and chill 30 minutes or longer.

Drop dough by rounded teaspoonfuls 2 inches apart onto ungreased baking sheets. Mist the bottom of a 3-inch flat bottom glass with water and dip glass in extra sugar. Press the top of each cookie lightly with glass bottom to flatten. Mist and sugar glass before pressing each cookie. Bake at 400 degrees for 8 minutes or until lightly browned. Cool on baking sheets 2 minutes. Remove to wire racks to cool completely. Store at room temperature in airtight containers or freeze. Yield: 4 dozen cookies.

Starlight Sugar Crisps

1	package dry yeast (1 tablespoon)	2	eggs, beaten
¼	cup lukewarm water	½	cup sour cream
3¾	cups sifted plain flour	1	teaspoon vanilla
1½	teaspoons salt	1½	cups sugar
1	cup butter	2	teaspoons vanilla

Mix yeast with lukewarm water. Sift flour and salt into a mixing bowl. With 2 knives, cut in butter until particles are the size of small peas. Blend in eggs, sour cream, vanilla and softened yeast. Mix thoroughly. Cover and chill at least 2 hours. Dough can be refrigerated up to 4 days.

Combine sugar and vanilla. Sprinkle ½ cup of vanilla sugar mixture over a pastry cloth or board. Roll out half of chilled dough over vanilla sugar into a 16x8-inch rectangle. Sprinkle with about 1 tablespoon more of vanilla sugar. Fold one end of dough over center. Fold other end over to make 3 layers. Turn a quarter turn around, then repeat rolling and folding twice, sprinkling board and dough with extra vanilla sugar as needed. Roll out to a 16x8-inch rectangle about ¼-inch thick. Cut into 4x1-inch strips. Twist each strip 2 or 3 times and place on ungreased baking sheets. Repeat entire process with remaining dough. Bake at 275 degrees for 15 to 20 minutes or until light and golden brown. Yield: About 5 dozen twists.

Suzanne's Favorite Cookies

½	cup butter	½	teaspoon salt
½	cup cooking oil	½	teaspoon cream of tartar
½	cup brown sugar	½	teaspoon baking soda
½	cup granulated sugar	½	cup crispy rice cereal
1	egg	½	cup flaked coconut
1	teaspoon vanilla	½	cup nuts
1¾	cups all-purpose flour	½	cup oatmeal

Cream butter, oil and both sugars. Beat in eggs and vanilla. In a separate bowl, sift together flour, salt, cream of tartar and baking soda. Add dry ingredients to creamed mixture. Stir in cereal, coconut, nuts and oatmeal. Drop dough by teaspoonfuls onto a greased baking sheet. Bake at 350 degrees for 12 minutes or until lightly browned. Yield: About 50 cookies.

Amaretto Bread Pudding

1	pound bread, broken into pieces (I like challah)	3	eggs, room temperature
1	quart half-and-half	2	tablespoons almond extract
2	tablespoons unsalted butter, softened	1	cup white raisins
1½	cups sugar	¾	cup sliced almonds

Combine bread and half-and-half in a large bowl. Cover and let stand 1 hour. Use 2 tablespoons softened butter to grease a 9x13-inch baking dish. Whisk sugar, eggs and almond extract together. Stir mixture into soaked bread. Gently fold in raisins and almonds. Transfer mixture to prepared dish. Bake in center of oven at 325 degrees for 50 minutes or until firm. Cool. Serve with Amaretto Sauce (recipe follows). Yield: 8 to 10 servings.

Amaretto Sauce

1	cup powdered sugar	1	egg, well beaten
½	cup unsalted butter	¼	cup amaretto liqueur

Stir sugar and butter in the top of a double boiler over simmering water until butter melts, sugar dissolves and mixture is very hot. Remove from over water and whisk in egg. Return to double boiler and cook, whisking, a few more minutes. Remove from double boiler and whisk until cooled to room temperature. Mix in liqueur.

Amaretto Soufflé Cheesecake

¼	cup finely ground amaretti cookies (Italian almond macaroons)	1	tablespoon all-purpose flour
1½	(8-ounce) packages cream cheese, softened	3	eggs, separated
		¼	cup sour cream
½	cup sugar	3	tablespoons amaretto liqueur
		¼	teaspoon salt

Add cookie crumbs to a generously greased 9-inch springform pan, shaking pan to coat bottom and sides with crumbs. In the bowl of an electric mixer, beat together cream cheese, sugar and flour until light and fluffy. Beat in egg yolks, sour cream, liqueur and salt until smooth. In a separate bowl, beat egg whites until soft peaks form. Fold one-third of whites into cream cheese mixture to lighten, then fold in remaining whites gently but thoroughly. Pour filling into pan. Bake at 350 degrees in center of oven for 30 minutes or until just set. Cool completely in pan on a wire rack. Chill, covered, for at least 4 hours before serving.

Bananas Foster Bread Pudding

1	(12-inch) loaf French bread, cut into large cubes	1	teaspoon nutmeg
1	quart heavy cream	1	banana, coarsely chopped
8	eggs, lightly beaten	1	tablespoon dark rum
½	cup sugar	1	tablespoon banana liqueur
1	teaspoon cinnamon		Cinnamon sugar
			Butter

Place bread in a greased 2-quart baking dish. Mix cream, eggs, sugar, cinnamon, nutmeg, banana, rum and liqueur. Pour mixture over bread and stir bread around until well coated. Let stand 15 minutes. Sprinkle with cinnamon sugar and dot with butter. Bake, covered, at 325 degrees for 30 minutes. Uncover and bake 30 minutes longer. Serve warm with Banana Foster Sauce (recipe follows). Yield: 6 servings.

Banana Foster Sauce

1	pound light brown sugar	3	cups heavy cream
	Juice of 1 lemon	½	cup dark rum
	Juice of 1 orange	¼	cup banana liqueur
1	teaspoon cinnamon	½	cup butter
¼	teaspoon nutmeg	2	tablespoons cornstarch

Combine all sauce ingredients in a large saucepan. Bring to a boil over low heat, stirring until sauce reduces and thickens. Use ½ cup sauce for each serving of bread pudding. Yield: 4 cups sauce.

Basic Cheesecake

Pastry

1 cup all-purpose flour	Dash of vanilla
¼ cup sugar	1 egg yolk
1 teaspoon lemon zest	½ cup butter, softened

Filling

5 (8-ounce) packages cream cheese, softened	1½ teaspoons orange zest
	¼ teaspoon vanilla
1¾ cups sugar	5 eggs
3 tablespoons all-purpose flour	2 egg yolks
1½ teaspoons lemon zest	¼ cup heavy cream

Combine flour, sugar, lemon zest and vanilla in a large mixing bowl. Make a well in the center. Add egg yolk and butter to well and mix with your hands until well blended, adding a little cold water if needed to make a workable dough. Wrap dough in plastic and chill 1 hour. Grease the base and sides of a 9-inch springform pan and remove the base. Roll out one-third of the dough to ⅛-inch thick and fit over the base of the pan. Trim by running a rolling pin over the edges. Bake at 400 degrees for 15 minutes or until golden; cool.

To prepare filling, beat cream cheese in a large mixing bowl with an electric mixer. Add sugar, flour, lemon and orange zests and vanilla and beat well. Add eggs and egg yolks, one at a time, beating lightly after each addition. Add cream and beat lightly. Set filling aside.

Place top of springform pan over base and secure. Roll remaining dough to ⅛-inch thick. Cut dough into strips to fit almost to the top of the sides of the pan and press so the strips line the sides completely. Fill pan with cheese filling. Bake at 550 degrees for 10 minutes. Reduce heat to 200 degrees and bake 1 hour longer. Cool in pan on a wire rack, then refrigerate until chilled. To serve, carefully release and remove sides of pan. If desired, top cheesecake with Strawberry Glaze, Cherry Sauce Topping or Pineapple Glaze (recipes below). Cut cake into 12 wedges. Yield: 12 servings.

Strawberry Glaze

1 quart strawberries, stemmed	1½ tablespoons cornstarch
¾ cup sugar	1 teaspoon butter
¼ cup cold water	Red food coloring
Dash of salt	

Crush enough small, uneven-sized berries to measure 1 cup; press through a strainer. Leave remaining berries whole and reserve for top of cake. Combine crushed berries, sugar, water, salt and cornstarch in a saucepan. Boil 2 minutes, stirring constantly. Stir in butter. Add food coloring to reach desired shade. Cool slightly. Arrange whole berries on top of cheesecake. Carefully spoon strawberry glaze on cake; cool.

Basic Cheesecake continued

Cherry Sauce Topping

½ cup sugar
2 tablespoons cornstarch
   Dash of salt

1 (20-ounce) can pitted tart red cherries, or frozen, thawed

Combine sugar, cornstarch and salt in a saucepan. Add cherries and cook, stirring constantly, until mixture is thick and bubbly. Simmer 10 minutes. Chill thoroughly. Spoon over cake.

Pineapple Glaze

2 tablespoons sugar
4 teaspoons cornstarch
2 (8¼-ounce) cans crushed pineapple in heavy syrup, undrained

2 tablespoons lemon juice
2 drops yellow food coloring (optional)

Combine sugar and cornstarch in a small saucepan. Stir in undrained pineapple, lemon juice and yellow food coloring. Bring to a boil over medium heat. Boil 1 minute or until thickened and translucent. Cool and spoon over cake.

Amaretto Soufflé

5 eggs
½ cup powdered sugar
2 (¼-ounce) packages unflavored gelatin

1½ ounces amaretto liqueur
1 pint heavy cream, whipped
1-2 (16-ounce) cans black cherries

Whip eggs with powdered sugar until stiff. Dissolve gelatin in liqueur and heat until lukewarm. Add dissolved gelatin to egg mixture. Fold in whipped cream. Fill bottoms of serving glasses with cherries. Fill glasses to the top with soufflé mixture. Chill and serve.

Served in champagne glasses, this is good for a bridesmaid luncheon. Top each serving with a black cherry and toasted sliced almonds.

Black Cherry and Port Sauce

1 (12-ounce) jar black cherry preserves
2 tablespoons unsalted butter

¼ cup tawny port
1 tablespoon fresh lemon juice

Combine all ingredients in a saucepan and bring to a boil, stirring constantly. Simmer, stirring occasionally, for 5 minutes. Cool sauce and purée in a blender. Refrigerate sauce, covered, for 1 hour or until cold, or up to 1 week. Serve chilled or at room temperature over pound cake or ice cream.

Bread Pudding Soufflé with Whiskey Sauce

Bread Pudding

¾	cup sugar	1	teaspoon pure vanilla extract
1	teaspoon cinnamon	5	cups day old French bread, cut into
	Pinch of freshly grated nutmeg		1-inch cubes
3	medium eggs	⅓	cup golden raisins
1	cup heavy cream		

Whiskey Sauce

1½	cups heavy cream	⅓	cup sugar
2	teaspoons cornstarch	⅓	cup bourbon
2	tablespoons cold water		

Meringue

9	medium egg whites, at room temperature	¼	teaspoon cream of tartar
		¾	cup sugar

To make pudding, combine sugar, cinnamon and nutmeg in a large bowl. Beat in eggs until smooth. Beat in cream. Add vanilla. Stir in bread and allow bread to soak up egg mixture. Scatter raisins in a greased 8-inch square baking pan. Pour bread mixture over raisins. Bake at 350 degrees for 25 to 30 minutes or until pudding has a golden color and is firm to the touch. If a toothpick inserted in the pudding comes out clean, the pudding is done. It should be moist, not runny or dry. Cool to room temperature.

For the sauce, bring the cream to a boil in a saucepan. Combine the cornstarch and cold water and add to boiling cream, stirring constantly. Return mixture to a boil. Reduce heat and cook and stir about 30 seconds, being careful not to burn mixture. Stir in sugar and bourbon. Cool to room temperature.

To make meringue, be certain that mixing bowl and whisk are clean and that egg whites are completely free of yolk. This dish needs a good, stiff meringue and the egg whites will whip better if the chill is off them. In a large bowl or mixer, whip egg whites with cream of tartar until foamy. Gradually add sugar and continue to whip until shiny and thick. Test with a clean spoon. If the whites stand up stiff when you pull out the spoon, like shaving cream, the meringue is ready. Do not overwhip, or the whites will break down and the soufflé will not work.

In a large bowl, break half the bread pudding into pieces using your hands or a spoon. Gently fold in a quarter of the meringue, being careful not to lose the air in the whites. Divide mixture among six 6-ounce greased ceramic ramekins. Place remaining bread pudding in the bowl, break into pieces and carefully fold in remaining meringue. Top off soufflés with this lighter mixture, to about 1½ inches above the top edge of the ramekins. With a spoon, smooth and shape the tops into a dome over the ramekin rim.

Bread Pudding Soufflé with Whiskey Sauce continued

Bake at 350 degrees immediately for about 20 minutes or until golden brown. Serve immediately. Using a spoon at the table, poke a hole in the top of each soufflé. Spoon whiskey sauce into each soufflé. Yield: 6 servings.

New Orleans French bread is very light and tender. Outside New Orleans, use only a light bread. If the bread is too dense, the recipe won't work. A good Italian bread is the most comparable.

Caramel Pots de Crème

6	egg yolks	1	cup whole milk	
2	cups heavy cream		Sweetened whipped cream for garnish	
1	cup sugar		(optional)	
¼	cup water			

Whisk together egg yolks and cream in a large mixing bowl; set aside.

Place sugar in a heavy saucepan. Add water and cook over high heat, without stirring, until mixture starts to brown. Reduce heat to medium and swirl the pan to even out the color. Cook 5 minutes longer or until dark golden brown, swirling occasionally. The mixture may be a bit lumpy, but do not worry. Carefully add milk to hot sugar mixture (it may spatter). Cook over medium heat, without stirring, but continue to swirl pan occasionally for 5 minutes or until mixture becomes smooth. Remove pan from heat. Whisk hot caramel into egg yolk mixture until well combined. Pour mixture into 6 ramekins, custard cups or traditional pot-de-crème cups (which come with lids) and set them in a baking dish. Add hot water to baking dish to halfway up the ramekins. Remove any bubbles on the surface of the custards with a spoon, otherwise there will be holes in the custards. Cover baking dish loosely with foil, or if using pots-de-crème cups, put on lids. Place pan on lowest oven rack. Bake at 325 degrees for 50 to 60 minutes or until custards are set but still tremble slightly when shaken. If custards are not done, return to oven and continue to bake, checking for doneness after 15 minutes.

Uncover custards and remove from water bath. Cool at room temperature for 30 minutes, then refrigerate before serving for at least 3 hours. Serve in ramekins, each topped with a small dollop of whipped cream. Yield: 6 servings.

Cherries Jubilee

4	tablespoons unsalted butter	¼	cup kirsch
1	pound fresh Bing cherries, pitted		Vanilla ice cream
¼	cup sugar		

Melt butter in a large skillet over medium heat. Add cherries and sugar and stir to combine. Cook 5 minutes or until cherries are tender and sugar is dissolved. Remove from heat and pour kirsch over cherries. Carefully ignite liquid with a long match. When flames go out, spoon cherries over ice cream. Yield: 4 to 6 servings.

Chocolate Turtle Cheesecake

2	cups vanilla wafer crumbs	½	cup sugar
6	tablespoons butter, melted	1	teaspoon vanilla
1	(14-ounce) bag caramels	2	eggs
1	(5-ounce) can evaporated milk	½	cup semisweet chocolate pieces, melted
1	cup chopped pecans, toasted		Whipped cream, chopped pecans and
2	(8-ounce) packages cream cheese, softened		maraschino cherries for garnish (optional)

Combine wafer crumbs and butter and press into the bottom and up the sides of a 9-inch springform pan. Bake at 350 degrees for 10 minutes. Melt caramels with milk in a 1½-quart heavy saucepan over low heat, stirring frequently, until smooth. Pour mixture over crust and top with pecans. Blend cream cheese, sugar and vanilla with an electric mixer on medium speed until well blended. Add eggs, one at a time, mixing well after each addition. Blend in chocolate. Pour mixture over pecans. Bake at 350 degrees for 40 minutes. Loosen sides of pan and cool before removing sides. Chill. Garnish as desired, or top with Turtle Cheesecake Topping (recipe follows). Yield: 12 servings.

Turtle Cheesecake Topping

1	cup brown sugar	2	tablespoons heavy cream
4	tablespoons butter, melted	1½	cups pecan halves for garnish

Melt together sugar, butter and cream. Cool slightly, but not completely. Pour over top of chilled cheesecake. Arrange pecan halves around rim of cake. Refrigerate until ready to serve.

Chocolate Eclairs

Shells

½	cup boiling water	½	cup all-purpose flour
4	tablespoons butter	2	eggs

Cream Filling

½	cup sugar	1	egg, beaten
¼	cup flour	1½	tablespoons butter
½	teaspoon salt	½	teaspoon lemon extract
1½	cups hot scalded milk		

Frosting

1	cup finely chopped dark or milk chocolate	½	cup heavy cream

Pour boiling water over butter in a saucepan. Bring to a boil and stir until butter melts. Add flour all at once and stir constantly with a wooden spoon until mixture leaves the sides of the pan and forms a ball. Remove from heat. Immediately add unbeaten eggs, one at a time, beating to a smooth paste after each one. Beat mixture until smooth and velvety. Drop by heaping tablespoonfuls, drawing out into finger-length mounds of uniform shape and height, onto a greased baking sheet, spacing each 3 inches apart. Bake at 450 degrees for 15 minutes or until well puffed and delicately browned. Reduce heat to 300 degrees and bake 30 to 40 minutes longer. This will bake the centers thoroughly, but outside should not brown further. Remove to a wire rack to cool. When cool, cut off tops with a sharp knife and fill with cream filling. Ice with chocolate icing.

To make filling, mix sugar, flour and salt in the top of a double boiler. Gradually stir in hot milk and cook over direct heat, stirring constantly, until thickened. Stir a little of hot mixture into beaten egg, then return to hot mixture and place over boiling water. Cook, stirring constantly, for 2 minutes. Remove from heat and stir in 1½ tablespoons butter and lemon extract; cool. Fill eclairs with cooled cream filling. For best flavor and crispness, filled eclairs should be served the same day they are baked.

For frosting, place chocolate in a large bowl. Carefully bring cream to a boil a small saucepan over medium heat. Pour hot cream over chocolate and stir until melted and smooth. Strain and cool slightly before using. Yield: 1 cup frosting.

Old Fashioned Chocolate Icing

4	tablespoons butter, softened	3	tablespoons cream
1½	cups sifted powdered sugar	½	teaspoon vanilla
¼	cup unsweetened cocoa powder		

Cream butter until smooth. Sift sugar and cocoa together. Add sugar mixture to butter alternately with cream and vanilla and blend thoroughly. Spread icing immediately over eclairs.

Chocolate Ganache

1	cup heavy cream	10	ounces semisweet or bittersweet chocolate, chopped

Gently warm the cream in a small saucepan over medium heat until small bubbles begin to appear at the edges. Remove from heat and stir in chocolate until melted and smooth. Do not stir so vigorously that bubbles form.

Alternatively, place chocolate in a food processor fitted with a metal blade or a blender. Pour hot cream over chocolate and allow to stand 15 seconds. Cover to prevent spattering and process or blend until smooth.

If there are any visible lumps, strain mixture through a fine-mesh sieve. Ganache will keep in a covered container in the refrigerator for up to 1 month, or frozen for up to 6 months. To reheat, warm sauce in a small heatproof bowl set over a pan of hot water or in a microwave on full power for 20 to 30 seconds. Yield: About 3 cups.

Cold Lemon Soufflé

1	(¼-oucne) envelope unflavored gelatin	2	teaspoons lemon zest
¼	cup cold water	1½	cups sugar, divided
5	eggs, separated	1	cup heavy cream
¾	cup lemon juice	1	(10-ounce) package frozen raspberries

Sprinkle gelatin over cold water; set aside. Combine egg yolks, lemon juice, lemon zest and ¾ cup sugar in the top of a double boiler. Cook mixture over simmering water for 20 minutes. Remove custard from heat and stir in dissolved gelatin. Refrigerate or freeze for 15 minutes or until cool. When cool, beat egg whites until peaks form. Gradually beat in remaining ¾ cup sugar. Whip cream until stiff. Fold together whipped cream, egg whites and cooled lemon mixture. Pour mixture into a 2-quart dish. Cover and chill.

Purée raspberries in a blender. When ready to serve, spoon raspberries over soufflé. Yield: 6 servings.

This makes a lovely dessert for a bridesmaid luncheon. Spoon into tall glass dishes or champagne glasses layered with raspberry purée.

Chocolate Mousse

3	eggs, separated		1	cup heavy cream
1½	tablespoons water			Pinch of salt
2	tablespoons cognac or Kahlúa liqueur		1	tablespoon superfine sugar
4	ounces Tobler extra bittersweet chocolate, melted			(omit if using Kahlúa)

In a heavy saucepan or double boiler, whisk egg yolks and water over very low heat until yolks start to thicken. Whisk in liqueur and continue whisking until mixture starts to thicken to a consistency of a hollandaise sauce. Remove from heat and fold in melted chocolate. Pour into a mixing bowl. In a separate bowl, beat cream until stiff peaks form. Fold cream into chocolate mixture. Beat egg whites with salt until soft peaks form. Beat sugar into egg whites, if using, until whites barely form stiff peaks. Fold a small amount of whites into chocolate mixture to lighten, then fold in remaining whites. Spoon into a serving bowl or individual charlotte molds. Yield: 6 servings.

Creamy Caramel Flans

¾	cup sugar		1	teaspoon vanilla
4	eggs		⅛	teaspoon salt
1¾	cups water			Sugar Garnish (optional), recipe below
1	(14-ounce) can sweetened condensed milk			

Cook and stir sugar in a heavy skillet over medium heat until melted and caramel-colored. Pour melted sugar into eight ungreased 6-ounce custard cups, tilting to coat bottoms.

In a bowl, beat eggs with and electric mixer or a wire whisk. Stir in 1¾ cups water, milk, vanilla and salt until well blended. Pour mixture into prepared custard cups. Set cups in a shallow baking pan (a paella pan is perfect). Fill pan with 1 inch of hot water. Bake at 350 degrees for 25 minutes or until a knife inserted near the center comes out clean. Cool, then chill.

To serve, invert flans onto individual serving plates. Garnish as desired. Refrigerate leftovers. Yield: 8 servings.

Sugar Garnish

1	cup sugar		¼	cup water

Fill a medium metal bowl half full with ice. Combine sugar with water in a saucepan and stir. Cover pan and bring to a boil. Cook over high heat until amber in color. Immediately put pan in ice for 1 minute. Using a spoon, carefully drizzle sugar decoratively over foil. Allow to cool. Peel from foil and place on flans just before ready to serve.

Cream Cheese and Lemon Flan

1	pie pastry for a 10-inch tart	1	(8-ounce) package cream cheese, softened
4	eggs		
¼	teaspoon salt	¼	cup sugar
½	cup heavy cream		Pinch of nutmeg
	Zest of 1 lemon	1	tablespoon vanilla
¼	cup fresh lemon juice, or more to taste		

Topping

4-5	tablespoons sugar	4-5	tablespoons chopped walnuts

Line a 10-inch tart pan with pastry dough and prick all over several times. Line pastry crust with lightweight foil and fill with pie weights or dried beans. Bake at 400 degrees for 10 minutes or until pastry below the foil is set. Remove foil and weights or beans. Prick crust again lightly and bake 5 minutes longer or until just beginning to brown and just starting to shrink from the pan. Remove from oven; increase oven temperature to 425 degrees.

Meanwhile, in a food processor or blender, combine eggs, salt, cream, zest, lemon juice, cream cheese, sugar, nutmeg and vanilla. Process until smooth.

In a small bowl, prepare topping by combining sugar and walnuts.

Slide out the oven rack and place tart pan containing partially baked crust on rack. Pour lemon filling into crust; do not overfill or the flan might spill during baking. Bake at 425 degrees for 10 minutes or just until filling has partially set. Sprinkle sugar-walnut topping over the surface and bake 10 minutes longer. Reduce oven temperature to 350 degrees. Bake another 15 minutes or until flan is puffed and lightly browned and the bottom of the crust is browned. Cool to warm before serving, or serve cold. Yield: 10 servings.

You can use a frozen pie shell, or prepare the flan in a baking dish with no pastry shell.

Cointreau Strawberry Sauce

3	tablespoons butter	½	cup sugar
3	tablespoons orange zest	3	pints strawberries, stemmed and puréed
¼	cup orange juice concentrate	3	tablespoons Cointreau
2	tablespoons lemon juice	2	tablespoons cognac

Combine butter, orange zest, orange juice concentrate, lemon juice, sugar and puréed strawberries in a 3-quart saucepan. Bring to a boil, stirring constantly. Add Cointreau and cognac. Simmer 5 minutes, stirring constantly. This sauce is especially good when served with cheesecake. Yield: 2 cups.

Crème Brûlée

1	quart heavy cream		Dash of vanilla
8	egg yolks	½	cup brown sugar, sifted
½	cup granulated sugar		

Heat cream in the top of a double boiler over hot water until cream reaches the boiling point. Meanwhile, beat egg yolks lightly. Beat granulated sugar into yolks. Flavor with a touch of vanilla. Slowly add hot cream to egg mixture, beating constantly with a wooden spoon. Return egg/cream mixture to top of double boiler and cook, stirring constantly, until mixture coats spoon with a thin film; do not overcook or the eggs will curdle. Pour mixture into a heatproof serving dish or ramekins and refrigerate 6 to 8 hours.

When ready to serve, sprinkle top of crème with sifted brown sugar and place under a broiler for 1 minute or until sugar is glazed. Cool before serving. Yield: 8 servings.

Easy Peach Cobbler

½	cup butter	1	cup self-rising flour
6	cups sliced peaches, sweetened	1	cup milk
1	cup sugar		

Melt butter in a casserole dish. Add peach slices. Combine sugar, flour and milk and pour over peaches. Bake at 425 degrees for 30 minutes or until crust rises to the top and browns. Yield: 6 to 8 servings.

Fluffy Meringue

½	cup sugar	⅛	teaspoon cream of tartar
⅛	teaspoon salt	2	egg whites, stiffly beaten
¼	cup water	⅛	teaspoon almond extract

Combine sugar, salt, water and cream of tartar in a saucepan. Cook to thread stage (232 degrees). Gradually pour hot mixture over beaten egg whites, beating constantly. Continue beating until mixture holds its shape. Add almond extract.

Crêpes Suzettes

Dessert Crêpes

½	cup flour	1	tablespoon kirsch or Grand Marnier liqueur
¼	cup milk		
¼	cup water	1	tablespoon sugar
1	egg		Pinch of salt
1	egg yolk		Orange Butter (recipe below)
1½	tablespoons butter, melted, plus extra for cooking		Orange Sauce (recipe below)
			Grand Marnier liqueur

Place flour in a mixing bowl. Drizzle milk and water into flour while whisking to make a perfectly smooth blend. (If using regular flour, pour batter through a fairly thin-meshed sieve after mixing to remove any lumps.) Whisk in egg, egg yolk, butter, liqueur, sugar and salt. Cover batter and refrigerate at least 2 hours.

Heat a nonstick 6-inch skillet until drops of water dance on it, then brush lightly with melted butter. Pour ¼ cup batter into the center of the skillet and tilt in all directions so that batter covers the pan with a light coating; pour out any excess batter.

After 30 seconds or so, the bottom of the crêpe should be lightly browned; lift an edge with the spatula to check. Shake the pan by its handle to dislodge crêpe. Turn crêpe over with fingers or a spatula, or flip it over by a toss of the pan. Cook 15 to 20 seconds. (This is the side not seen, cook only to a spotty brown). Transfer crêpes as they get done to a plate. Allow to cool completely before stacking to prevent sticking. Slip crêpes into a plastic bag and refrigerate up to 2 days, or freeze for several weeks. Yield: Ten 5½-inch crêpes.

To serve, spoon about 1 tablespoon orange butter onto each crêpe, spreading evenly to outer edges. Fold crêpes in half, then into quarters. Spoon half of orange sauce into a chafing dish. Arrange quartered crêpes in sauce. Spoon remaining sauce over crêpes. Place in a 250 to 300 degree oven until thoroughly heated. Just before serving, heat Grand Marnier, ignite and pour over crêpes.

Orange Butter

¾	cup unsalted butter, softened	⅓	cup Grand Marnier or other orange flavored liqueur
½	cup sugar		
		¼	cup orange zest

Cream butter and sugar until light and fluffy. Blend in liqueur and orange zest. Yield: 2 cups.

Orange Sauce

½	cup unsalted butter, melted	⅔	cup orange juice
¾	cup sugar	2	oranges, peeled and sectioned
2	tablespoons orange zest	¼	cup Grand Marnier liqueur

Combine butter, sugar, orange zest and juice in a skillet. Cook over low heat for 10 minutes, stirring frequently. Add orange sections and liqueur. Yield: 2¾ cups.

Fresh Berry Cobbler

4 cups fresh berries, such as blackberries, raspberries or blueberries
1¼ cups sugar, divided
¼ cup water

½ cup butter
1 cup self-rising flour
1 cup milk

Combine berries, ¼ cup sugar and water in a saucepan. Bring to a boil; this releases the juices from the berries. Melt butter in a casserole dish. Pour fruit over melted butter. Mix flour, milk and remaining 1 cup sugar and pour over fruit. Bake at 350 degrees until topping is browned. Yield: 6 servings.

Fresh Peach Ice Cream

5 peaches (about 1¼ pounds)
1½ cups sugar
1½ cups milk

1½ cups heavy cream
1 teaspoon vanilla

Have a bowl of ice and cold water ready. Blanch peaches in boiling water for 1 minute and transfer to ice water to stop cooking. Peel peaches and remove pits. Purée peaches in a food processor or blender.

In a large bowl, combine sugar, milk and cream and stir until sugar dissolves. Stir in peach purée and vanilla. Freeze mixture in an ice cream maker. Yield: 1½ quarts.

Frozen Pineapple Torte

3 eggs, separated
Dash of salt
½ cup plus 2 tablespoons sugar
1 (9-ounce) can crushed pineapple, drained, juice reserved

2 tablespoons lemon juice
1 cup heavy cream, whipped
2 cups vanilla wafer crumbs

Beat egg yolks in the top of a double boiler. Add salt, ½ cup sugar, reserved pineapple juice and lemon juice. Cook over hot water until mixture coats a spoon. Add crushed pineapple and cool. Beat egg whites until stiff. Gradually beat remaining 2 tablespoons sugar into egg whites. Fold egg whites and whipped cream into custard mixture. Coat sides and bottom of a greased freezer-proof 4x8-inch dish with crumbs. Pour custard into dish and cover with remaining crumbs. Freeze 3 to 4 hours, or up to 24 hours. Yield: 6 servings.

Fresh Strawberry Mousse

1	pint strawberries	¼	cup sugar
1	(3-ounce) package strawberry flavored gelatin	2	cups heavy cream
		1	strawberry fan for garnish

Mash strawberries; drain, reserving juice. Set pulp aside. Add water to reserved juice to equal 1½ cups liquid. Bring juice mixture to a boil in a saucepan. Add gelatin and stir until dissolved. Chill until mixture is the consistency of unbeaten egg whites.

Combine strawberry pulp and sugar and stir well. Stir pulp mixture into gelatin mixture. Pour heavy cream into a chilled bowl and whip until small peaks appear. Fold in strawberry mixture. Spoon into a lightly greased 7-cup mold. Chill until set. Serve with a fresh strawberry fanned on top as a garnish. Yield: 10 to 12 servings.

Fried Pies

Filling

2	cups cooked, drained and mashed dried fruit, such as apples or peaches or a mixture	4	tablespoons butter
		⅓	cup sugar

Pastry

3	cups flour	1	egg, beaten
¼	cup sugar	1	tablespoon water
1	teaspoon salt	¼	teaspoon vinegar
¾	cup vegetable shortening		

Combine filling ingredients in a saucepan. Heat and stir until butter and sugar melt. Set aside to cool.

To make pastry, mix flour, sugar and salt. Using a pastry blender, cut in shortening until mixture resembles cornmeal. Combine egg, water and vinegar and sprinkle over flour mixture. Mix until dough clings together and forms a ball. Add slightly more water if needed to make a ball. Divide dough in half and roll each half very thin. Cut dough into 5-inch diameter circles. Combine pastry scraps and repeat until all dough is used. Place 2 tablespoons cooled fruit filling on each circle. Fold pastry in half to encase fruit. Crimp edges with a fork. Prick top of dough twice with a fork for ventilation.

To fry, heat ¼-inch depth of oil in a skillet to 375 degrees. Gently place pies, a few at a time, in hot oil. Cook until brown on both sides, turning once. Drain on paper towels. For extra richness, brush sides of each cooked pie with melted butter and sprinkle lightly with granulated sugar. Serve hot or cold.

To bake, melt ½ cup butter. Generously brush both sides of each pie with melted butter. Place on a lightly greased baking sheet. Bake at 350 degrees for 30 minutes or until brown. Cool on a wire rack.

Fresh Peach Trifle

1	(14-ounce) can sweetened condensed milk	1	angel food cake
			Sherry (I use peach Schnapps)
1½	cups water	1½	pounds fresh peaches, peeled and sliced
1	(3-ounce) package dry instant vanilla pudding mix	½	cup raspberry or strawberry preserves
2	cups heavy cream, whipped		Toasted almonds or pecans

Combine milk and water in a bowl. Mix in pudding and refrigerate 5 minutes. Fold in whipped cream. Crumble cake into a separate bowl. Sprinkle cake with sherry. Place half of cake crumbs in the bottom of a trifle bowl. Top with half the sliced peaches. Pour half of custard mixture over peaches. Spread or spoon raspberry preserves over custard. Repeat cake, peach and custard layers, ending with custard. Garnish with nuts. Chill before serving. Yield: 8 to 12 servings.

Hot Fudge Sauce

½	cup unsweetened cocoa powder	¼	teaspoon salt
1	cup sugar	3	tablespoons butter
1	cup light corn syrup	1	teaspoon vanilla
½	cup light cream		

Combine all ingredients except vanilla in a saucepan. Cook over medium heat, stirring constantly, until mixture comes to a full rolling boil. Boil briskly for 3 minutes, stirring occasionally. Remove from heat and stir in vanilla. Yield: 2½ cups.

Irish Cream Sauce

¾	cup French vanilla ice cream	⅓	cup heavy cream, whipped
3	tablespoons Irish cream liqueur		

Place ice cream in a microwave-safe bowl. Microwave on high powder for 30 seconds or until just melted. Stir in liqueur. Fold in whipped cream. Store in refrigerator. Yield: 1¼ cups.

Grand Marnier Soufflés with Crème Anglaise

¾   stick (6 tablespoons) unsalted butter plus additional for buttering ramekins

1   cup sugar plus additional for coating ramekins

¼   cup plus 2 tablespoons all-purpose flour

1   cup whole milk

7   large egg yolks

¼   teaspoon vanilla

⅛   teaspoon oil

2   tablespoons Grand Marnier liqueur

8   large egg whites

Preheat oven to 400 degrees. Generously butter eight 1 cup (3½x2 inch) ramekins and coat with sugar, knocking out excess sugar. In a 1½ quart heavy saucepan, melt ¾ stick butter over moderately low heat and whisk in flour. Cook roux, whisking for 3 minutes. Add milk and cook over moderate heat, whisking, until mixture is very thick and pulls away from sides of pan. Transfer mixture to a bowl and cool 5 minutes. In a large bowl, whisk together yolks, vanilla, oil, and a pinch salt; whisk in milk mixture and Grand Marnier, whisking until smooth.

In a large bowl with an electric mixer beat whites until they hold soft peaks. Beat in 1 cup sugar, a little at a time, and beat meringue until it just holds stiff peaks. Whisk about one fourth meringue into yolk mixture to lighten and with a rubber spatula fold in remaining meringue gently but thoroughly.

Spoon batter into ramekins, filling them just to rim; arrange ramekins at least 1½ inches apart in a large baking pan. Add enough hot water to pan to reach halfway up sides of ramekins and bake soufflés in middle of oven 20 minutes, or until puffed and tops are golden.

Crème Anglaise

1   cup half-and-half

½   cup heavy cream

2   large egg yolks

3   tablespoons sugar

1   teaspoon cornstarch

In a 1½ quart heavy saucepan bring half-and-half and heavy cream to boil. While cream mixture is heating, whisk together in a bowl yolks, sugar and cornstarch until slightly thickened and pale, about 2 minutes. Add hot cream mixture in a stream, whisking, and transfer custard to pan. Cook custard over moderately low heat, stirring constantly with a wooden spoon, until a thermometer registers 180 degrees (about 2 minutes; do not let custard boil). Transfer custard to cleaned bowl and cool until warm, stirring occasionally. Crème anglaise may be made 2 days ahead and chilled, covered. Reheat sauce if desired. Makes about 1⅔ cups.

To serve: Spoon the crème anglaise over the top of the soufflés or you may punch a hole in the top of the soufflés and fill with custard. Yield: 8 servings

Home Churned Ice Cream

There is nothing so refreshing on a hot summer day as an ice cream freezer full of homemade churned ice cream. What Fourth of July celebration or child's summer birthday is complete without it?

In the United States, ice creams often are referred to as custard, French, or Philadelphia style. The base of custard or French style ice cream is made by cooking cream or milk, sugar, egg or egg yolks and flavorings. This style has a rich and smooth texture. Philadelphia style ice cream, on the other hand, is made without eggs, resulting in a product that is not nearly as rich and creamy. Its base is made simply by heating the cream and milk to incorporate the sugar and other ingredients.

When preparing to freeze the custard, make sure the base is very cold before it is added to the machine's canister. If possible, let the base chill in the refrigerator for at least 4 hours to ensure it is properly cooled and the flavors are fully developed. Fill the canister no more than two-thirds full to allow space for the base to expand as it freezes.

The ice cream is properly frozen when it looks like slightly grainy soft-serve ice cream.

You can flavor ice cream in a number of ways. Ingredients such as vanilla beans, tea, coffee or spices are steeped in the liquid of the custard base, infusing it with their flavors.

Ingredients such as caramel, ganache or fruit purées can be folded into the ice cream at the end of the churning stage for a rippled or marbled effect. Pieces of poached fruit, nuts, chopped chocolate and crushed candy bars can add an element of texture to ice cream.

When I add peaches or other fruit to the ice cream, I always, before freezing, purée the fruit because I do not like the big frozen lumps in the ice cream. After placing the ice cream mixture in the canister, alternate layers of finely crushed ice and rock salt around the canister until it reaches the top of the outside container.

Hand churn or plug in, if using an electric churn. When hand churning, the handle will become very hard to turn when the ice cream is ready. Electric churns will automatically turn off when the ice cream is frozen. Cover the top of the whole container with a heavy towel and set aside for at least 30 minutes before removing the canister from the ice. Open the canister and remove the dasher (the mixer in the center). Serve and enjoy!

Lemon Curd

6	eggs, lightly beaten	¾	cup fresh squeezed lemon juice (about 4 lemons)
2	egg yolks, lightly beaten	1	cup butter, softened
2	cups sugar	¼	cup lemon zest

Combine all ingredients in the top of a double boiler. Cook over low heat, stirring frequently, for 25 minutes or until thickened. Remove from heat and cool. Store tightly covered in the refrigerator.

Use as a filling for small tart shells, layer cake squares, between cake layers or to fill small muffin cakes with the centers scooped out. Yield: 4 cups.

Lemon Ice Cream

2	quarts half-and-half	2	tablespoons lemon zest
4	cups sugar	1	cup fresh lemon juice (about 6 lemons)

Combine all ingredients. Freeze in an ice cream maker. If there is any leftover, pour into a plastic freezer container and freeze. Yield: 1 gallon, 10 to 12 servings.

Molten Chocolate Cake

½	cup unsalted butter, plus more for greasing ramekins	¼	cup sugar
			Pinch of salt
6	ounces bittersweet chocolate, chopped	2	tablespoons all-purpose flour, plus more for dusting
2	eggs		
2	egg yolks		

Butter and flour four 6-ounce ramekins, tapping out excess flour. Melt butter and chocolate in the top of a double boiler set over simmering water. In a medium bowl using a handheld electric mixer, beat eggs, egg yolks, sugar and salt on high speed until pale and thickened. Whisk chocolate mixture until smooth, then quickly fold chocolate into egg mixture along with flour. Mix just until incorporated.

Spoon the batter into prepared ramekins and set on a baking sheet. Bake at 450 degrees for 12 minutes or until the sides of the cakes are firm but the centers are soft. Cool cakes 1 minute. Run a knife around the edge of each cake. Cover with an inverted dessert plate and turn cake over. Let cakes stand a few seconds before unmolding. Serve immediately with vanilla ice cream. Yield: 4 servings.

Meringue Nests

½	cup egg whites	½	teaspoon vanilla	
⅛	teaspoon salt		Whipped cream for garnish	
¾	cup sugar			

Combine egg whites and salt and beat with an electric mixer on high speed until stiff. Add sugar, 1 tablespoon at a time, beating well after each addition. Stir in vanilla. Line a baking sheet with parchment paper. Draw circles on the paper the size you want nests to be; usually about 4 inches. Spoon meringue onto paper in equal amounts. Make a deep well in the center of each mound, building up the sides with the back of spoon to form nests. Bake at 300 degrees for 12 to 15 minutes or until meringues are delicate golden color. Reduce oven temperature to 250 degrees and bake 30 to 40 minutes longer or until dry and light brown in color. Turn off oven and leave shells in oven with door closed for 1 to 2 hours. Remove from oven and cool completely. Fill cooled nests with Lemon or Chocolate Filling (recipes below). Garnish with whipped cream. Yield: 6 regular or 8 to 10 small nests.

Lemon Filling

3	egg yolks, beaten		Zest of 1 lemon
⅔	cup sugar	2	cups heavy cream, whipped
¼	cup lemon juice		

Combine egg yolks, sugar, lemon juice and zest in the top of a double boiler. Stir well and cook over boiling water until thickened; cool. Set aside ½ cup whipped cream for garnish. Fold remaining whipped cream into lemon mixture.

Chocolate Filling

2	cups milk	¼	teaspoon salt
2	(1-ounce) squares unsweetened chocolate	3	egg yolks, lightly beaten
¼	cup cornstarch	2	tablespoons butter
1	cup sugar, divided	½	teaspoon vanilla

Scald milk in a saucepan. Add chocolate to hot milk and stir until melted. Mix cornstarch, ⅔ cup sugar and salt in the top of a double boiler. Gradually stir in milk mixture. Cook over boiling water for 10 minutes or until thickened, stirring constantly. Slowly add a small amount of hot mixture into egg yolks, then stir back into remaining hot sauce. Cook 5 minutes. Cool to warm. Stir in butter and vanilla.

Old Fashioned Banana Pudding

4	eggs	4	cups milk, scalded
⅓	cup cornstarch	1	teaspoon vanilla
½	teaspoon salt	3	dozen vanilla wafers
1½	cups sugar, divided	6-8	ripe bananas, divided

Separate eggs, placing whites in a copper pan to make meringue. Beat yolks in a separate bowl and set aside. Mix cornstarch, salt and 1 cup sugar in a heavy saucepan. Add scalded milk. Cook and stir over medium heat until mixture begins to thicken. Remove from heat. Pour a small amount of hot mixture into beaten egg yolks, beating constantly, then add back into hot mixture. Return to heat and cook and stir until smooth and thick. Remove from heat. Stir in vanilla.

Place a layer of vanilla wafers in a large casserole dish. Slice 3 to 4 bananas over the wafers. Pour half of pudding mixture over the bananas. Repeat layers, smoothing top pudding layer.

Prepare a meringue by beating egg whites until frothy. Add remaining ½ cup sugar and continue to beat until stiff peaks form. Spread meringue over top of pudding. Bake at 325 degrees until meringue is browned. Yield: 8 to 10 servings.

Peaches Foster

4	large ripe peaches (2 pound total)	⅓	cup dark rum
4	tablespoons unsalted butter	¼	teaspoon cinnamon
6	tablespoons light brown sugar	⅛	teaspoon salt

Have ready a large bowl of ice and cold water. Blanch peaches in boiling water for 15 seconds. Using a slotted spoon, transfer peaches immediately to ice water bath to cool completely. Remove skin with a paring knife. Slice peaches into ½-inch thick wedges, discarding pits.

Melt butter in a 10- to 12-inch heavy skillet over medium heat. Stir in brown sugar, rum, cinnamon and salt until smooth. Add peach slices. Simmer, stirring and turning peaches over occasionally for 3 to 5 minutes or until tender. Cool until warm. Serve over scoops of vanilla ice cream. Yield: 8 servings.

Peaches in sauce can be made up to 2 hours ahead. Reheat to warm before serving.

Poached Pears with Chocolate Sauce

6	large Bartlett, Comice and Anjou pears, slightly underripe	⅔	cup brown sugar
2	cups sweet white wine, or 1 cup each white grape juice and water		Strips of zest from 1 orange
6	whole cloves	3	cups white chocolate ice cream or chocolate ganache

Select a heavy pan (preferable enamelware) with a tight-fitting lid that can accommodate all the pears placed upright. Using a sharp paring knife, peel pears. Slice off the very bottom of each pear so it will stand straight. Using an apple corer or other sharp-edged tool, scoop out the seeds and part of the core from the bottom of each pear. Add wine, cloves, brown sugar and orange zest to pan. Stir to dissolve sugar slightly. Add pears. Do not worry that the pears are not covered by liquid. Cover pan and cook over medium heat until the liquid comes to a gentle simmer. Continue simmering 20 to 30 minutes or until paring knife inserted in the side of the pears goes in easily. The cooking time will depend upon the type, size and ripeness of the pears; do not overcook or they will fall apart. Using a slotted spoon, gently transfer the pears to a large serving dish or to individual dishes. Cool 1 hour or to room temperature.

Blot pears with paper towels to remove excess moisture. Heat chocolate ice cream or ganache to the consistency of very thick cream. Spoon a pool of chocolate sauce around each pear on individual serving plates. Yield: 6 servings.

Raspberry Purée

2½	cups fresh raspberries, or one 10-ounce package frozen unsweetened raspberries, thawed	½	cup superfine sugar
		¼	cup framboise or other raspberry-flavored liqueur (optional)

Combine all ingredients in a blender or food processor fitted with a metal blade. Purée until smooth. If a seedless sauce is desired, strain purée through a sieve. This sauce will keep for up to 2 weeks in the refrigerator, or can be frozen for up to 6 months. Yield: 3 cups.

Raspberry Swirl Parfaits

2	(10-ounce) packages frozen raspberries in light syrup, thawed	2½	tablespoons honey
½	cup walnuts	¾	cup heavy cream, well chilled
3	eggs		Fresh raspberries and mint leaves for garnish
2½	tablespoons sugar		

Purée raspberries with syrup in a food processor. Force purée through a fine sieve into a heavy saucepan, pressing hard on solids. Boil purée, stirring occasionally, until reduced to 1 cup. Cool purée and chill. Lightly toast walnuts, cool completely and chop. In the top of a double boiler with a handheld electric mixer, beat together eggs, sugar and honey until well combined. Set over simmering water and beat mixture until pale and thick and until an instant read thermometer registers 160 degrees. Set pan over ice water and beat until cold. In a separate bowl with clean beaters, beat cream until it just holds stiff peaks. Gently fold cream and walnuts into egg mixture until thoroughly mixed. Alternately spoon raspberry purée and egg mixture into six 6-ounce glasses and swirl with a wooden skewer. Cover and freeze parfaits for at least 8 hours or up to 2 days. Let parfaits stand at room temperature for 15 minutes before serving. Garnish with raspberries and mint leaves. Yield: 6 servings.

This is a lovely dessert to serve at a bridesmaid luncheon.

Strawberries with Brown Sugar Sour Cream

1½	cups sour cream	1½	quarts strawberries, washed and stemmed
2	tablespoons light brown sugar		
½	teaspoon vanilla		

Combine sour cream, brown sugar and vanilla in a small bowl. Divide berries among 6 individual dessert dishes. Top each with a dollop of brown sugar sour cream. Yield: 6 servings.

If serving as a snack, place strawberries in a large bowl and sour cream mixture in a smaller bowl. Dip strawberries into sour cream mixture.

When washing strawberries, always wash under running water and place on a paper towel to dry. Do not leave strawberries in water to cover. They will absorb the water.

Strawberries Zabaglione

2	egg yolks	1	cup heavy cream
2	tablespoons granulated sugar	¾	cup sifted powdered sugar
2	tablespoons Marsala wine	30	large strawberries

Combine egg yolks, granulated sugar and wine in the top of a double boiler. Beat with an electric mixer at medium speed until well blended. Place over boiling water and reduce heat to low. Cook about 5 minutes or until soft peaks form, beating constantly at medium speed. Remove from heat. Spoon mixture into a medium bowl and place in a large bowl of ice. Beat about 2 minutes or until cool. Refrigerate 30 minutes. Combine cream and powdered sugar in a small bowl and refrigerate 30 minutes. Add cream mixture to cooked mixture and beat until stiff.

Cut 2 perpendicular slices down the pointed end of each strawberry, cutting to within ½-inch of stem end. Carefully spread out quartered sections of strawberry to form a cup. Fill each strawberry with cream mixture using a pastry bag. Refrigerate until ready to serve. Yield: 10 to 15 servings.

Strawberry Shortcake

3	cups all-purpose flour	1½	teaspoons orange zest (optional)
⅓	cup sugar	1	cup sour cream
1	tablespoon baking powder	1	cup milk
¾	teaspoon baking soda		Fresh strawberries
¾	teaspoon salt		Whipped cream
¾	cup unsalted butter, chilled and cut into bits		

Whisk together flour, sugar, baking powder, baking soda and salt in a large bowl. Cut in butter until mixture resembles coarse meal. In a small bowl, whisk together zest, sour cream and milk and add to flour mixture. Stir until mixture just forms a soft and sticky dough. Drop into 12 mounds at 1-inch intervals onto greased baking sheets. Pat dough to ½-inch thickness. Bake at 350 degrees for 12 to 15 minutes or until pale golden.

Serve with fresh strawberries and whipped cream.

Tiramisu

6	egg yolks	6	ounces tiramisu liqueur
1¼	cups sugar, plus extra to sprinkle on top	1	cup strong espresso coffee
		48	ladyfingers
1¼	cups mascarpone cheese		Unsweetened cocoa powder
1¾	cups heavy cream		

Beat egg yolks with sugar in the top of a double-boiler until smooth and lemon-yellow. Bring water in base of double-boiler to a boil, then reduce heat to low. Cook, stirring constantly, for 10 minutes. Remove from heat. Stir in cheese and beat well. Cool to room temperature. Beat cream until soft peaks form. Fold cream into cheese mixture.

Mix liqueur and coffee. Brush coffee mixture over ladyfingers until they are well saturated, but not falling apart. Line the sides and bottom of a 3-quart soufflé dish with 36 ladyfingers. Pour in half the cheese filling. Layer remaining ladyfingers on top. Cover with remaining filling and smooth top with a rubber spatula. Combine extra sugar and cocoa to taste and sprinkle over top. Cover and chill overnight. Serve directly from soufflé dish. Yield: 10 servings.

Tiramisu liqueur is available in many liquor stores. You may substitute Marsala wine or rum (but it will not be as good).

Vanilla Ice Cream

1	pint half-and-half	1	(14-ounce) can sweetened condensed milk
1	pint heavy cream	2	tablespoons vanilla

Combine all ingredients and freeze in an ice cream maker. Yield: 1½ quarts.

Strawberry or other fruit flavors

3	cups half-and-half	1	cup mashed or puréed fruit
1	(14-ounce) can sweetened condensed milk	1	tablespoon vanilla

Combine all ingredients and freeze in an ice cream maker.

Caramel Pumpkin Pie

Crust

1⅓	cups all-purpose flour	6	tablespoons unsalted butter, chilled and cut into ½-inch cubes
1	tablespoon sugar		
½	teaspoon salt	2	tablespoons (or more) ice water

Filling

⅔	cup sugar	1	egg yolk
2	tablespoons water	1	cup canned solid pack pumpkin
2	tablespoons unsalted butter	2	teaspoons ground cinnamon
¾	cup half-and-half	¾	teaspoon ground ginger
⅔	cup heavy cream	¼	teaspoon ground cloves
2	eggs	¼	teaspoon salt

To make crust, mix flour, sugar and salt in a food processor. Add butter while pulsing processor on and off. Process until coarse meal forms. Add 2 tablespoons ice water and process until moist clumps form, adding more water, 1 teaspoon at a time, if mixture is dry. Form dough into a disk. Wrap in plastic and refrigerate 1 hour. Roll out dough on a floured surface to a 12-inch circle. Transfer to a 9-inch pie pan. Fold overhang under and crimp edges decoratively. Chill 1 hour.

Bake chilled crust at 375 degrees for 15 minutes or until edges begin to brown. Press crust while baking with back of a fork if bubbles form. Cool slightly. Reduce oven temperature to 350 degrees.

For filling, combine sugar and water in a medium saucepan. Stir over medium heat until sugar dissolves. Increase heat and boil without stirring for about 7 minutes or until sugar turns dark amber, occasionally swirling pan and brushing down pan sides with a wet pastry brush. Remove from heat. Whisk in butter, 1 tablespoon at a time; mixture will bubble. Stir in half-and-half and cream and stir until all caramel bits dissolve. Whisk eggs and egg yolk together in a bowl. Whisk pumpkin, cinnamon, ginger, cloves and salt into eggs. Gradually whisk caramel mixture into pumpkin mixture. Transfer filling to crust. Bake at 350 degrees for 50 minutes or until puffed and set in the center. Cool pie on a rack. Yield: 8 servings.

Place a slice of apple in hardened brown sugar or place in microwave to soften it back up.

Cherry Cobbler

Filling

6	cups fresh or frozen pitted tart cherries	1	tablespoon Frangelico or amaretto liqueur
1	cup sugar		
1½	tablespoons cornstarch	1	teaspoon vanilla

Topping

5	tablespoons unsalted butter, chilled and cut into pieces	1½	teaspoons baking powder
		½	teaspoon salt
1	cup all-purpose flour	½	cup milk
2	tablespoons yellow cornmeal	½	teaspoon vanilla
¼	cup sugar		

If using fresh cherries, pit them. In a large heavy saucepan, whisk together sugar and cornstarch. Add cherries, liqueur and vanilla and bring to a boil over medium heat, stirring occasionally. Simmer and stir 2 minutes. Transfer to a shallow 2-quart baking dish.

For topping, use a pastry blender or food processor to blend or pulse together butter, flour, cornmeal, sugar, baking powder and salt until mixture resembles coarse meal. If using a food processor, transfer mixture to a bowl. Add milk and vanilla and stir with a fork until mixture forms a dough.

Drop topping by rounded tablespoons onto filling, but do not completely cover filling. Bake at 375 degrees in center of oven for 40 minutes or until topping is golden and cooked through. Transfer to a rack to cool slightly. Serve warm with ice cream. Yield: 8 servings.

Light Sweet Potato Pie

1	pound sweet potatoes		Juice and zest of 1 lemon
½	cup butter, softened slightly	1	(5-ounce) can evaporated milk
1	cup light brown sugar		Whole milk
2	teaspoons cinnamon	2	ounces brandy (optional)
1	teaspoon nutmeg	1	(9-inch) pie crust, unbaked
4	eggs, separated		

Cook sweet potatoes in boiling water. When cool enough to handle, peel potatoes and mash. Measure out 2 cups mashed potatoes. Cream butter and brown sugar. Mix in 2 cups mashed sweet potatoes. Beat in cinnamon, nutmeg, egg yolks and lemon juice and zest. Combine evaporated milk with enough whole milk to measure 1 cup total. Beat milk mixture and brandy into potato filling. Beat egg whites until stiff and fold into filling. Pour filling into pie crust. Bake at 400 degrees for 10 minutes. Reduce temperature to 325 degrees and bake 40 to 45 minutes or until set.

Chocolate Cream Pie

Crumb Crust

6   tablespoons unsalted butter
45   vanilla wafers

⅓   cup sugar

Filling

5   ounces bittersweet chocolate, chopped
4   ounces unsweetened chocolate, chopped
1   cup sugar
½   cup cornstarch
¾   teaspoon salt
6   egg yolks

4½   cups milk
3   tablespoons unsalted butter, cut into pieces
1½   teaspoons vanilla
    Whipped cream and grated chocolate or chocolate curls for garnish

Melt butter and cool slightly. In a food processor, finely grind enough vanilla wafers to measure 2 cups crumbs. In a bowl, stir together crumbs, butter and sugar. Press mixture evenly onto the bottom and up the sides of a 10-inch pie pan. Bake at 350 degrees in center of oven for 15 to 20 minutes or until crisp. Cool on a rack.

For filling, melt both chocolates, stirring until smooth, in a metal bowl set over a pan of barely simmering water, or in a double boiler. In a heavy 3-quart saucepan, whisk together sugar, cornstarch, salt and egg yolks until well combined. Whisk in milk in a steady stream. Bring mixture to a boil, whisking constantly, over medium heat. Simmer 1 minute or until thickened. Using a rubber spatula, force filling through a fine sieve into a bowl. Whisk in melted chocolate, butter and vanilla until smooth. Pour filling into cooled crust. Cover surface of pie with plastic wrap and chill. Spoon whipped cream decoratively onto pie and sprinkle with grated chocolate or chocolate curls. Yield: 8 servings.

Fudge Pie

1   cup butter, melted
1   cup sugar
¼   cup unsweetened cocoa powder
¼   cup flour

2   eggs, beaten
1   teaspoon vanilla
¼   cup chopped nuts (optional)
1   (9-inch) prepared pie crust, unbaked

Combine butter, sugar, cocoa and flour and stir well. Add eggs, vanilla and nuts. Stir until well blended. Place into prepared pie crust. Bake at 375 degrees for 25 to 30 minutes or until center shakes slightly like a custard, but is not firm; do not overcook. Serve warm with a scoop of vanilla ice cream or whipped cream. Yield: 6 to 8 servings.

Daiquiri Pie

18	squares graham crackers	3	tablespoons fresh lime juice
6	tablespoons butter, melted	1	tablespoon fresh lemon juice
1	(14-ounce) can sweetened condensed milk	¼	teaspoon salt
4	tablespoons light rum, divided	1½	cups heavy cream, divided
1	tablespoon lime zest	1	tablespoon sugar

Process graham crackers in a food processor into crumbs. Add melted butter and process briefly. Press mixture into the bottom and up the sides of a 9-inch pie pan or tart pan with removable bottom. Bake at 350 degrees for 8 minutes; set aside to cool.

To prepare filling, beat milk, 3 tablespoons rum, lime zest, lime juice, lemon juice and salt in a medium bowl. Chill 5 minutes. In a separate bowl, whip ½ cup cream. Stir 2 to 3 spoonfuls of filling into whipped cream, then gently fold back into filling. Spoon filling into cooled crust and refrigerate at least 2 hours.

Before serving, whip remaining 1 cup cream. When soft peaks form, beat in sugar and remaining 1 tablespoon rum. Spoon a dollop of whipped cream on each serving. Yield: 6 to 8 servings.

You may freeze this pie (3 hours).

Perfect Pie Pastry

4	cups all-purpose flour	½	cup water
1	tablespoon sugar	1	tablespoon vinegar
2	teaspoons salt	1	egg
1¾	cups vegetable shortening		

Combine flour, sugar and salt in a large bowl. Cut in shortening with 2 knives until crumbly, or mix in a food processor. In a small bowl, beat together water, vinegar and egg. Combine the two mixtures and stir with a fork until all ingredients are moistened. Divide dough into 5 portions. Shape each portion into a flat round disk with hands. Wrap each disk separately with plastic and chill at least 1 hour before rolling out dough. May also freeze wrapped dough disk at this point for later use. Yield: 5 pie crusts.

I always keep some of these in the freezer; just thaw and roll out. If I am making a one-crust pie, I place the rolled out pie crust back in the freezer for about 5 minutes before I bake.

Fresh Cherry Pie

Crust

⅓	cup whole milk	½	teaspoon salt
1	tablespoon white vinegar	1	cup vegetable shortening, chilled and
2	cups all-purpose flour		cut into ½-inch cubes

Filling

5	cups fresh or frozen pitted cherries	½	teaspoon salt
1	cup plus 3 tablespoons sugar, divided	2	tablespoons fresh lemon juice
¼	cup quick-cooking tapioca	2	tablespoons vanilla

Whisk milk and vinegar in a small bowl to blend. Whisk flour and salt in a medium bowl. Rub shortening into flour mixture with fingertips until mixture resembles coarse meal. Stir in milk mixture with a fork. Briefly knead in bowl until dough just comes together. Gather into a ball and divide into 2 pieces, one slightly larger than the other. Flatten each into a round disk. Wrap disks separately in plastic and refrigerate 30 minutes.

If using fresh cherries for filling, pit them. In a small bowl, stir together 1 cup, 2 tablespoons sugar, tapioca and salt. In a large heavy skillet, cook and stir cherries and lemon juice over medium-high heat for 2 minutes or until slightly softened. With a slotted spoon, transfer cherries to a heatproof bowl. Add sugar mixture to cherry juice in skillet and simmer, stirring, for 3 minutes or until thickened. Stir cherry sauce and vanilla into cherries and cool.

Roll out larger disk of dough between 2 sheets of wax paper. Lift top paper to loosen, then turn over and lift the other side to loosen. Transfer crust to a 9-inch pie pan. Roll out remaining disk of dough to a 12x8-inch rectangle. Using a pastry wheel or sharp knife, cut lengthwise into strips. On a fresh piece of wax paper, make a circle the size of the pie dish. Use the dough strips to make a latticed top for the pie on circle of wax paper. Chill slightly for easier handling, if necessary. Brush the edges of the bottom crust with water. Brush the lattice top with water and sprinkle with remaining 1 tablespoon sugar. Spoon filling into bottom crust. Carefully place latticed top over filling. Flute edges. Place pie on a pizza pan or foil and place in middle rack of oven. Bake at 400 degrees for 45 minutes or until pastry is golden and filling just begins to bubble. Cool slightly. Serve warm with ice cream. Yield: 8 servings.

If preferred, thicken cherry juice with ¼ cup cornstarch dissolved in a small amount of water instead of the tapioca.

I always place juicy pies that may run over on a pizza pan or foil so filling does not get in the oven.

Jimmy Ruth's Chocolate Bar Pie

6	chocolate bars with almonds	1	cup heavy cream, whipped
16	marshmallows	1	pie crust, baked
½	cup milk		

Melt together chocolate bars and marshmallows with milk. Cool. Fold in whipped cream. Pour chocolate filling into baked pie crust. Chill before serving. Yield: 6 to 8 servings.

Lemon Meringue Pie

7	tablespoons cornstarch	1	tablespoon grated lemon peel
1½	cups sugar	2	cups boiling water
½	teaspoon salt	4	eggs, separated
2	tablespoons butter	¼	cup lemon juice

Combine cornstarch, sugar and salt. Add the water. Cook until thick, stirring constantly. Cover and place over boiling water for about 10 minutes, stirring occasionally. Beat egg yolk slightly, add a little of the hot mixture, stir and pour back into cornstarch mixture. Cook 2 minutes, stirring constantly. Remove from heat and stir in lemon juice, butter, and grated lemon peel. Pour into cooled baked pastry shell.

Meringue

In a small boiler cook until clear and thick:

2	tablespoons sugar	½	cup cold water
1	tablespoon cornstarch		

Set this aside to cool completely. This step is not always necessary, but when the weather is humid it will prevent the meringue from getting little moisture beads. Beat 4 egg whites with ¼ teaspoon cream of tartar and pinch of salt until soft peaks are formed. Gradually add 8 tablespoons sugar and beat well (until sugar has dissolved). Beat the cooled cornstarch mixture into the meringue. Add 1 teaspoon of lemon juice. Spread over hot lemon filling, and bake about 25 to 30 minutes at 300 degrees, or until brown.

Note: Eggs separate better when they are cold. Separate immediately after removing from the refrigerator. The whites beat higher when they are at room temperature and when beaten in a copper container. You can purchase a copper liner for your mixer bowl or purchase a copper bowl. Do not let any yolk mix with the white of the egg. It is usually better to separate the yolk from the white in a smaller bowl and then place the whites into the bowl for beating. Place the yolks in a small bowl to be added to the filling.

Lemon Tart Brûlée

Crust

1	cup all-purpose flour	6	tablespoons unsalted butter, chilled
¼	cup powdered sugar		and cut into ½-inch pieces
2	tablespoons granulated sugar	2	tablespoons heavy cream, chilled
⅛	teaspoon salt	1	egg white, beaten

Filling

¾	cup plus 2 tablespoons sugar	½	cup fresh lemon juice
¾	cup heavy cream	1	tablespoon lemon zest
2	eggs		Pinch of salt
4	egg yolks		

To make crust, blend flour, both sugars and salt in a food processor. Add butter and pulse on and off until mixture resembles coarse meal. Mix in cream. Turn dough out onto a work surface. Gather dough into a ball and flatten into a disk. Wrap in plastic and refrigerate 1 hour.

Roll dough out on a lightly floured surface to a 13-inch round. Transfer to a 9-inch tart pan with a removable bottom. Trim dough, leaving a ½-inch overhang. Fold overhang under, folding to form a double-thick sided crust. Chill 15 minutes. Bake at 350 degrees for 18 minutes or until golden, pressing with the back of a fork if crust bubbles. Brush inside of hot crust twice with egg white.

For filling, whisk together ¾ cup sugar, cream, eggs, egg yolks, lemon juice, lemon zest and salt in a bowl. Pour filling mixture into crust. Bake at 350 degrees for 30 minutes or until set. Cool 1 hour or until completely cooled.

Sprinkle remaining 2 tablespoons sugar over tart. Cover crust of tart with foil to protect from heat. Broil tart 3 minutes, watching closely, or until sugar caramelizes in spots. Serve warm or at room temperature. Yield: 8 servings.

Sunrise Peach Pie

¾	cup sugar	3½	cups drained canned cling peach slices,
¼	cup flour		juice reserved
½	teaspoon cinnamon	2	pie crusts, unbaked

Combine sugar, flour, cinnamon and ½ cup reserved peach juice in a heavy saucepan. Cook and stir until thickened. Add peach slices. Fit one of the pie crusts into a pie pan. Pour peach filling over crust. Cut a hole in center of second crust and fit crust over filling. Slash top crust around hole to form sunrays. Bake at 425 degrees for 35 to 45 minutes. Yield: 6 to 8 servings.

Pecan Pie Dessert

Pastry

1½	cups all-purpose flour
⅛	teaspoon salt

½	cup unsalted butter, chilled and cut into small pieces
¼	cup cold water

Filling

1¼	cups light corn syrup
1	cup sugar
5	tablespoons unsalted butter
4	eggs

1½	teaspoons vanilla
1½	cups coarsely chopped pecans
⅓	cup sliced almonds, lightly toasted

Sauce

⅔	cup light brown sugar
⅔	cup light corn syrup
4	tablespoons unsalted butter

⅔	cup heavy cream
3	tablespoons bourbon

1	quart vanilla ice cream

To make pastry, combine flour, salt and butter in a food processor. Add water and process until mixed. Roll out pastry to fit in a 10-inch tart pan with a removable bottom. Place pastry in pan, fold down edges and shape into pan.

Combine all filling ingredients except almonds. Pour mixture into a tart pastry shell. Sprinkle with almonds. Bake at 350 degrees for 30 minutes or until set.

For sauce, bring sugar, corn syrup and butter to a boil in a saucepan. Add cream and bourbon and boil a few minutes. Refrigerate until ready to use. Bring to room temperature before serving.

To serve, place a slice of pie on an individual serving plate. Top with a scoop of vanilla ice cream. Pour sauce over the top.

Brush beaten egg white over a pie crust before baking to yield a glossy finish.

Pecan Pumpkin Pie

Pastry

1⅛	cups all-purpose flour
¼	teaspoon salt
2	tablespoons unsalted butter, chilled and cut into pieces

½	cup vegetable shortening, chilled and cut into pieces
2	tablespoons (about) ice water

Pumpkin Filling

¾	cup canned solid pack pumpkin
2	tablespoons light brown sugar
1	egg, beaten

2	tablespoons sour cream
⅛	teaspoon cinnamon
⅛	teaspoon freshly grated nutmeg

Pecan Topping

¾	cup light corn syrup
½	cup light brown sugar
3	eggs, lightly beaten
3	tablespoons unsalted butter, melted and cooled

2	teaspoons vanilla
¼	teaspoon freshly grated lemon zest
1½	teaspoons fresh lemon juice
¼	teaspoon salt
1⅓	cups pecans

Blend flour, salt, butter and shortening with a pastry blender in a bowl until mixture resembles meal. Add ice water, 1 tablespoon at a time, tossing with a fork until mixture forms a soft, but not sticky, dough. Form into a ball, wrap in plastic and chill. Roll out chilled dough between 2 sheets of wax paper. Transfer to a 9-inch pie pan and crimp edges. Chill.

For pumpkin filling, whisk together all ingredients until smooth. Spread filling evenly over chilled pastry crust.

To make pecan topping, stir together all ingredients except pecans. When well combined, stir in pecans. Spoon topping over pie, being careful not to disturb pumpkin layer.

Bake at 425 degrees in upper third of oven for 20 minutes. Reduce oven temperature to 350 degrees and bake 20 minutes longer or until filling is slightly puffed. Transfer to a wire rack to cool. Serve pie warm or at room temperature. If made ahead, reheat at 350 degrees for 10 minutes. Yield: 6 to 8 servings.

Pumpkin Chiffon Pie

3	eggs, separated	½	teaspoon ground cinnamon
1	cup sugar, divided	½	teaspoon salt
1¼	cups canned pumpkin	1	(¼-ounce) envelope unflavored gelatin
½	cup milk	¼	cup cold water
½	teaspoon ground nutmeg	1	(9-inch) pie crust, baked and cooled
½	teaspoon ground ginger		Whipped cream for garnish

Lightly beat egg yolks in the top of a double boiler. Add ½ cup sugar, pumpkin, milk, nutmeg, ginger, cinnamon and salt. Cook over boiling water until thickened. Soften gelatin in cold water. Add softened gelatin to hot pumpkin mixture and mix thoroughly; cool. Beat egg whites with remaining ½ cup sugar until stiff. When pumpkin mixture begins to thicken as it cools, fold in egg whites. Pour pumpkin filling into pie crust and chill in refrigerator. Garnish with whipped cream just before serving. Yield: 6 to 8 servings.

This pie is delicious served in a gingersnap crust.

Sweet Potato Pecan Pie

1	frozen deep dish pie crust, thawed	¼	teaspoon allspice
1	(1-pound) red-skinned sweet potato	¼	teaspoon salt
½	cup light brown sugar	¾	cup light corn syrup
2	tablespoons unsalted butter, melted	2	eggs
1	tablespoon vanilla	1	cup pecan halves
½	teaspoon cinnamon		

Prick crust all over with a fork. Bake at 400 degrees for 8 minutes or until pale golden; set aside. Reduce oven temperature to 350 degrees.

Pierce sweet potato with a fork. Cook potato in microwave on high power for 6 minutes per side or until tender. Cut potato in half and scoop flesh into a medium bowl. Mash and measure out 1 cup mashed potato. Place potato in a large bowl. Whisk in brown sugar, butter, vanilla, cinnamon, allspice and salt. Spread filling mixture over baked crust. Whisk corn syrup and eggs together in a bowl until blended. Stir in pecans. Pour syrup mixture over filling. Bake at 350 degrees for 45 minutes or until filling is set, puffed and brown. Cool pie completely. Serve at room temperature. Yield: 8 servings.

Party Foods

Apricot-Cream Cheese Dreams

1 (8-ounce) package cream cheese, softened	½ cup apricot preserves White bread

Mix cream cheese and preserves together. Spread mixture on a slice of bread. Top with a second slice of bread. Trim away crusts and cut sandwiches into small squares or triangles. Yield: About 20 small sandwiches.

Calla Lily Sandwiches

1 (2-ounce) package slivered almonds	1 (8-ounce) package cream cheese, softened
2-3 drops yellow food coloring	
1 king-size loaf white sandwich bread	2 tablespoons orange marmalade

Combine almonds and food coloring in a jar. Cover with a lid and shake vigorously until almonds are evenly coated.

Roll each slice of bread to ⅛-inch thickness with a rolling pin. Cut each slice with a 2½-inch biscuit cutter. Combine cream cheese and marmalade. Spread about 1 teaspoon on each bread round. Pinch edges of one portion of circle together to form a calla lily. Press a tinted slivered almond into the pinched portion to represent the flower's stamen. Yield: 2 dozen.

Cheese Puffs

1 loaf white bread, unsliced	½ cup butter
1 (3-ounce) package cream cheese	2 egg whites, stiffly beaten
4 ounces extra sharp Cheddar cheese	

Trim crusts from bread and cut loaf into 1-inch cubes. Melt cheeses and butter in the top of a double boiler over hot water until thickened. Remove from heat and fold in stiffly beaten egg whites. Dip bread cubes into cheese mixture until well coated and place on a baking sheet. Refrigerate overnight.

Just before ready to serve, bake puffs at 400 degrees for 12 to 15 minutes or until puffy and golden brown.

Chicken Salad Filling

1	cup diced cooked chicken	4-6	tablespoons mayonnaise
¼	cup finely chopped celery	½	teaspoon salt
1	tablespoon minced onion	⅛	teaspoon white pepper

Combine all ingredients and mix well. Spread filling over bread with trimmed crusts. Cut into small sandwiches. Yield: About 20 small sandwiches.

These sandwiches may be garnished by tinting cream cheese pink and green. Use the pink to make tiny rosettes on top of the sandwiches. Use the green for leaves.

Chicken Salad Mini Cream Puffs

Mini Cream Puffs

¼	cup butter or margarine	⅛	teaspoon salt
½	cup water	2	eggs, at room temperature
½	cup all-purpose flour		

Chicken Salad Filling

2	cups finely chopped cooked chicken	1	teaspoon fresh lemon juice
½	cup finely minced celery	1	teaspoon sugar
1	apple, unpeeled and finely chopped	½	teaspoon salt
2	tablespoons finely diced pimento	½	teaspoon freshly ground black pepper
5	tablespoons mayonnaise	1	tablespoon finely chopped green onion
5	tablespoons sour cream		

Bring butter and water to a boil in a 1-quart saucepan over high heat. As soon as butter is melted, add flour and salt all at once, stirring constantly with a wooden spoon until dough forms into a ball. Remove from heat and cool 5 minutes. Add eggs, one at a time, beating well after each addition. Mix until dough forms a "round mass". Drop by scant teaspoonfuls onto lightly greased baking sheets. Bake at 425 degrees for 10 minutes. Reduce oven temperature to 375 degrees and bake 10 to 15 minutes or until puffs are golden brown and no moisture is evident. Cool completely on a wire rack. Cut off top third of puffs. Scoop out any mixture that may be in center. Fill with chicken salad and replace top.

To make chicken salad, combine chicken, celery, apple and pimento in a bowl. In a separate bowl, combine mayonnaise, sour cream, lemon juice, sugar, salt, pepper and onion. Pour dressing mixture over chicken mixture and toss gently to blend. Spoon filling into puffs and place on a baking sheet. Bake at 400 degrees for 5 to 7 minutes. Yield: About 40 puffs.

Cucumber Bites

1   (8-ounce) package cream cheese,
     softened
1   cucumber, peeled, seeded, minced and
     squeezed dry
2   green onions, finely minced

1   loaf thinly sliced fine grain bread
2-3 cucumbers, thinly sliced
1   (3-ounce) package cream cheese,
     softened

Combine 8-ounce package cream cheese, minced cucumber and green onions; chill. Cut bread into small circles or hearts. Spread mixture over bread pieces. Top each with a thin slice of cucumber. Cover with wax paper and a slightly damp kitchen towel and refrigerate until ready to serve. Use remaining 3-ounce package cream cheese to make piped rosettes for garnish. Yield: 3 dozen.

Curried Chicken Balls

½   (8-ounce) package cream cheese,
     softened
2   tablespoons mayonnaise
1   cup chopped pecans

1   tablespoon chopped chutney
1   teaspoon curry powder
1   cup chopped cooked chicken
1   cup grated coconut, toasted

Combine all ingredients except coconut. Shape mixture into small balls. Roll balls in coconut and place on a tray. Refrigerate until serving. Yield: 30 balls.

Mints with Cream Cheese

¼   (8-ounce) package cream cheese,
     softened
⅓   teaspoon oil of peppermint
     (available at drug stores)

Food coloring as choice
1⅔ cups powdered sugar
Granulated sugar

Mash cream cheese. Add peppermint oil and food coloring. Mix in powdered sugar. Knead mixture with hands until similar to pie dough. Roll mixture into marble-size balls. Place on top a small amount of granulated sugar. Press balls, sugar-side down, into molds and remove immediately.

Mints

1	(1-pound) box less ¼ cup powdered sugar	7	drops food coloring of choice
4	tablespoons butter, melted	7	drops oil of peppermint (available at drug stores)

Combine all ingredients with a fork until moistened. Place in rubber or plastic molds and remove immediately. Mints freeze well.

Party Chicken

8	boneless, skinless chicken breasts	1	(10¾-ounce) can condensed cream of mushroom soup
8	slices bacon		
1	(2-ounce) package chipped beef	1	cup sour cream

Wrap chicken breasts in bacon. Cover bottom of a greased flat baking dish with chipped beef. Place wrapped chicken on beef. Combine soup and sour cream and pour over chicken. May be refrigerated at this point until ready to bake. Bake, uncovered, at 275 degrees for 3 hours. Yield: 6 to 8 servings.

Party Shrimp Mold

1	(10¾-ounce) can condensed tomato soup	½	cup heavy cream
		½	cup chopped olives
1	(8-ounce) package cream cheese		Salt to taste
1	tablespoon onion juice	1	tablespoon Tabasco sauce
1	tablespoon butter	1	tablespoon Worcestershire sauce
1	(¼-ounce) envelope unflavored gelatin	1	cup chopped green bell pepper
¼	cup cold water	½	cup chopped celery
½	cup mayonnaise	1	pound boiled shrimp, chopped

Heat undiluted soup in the top of a double boiler. Add cream cheese, onion juice and butter. While cheese is heating, dissolve gelatin in cold water. When cheese is melted and mixture is smooth, add gelatin and cool. Stir in mayonnaise, cream, olives, salt, Tabasco sauce, Worcestershire sauce, bell pepper, celery and shrimp. Turn mixture into a wet mold or a mold sprayed with nonstick spray. Refrigerate at least 2 hours. Yield: 4 to 6 servings.

Rolled Asparagus Sandwiches

25   spears asparagus
1   long loaf bread, thinly sliced

½   cup butter, softened

Cook asparagus until just tender; drain.

Remove crusts from slices of bread. Spread slices with butter. Place an asparagus spear on the edge of each slice of bread. Roll up securely and fasten with a wooden pick. Cover with plastic wrap and refrigerate several hours before using. Remove picks and cut into halves. Yield: About 50 sandwiches.

You can use white asparagus rolled in wheat bread or green asparagus rolled in white bread for these.

Shrimp Spread

2   cups raw shrimp, peeled
1   slice lemon
1   teaspoon red pepper flakes
1   sprig fresh dill
1   (3-ounce) package cream cheese,
     softened

1   small onion, grated
⅓   cup finely chopped celery
¼   teaspoon Tabasco sauce
⅛   teaspoon Worcestershire sauce
     White pepper
     Mayonnaise

Add shrimp with lemon slice, pepper flakes and dill to enough boiling water to cover. Cook just until water returns to a boil. Immediately remove from heat and let stand in hot water for about 3 minutes. Do not overcook. Drain and discard lemon and dill. Mince shrimp. Add cream cheese, onion, celery, Tabasco sauce, Worcestershire sauce and white pepper. Mix in enough mayonnaise to moisten. Chill several hours to allow flavors to blend.

Spread mixture on thin white sandwich bread that has had crusts trimmed. Roll or cut into small heart-shaped open faced sandwiches. Yield: 2 dozen.

The rolled sandwiches may be tied with pink ribbon for bridal parties.

Spinach Balls

1	(10-ounce) package frozen chopped spinach	¾	cup butter, melted
3	cups herb-seasoned stuffing mix	½	cup grated Parmesan cheese
1	large onion, finely chopped	1	tablespoon black pepper
6	eggs, well beaten	1½	teaspoons garlic salt
		½	teaspoon dried thyme

Cook spinach according to package directions; drain well and squeeze to remove excess moisture. Combine spinach with stuffing mix, onion, eggs, butter, cheese, black pepper, garlic salt and thyme. Form mixture into small balls and place on lightly greased baking sheets. Bake at 325 degrees for 15 to 20 minutes. Yield: 7 to 8 dozen.

Spinach balls can be frozen before baking. Place on a baking sheet and freeze until firm. When frozen, remove from baking sheet and store in plastic bags. Thaw slightly and bake at 325 degrees for 20 to 25 minutes.

Strawberries in Tuxedos

Purchase large strawberries with stems still on. You may order them from your produce supplier or purchase from a specialty market. Leave stems and leaves attached. Lightly wash strawberries and drain on a paper towels. (Never soak strawberries in water as they will absorb it. Lightly rinse under running water in a colander or by hand. I make one per guest. Let strawberries dry completely.)

Melt a good grade of white dipping chocolate. Dip strawberries to ½-inch below the leaves. Lay on side on wax paper to dry. Melt dark chocolate and dip each side of the strawberries to the top of the white chocolate, leaving a "bib" of the white chocolate to simulate a coat front. Using a pastry bag and a small writing tip, make a bow tie at the top of the white chocolate bib between the dark chocolate. Make 3 buttons under the bow tie using the decorator tip.

Tuna Mousse

1	(¼-ounce) envelope unflavored gelatin	½	cup mayonnaise
¾	cup milk	2	(7-ounce) cans or packages albacore tuna, finely chopped
1	(10¾-ounce) can condensed tomato soup	½	cup minced celery
1	(8-ounce) package cream cheese	½	cup chopped onion

Dissolve gelatin in milk; set aside. Heat soup and cream cheese and stir well until smooth. Remove from heat and add gelatin mixture. Fold in mayonnaise, tuna, celery and onion. Pour into a 4-cup mold and chill. Serve with crackers, celery or carrots.

Tuna Mold

1	(10¾-ounce) can condensed tomato soup	1	(7-ounce) bottle stuffed olives, chopped
1	(8-ounce) package cream cheese	½	cup finely chopped onion
1½	(¼-ounce) packages unflavored gelatin	½	cup finely chopped celery
2	(6-ounce) cans tuna, flaked	½	cup finely chopped bell pepper
		1	cup Durkee's dressing

Heat soup. Add cream cheese and mix until melted, whisking or mixing with a hand mixer until smooth. Dissolve gelatin in warm soup mixture; cool. Add tuna, olives, onion, celery, bell pepper and dressing. Mix well and pour into a well-greased fish mold; chill. When firm, turn out onto a platter and garnish with parsley. Use a small slice of a stuffed olive for the eye. Serve with crackers. Yield: 6 to 8 servings.

Watercress-Cucumber Sandwiches

1	bunch watercress, washed, stems trimmed and wilted leaves removed		Butter or cream cheese, softened
	Juice of 1 lemon	12	thin slices white bread
		1	cucumber, thinly sliced

Coarsely chop watercress and mix with lemon juice. Spread butter on bread. Pat mixture onto buttered bread. Garnish with cucumber slices, fanned out diagonally across open-faced sandwich. Cut in half lengthwise or diagonally.

If you prefer small cut sandwiches, 12 slices are needed. If you prefer open faced, 6 slices will work. You can make small cut sandwiches from this filling or serve open faced. I prefer open faced.

You can use boiled shrimp instead of the cucumbers. Use 1 small shrimp per slice of bread.

Watercress Sandwiches

7	bunches watercress, washed, stems trimmed and wilted leaves removed		Salt to taste
			Cayenne pepper, sparingly to taste
¼	cucumber, finely chopped	½	teaspoon Accent
1	(8-ounce) package cream cheese, softened	1¾	large loaves thinly sliced bread

Very finely chop watercress and mix with cucumber. Blend in cream cheese. Season with salt and cayenne pepper. Mix in Accent. Spread over bread slices. Yield: 100 party sandwiches; 25 large sandwiches cut into quarters.

Sauces & Garnishes

Amaretto Chocolate Sauce

½	cup granulated sugar	2	tablespoons amaretto, or 1 teaspoon
½	cup brown sugar		almond extract
1	(12-ounce) can evaporated milk	2	tablespoons butter
1	(12-ounce) package semisweet real		
	chocolate chips		

Combine both sugars and milk in a 2-quart saucepan. Cook over medium heat, stirring occasionally, for 4 to 6 minutes or until mixture comes to a boil. Add chocolate chips and stir 1 to 2 minutes or until melted. Remove from heat. Stir in amaretto and butter. Serve over ice cream, cake, desserts, etc. Store leftovers in the refrigerator. Yield: 3 cups.

Artichoke Sauce for Pasta

⅓	cup olive oil		Salt and pepper to taste
4	cloves garlic, minced		Hot cooked pasta, drained
2	shallots, chopped	1	small bunch parsley, chopped
6	artichokes, cooked fresh bottoms or	½	cup walnut halves, chopped
	canned	¼	cup grated Parmesan cheese
3	tablespoons dry white wine	2	tablespoons lemon juice

Heat olive oil in a saucepan. Add garlic and shallots and sauté 1 minute without browning. Add artichokes and wine and cook 2 to 3 minutes. Season with salt and pepper. Add cooked pasta, parsley and walnuts. Sprinkle with Parmesan cheese. Serve on warm plates. Yield: 4 servings.

If using fresh artichokes, use lemon juice to keep from browning.

Blender Hollandaise Sauce

3	egg yolks	¼	teaspoon cayenne pepper
2	tablespoons lemon juice	½	cup hot melted butter
¼	teaspoon salt		

Combine egg yolks, lemon juice, salt and cayenne in a blender. Cover and pulse blender on and off several times. Remove cover, switch blender to high speed and gradually add melted butter in a steady steam until just blended and thickened. Serve immediately, or keep warm by placing blender container in a pan of hot water. Yield: 1 cup.

Placing this in a thermos will keep it warm if you are entertaining.

Béarnaise Sauce

3	tablespoons tarragon vinegar	1	tablespoon cold water
1	teaspoon minced green onion	4	egg yolks
¼	teaspoon coarsely ground black pepper	½	cup butter, softened
	Dash of dried tarragon	1	teaspoon minced fresh parsley
	Dash of dried chervil or parsley	⅛	teaspoon salt

Combine vinegar, green onion, black pepper, tarragon and chervil in a saucepan. Bring to a boil over medium heat. Reduce heat to low and simmer until liquid is reduced by half. Pour mixture through a strainer, reserving liquid. Discard herb mixture. Combine vinegar liquid with cold water.

Beat egg yolks in the top of a double boiler with a wire whisk. Gradually add vinegar liquid in a slow steady stream. Bring water in bottom of double boiler to a boil. (Water should not be high enough to touch top pan.) Reduce heat to low. Add butter, 2 tablespoons at a time, beating constantly until butter melts. Continue beating until smooth and thickened. Remove from heat and stir in parsley and salt. Serve over beef, poultry or seafood. Yield: About 1 cup.

To rescue an overheated béarnaise sauce that has curdled, place 1 teaspoon of lemon juice and 1 tablespoon of the curdled sauce in a mixing bowl. Beat with a wire whisk until the mixture is thick and creamy. Gradually beat in the remaining sauce, 1 tablespoon at a time, making sure each addition has thickened before adding the next.

Bordelaise Sauce

2	tablespoons butter	¼	teaspoon dried thyme
2	tablespoons all-purpose flour	⅛	teaspoon salt
1	tablespoon minced green onions	⅛	teaspoon coarsely ground black pepper
1	tablespoon chopped fresh parsley	1	(10½-ounce) can beef broth
1	bay leaf	3	tablespoons dry red wine

Melt butter in a heavy saucepan over low heat. Add flour, stirring until smooth. Cook 1 minute, stirring constantly. Stir in green onion, parsley, bay leaf, thyme, salt and pepper. Gradually add broth and wine. Cook over medium-high heat, stirring constantly, until thickened and bubbly. Remove bay leaf. Serve over beef. Yield: 1½ cups.

Butter Rum Sauce

½   cup butter
1   (1-pound) package powdered sugar

Rum to taste

Melt butter. Slowly stir in powdered sugar. Add rum and heat until sauce bubbles. Use over pound cake or bread pudding.

Butterscotch/Caramel Sauce

2   cups sugar
1   cup light or dark corn syrup
2   tablespoons butter

Pinch of salt
1   (5⅓-ounce) can evaporated milk
1   teaspoon vanilla

Bring sugar, corn syrup, butter and salt to a hard boil, stirring constantly. Add milk and vanilla. Cook to desired consistency for pouring over ice cream, stirring constantly and being careful to not allow sauce to boil over. Sauce thickens as it cools and may be reheated.

Cranberry Walnut Sauce

2   (12-ounce) packages fresh cranberries,
      rinsed and drained
3⅓ cups sugar
1½ cups walnuts, toasted and coarsely
      chopped (about 6 ounces)

¼   cup Grand Marnier or other orange
      liqueur
Fresh lemon juice (optional)

Place cranberries in a 15x10x2-inch glass baking dish. Stir in sugar and cover dish with foil. Bake at 350 degrees for 1 hour, 15 minutes or until cranberries burst and sauce starts to thicken, stirring every 20 minutes. (Set your timer to 20 minutes each time you stir as a reminder.) Cool completely. Stir in walnuts and liqueur. Add lemon juice to taste, if desired. Transfer to a serving bowl. Sauce can be prepared up to 2 days ahead and stored in refrigerator. Yield: About 5 cups.

I halve this recipe because I also serve jellied cranberry sauce with a baked turkey.

Classic Pesto

4	cups fresh basil leaves	¼	cup freshly grated Parmesan cheese
½	cup olive oil	¼	cup freshly grated pecorino Sardo or
⅓	cup pine nuts		Parmesan cheese
2	cloves garlic	1	teaspoon coarse kosher salt

Combine basil, olive oil, pine nuts and garlic in a blender. Blend until a paste forms, stopping often to push down basil. Add both cheeses and salt and blend until smooth. Transfer to a small bowl. If making a day ahead, cover with ½ inch of olive oil and chill. Drain oil before serving. Yield: 1 cup.

This is delicious mixed with Minestrone Soup, or served over fish or in pasta dishes.

Cocktail Sauce

1	(14 ounce) bottle ketchup	3	tablespoons Worcestershire sauce
6	ounces chili sauce	3	drops Tabasco sauce
2	tablespoons white vinegar	¼	cup prepared horseradish
½	teaspoon salt	2	tablespoons grated onion

Combine all ingredients well. Store in a container in the refrigerator. Use on boiled shrimp, crab or other seafood.

Dill Sauce for Fish Steaks

3	egg yolks		Juice of 1 lemon
1	teaspoon cold water	1	tablespoon fresh dill, or 1 teaspoon
¾	pound clarified butter		dried

Whip egg yolks and cold water together in a stainless steel bowl. Place bowl over a pot of boiling water, being sure that water does not touch bottom of bowl. Continue whipping yolks until they form soft peaks and remove from heat. Slowly pour butter into egg yolks while whipping lightly. Blend in lemon juice and dill. Serve sauce over poached or baked fish steaks. Yield: 4 servings.

Epicurian Sauce

1	pint heavy cream	4	teaspoons prepared mustard
¼	cup mayonnaise	2	teaspoons salt
½	cup prepared horseradish	¼	cup chopped fresh parsley

Whip cream until stiff. Fold in mayonnaise, horseradish, mustard, salt and parsley until well blended. Serve chilled with roast beef or ham loaf. Very good served with cold sliced filet mignon for the holidays.

Fudge Sauce

1	(16-ounce) can chocolate syrup	½	cup butter
1	(14-ounce) can sweetened condensed milk		

Mix all ingredients and heat in a microwave or on stovetop until butter is melted. Stir to mix. Serve over ice cream or pound cake.

Hollandaise Sauce

4	egg yolks	⅛	teaspoon Worcestershire sauce
	Juice of 1 lemon	6	drops Tabasco sauce
	Zest of 1 lemon	¼	cup water
⅛	teaspoon salt	½	cup butter
⅛	teaspoon white pepper		

Combine egg yolks, lemon juice and zest, salt, pepper, Worcestershire sauce, Tabasco and water in the top of a double boiler. Add butter, a third at a time, allowing it to melt before next addition. Cook and stir until sauce thickens. Remove from heat. Avoid stirring again or sauce will curdle. Serve over broccoli, fish or eggs Benedict. Yield: 6 servings.

I often keep this sauce in a thermos to keep warm rather than reheating.

Horseradish Sauce

1	cup sour cream	4	teaspoons drained horseradish
½	cup mayonnaise		Minced garlic to taste
1	teaspoon lemon juice		Salt and white pepper to taste

Blend all ingredients. Chill 3 to 4 hours. Yield: 1½ cups.

Lemon Sauce

1	lemon	2	cups boiling water
1	cup sugar	2	tablespoons butter
2	tablespoons cornstarch		

Grate zest from the lemon and squeeze juice into a small container; set aside. Combine sugar and cornstarch in a small saucepan. Add boiling water, stirring constantly. Cook 8 to 10 minutes. Stir in lemon juice and zest. Add butter and stir until smooth. Transfer sauce to a serving dish. Serve with bread pudding or pound cake.

Lemon Velvet Butter Sauce

⅓	cup dry white wine	1	cup heavy cream
2	tablespoons finely chopped shallots	½	cup butter, cut into 8 pieces
4	teaspoons fresh lemon juice		Salt and white pepper to taste
1	tablespoon all-purpose flour		

Combine wine, shallots and lemon juice in a 10-inch skillet. Bring to a boil over medium-high heat. Continue to boil 4 to 5 minutes or until liquid has almost evaporated. Reduce heat to medium-low. Add flour and mix well. Slowly stir in cream with a wire whisk until well mixed. Cook, stirring constantly, for 1 to 2 minutes or until mixture boils. Stir in butter until melted. Season with salt and pepper. Serve over roasted or steamed vegetables. Yield: 1⅓ cups, or 12 servings.

Madeira Sauce

2	green onions, finely chopped	2	teaspoons tomato paste
1	tablespoon butter		Pinch of herbes de Provence
2½	tablespoons flour		Black pepper to taste
1	(10-ounce) can beef broth	3	tablespoons Madeira
½	bay leaf		

Sauté green onions in butter in a skillet until clear. Stir in flour. Cook 2 minutes to form a roux, stirring constantly. Stir in broth, bay leaf, tomato paste, herbes de Provence and pepper. Simmer 5 minutes, stirring constantly; strain. Stir in wine. Serve with beef tenderloin. Yield: 1¼ cups.

Mornay Sauce

1	egg yolk	2	tablespoons shredded Swiss cheese
2	tablespoons heavy cream	¼	teaspoon salt
1	cup Thin White Sauce (page 255)		Dash of white pepper
1	tablespoon minced onion		

Beat egg yolk and cream with a wire whisk; set aside. Combine warm white sauce and onion in a heavy saucepan. Cook over low heat, stirring constantly, for 3 to 4 minutes or until onion is tender. Gradually stir about a fourth of hot white sauce into yolk mixture. Add back into remaining hot white sauce, stirring constantly. Add cheese. Cook and stir until cheese melts. Season with salt and pepper. Serve over poached eggs, seafood or vegetables. Yield: 1 cup.

Parsley Garlic Sauce

2	egg yolks	¼	teaspoon dry mustard
1½	tablespoons lemon juice	⅛	teaspoon cayenne pepper
1	tablespoon minced fresh parsley		Dash of salt
2	cloves garlic, crushed	½	cup butter, softened
1	tablespoon chopped chives		

Combine egg yolks, lemon juice, parsley, garlic, chives, mustard, cayenne and salt in the top of a double boiler. Place over hot (not boiling) water and beat with a wire whisk until smooth. Add butter, 1 tablespoon at a time, beating constantly until melted. Continue beating until thickened. Serve over seafood, beef or vegetables. Yield: ¾ cup.

Mushroom Sauce

4	tablespoons unsalted butter		2	cups heavy cream
1	pound mushrooms, sliced		1	tablespoon finely sliced chives, plus
	Salt and pepper to taste			extra for garnish
1	shallot, finely chopped		1	tablespoon chopped fresh parsley
¼	cup sherry			

Heat butter in a large skillet over medium heat until foaming. Add mushrooms and sauté until golden brown. Season well with salt and pepper. Add shallot and cook 1 to 2 minutes. Stir in sherry and cook 1 minute, scraping bottom of pan with a wooden spoon to dislodge juices. Add cream, chives and parsley. Cook until sauce is reduced by a fourth. Taste and adjust seasonings as needed. Serve over meats or poached egg on ham. Yield: 6 servings.

A mixture of mushrooms is best, such as shiitake, morels, chanterelles, oyster and cremini.

Never soak mushrooms in water. They absorb water like a sponge. Use a brush to clean and if you do rinse, do it quickly under running water and wipe dry with paper towels.

Praline Sauce

1½	cups brown sugar		1	(5⅓-ounce) can evaporated milk
⅔	cup light corn syrup		¾	cup chopped pecans
4	tablespoons butter		⅛	teaspoon salt

Mix brown sugar, corn syrup and butter in a saucepan. Bring to a boil, stirring constantly. After reaching a boil, remove from heat and cool to lukewarm. Add milk, pecans and salt and mix well. Remove from saucepan and store in airtight jars. May be stored for several months in refrigerator and reheated as needed. This is especially good with pound cake or ice cream. Yield: 2 cups.

Raisin Sauce

¾	cup brown sugar		½	cup raisins
¼	cup granulated sugar		2	slices lemon, chopped
2	teaspoons cornstarch		2	teaspoons vinegar
1	cup water			

Mix both sugars and cornstarch in a saucepan. Stir in water until dissolved. Add raisins and lemon. Cook until thickened. Add vinegar. Serve with baked ham or ham steaks.

Raspberry Sauce

2	cups frozen or fresh raspberries		Juice of ½ lemon
½	cup powdered sugar	¼	cup crème de cassis liqueur or Kirsch

Combine raspberries, sugar and lemon juice in a saucepan. Simmer until thickened, stirring frequently. Strain to remove seeds, if desired. Stir in liqueur.

Rémoulade Sauce

¾   cup mayonnaise
2   teaspoons Dijon mustard
1½ teaspoons whole-grain mustard
1   teaspoon tarragon vinegar
¼   teaspoon Tabasco sauce
2   teaspoons tiny capers, drained and chopped

1   tablespoon chopped fresh flat-leaf parsley
1   green onion, with 3 inches of green, very thinly sliced
    Salt and freshly ground black pepper to taste

Combine all ingredients in a bowl. Cover and refrigerate until ready to use. Yield: 1 cup.

Shallot Herb Butter

½   cup unsalted butter, softened, divided
2   tablespoons finely chopped shallots
1   tablespoon finely chopped garlic

1   tablespoon chopped fresh flat-leaf parsley

Place 1 teaspoon butter in a skillet over low heat. Add shallot and garlic and cook and stir 3 to 4 minutes. Cool to room temperature. Place remaining butter in a small bowl and cream well. Add shallot mixture and parsley and mix well. Wrap in wax paper and refrigerate for up to 1 week, or freeze for up to 2 months.

Tartar Sauce

1   cup mayonnaise
1½ tablespoons minced or grated sweet pickle

1½ tablespoons minced fresh parsley
1½ tablespoons capers
1½ tablespoons minced or grated onion

Combine all ingredients and mix well. Chill several hours before serving. Yield: 1¼ cups.

Vanilla Custard Sauce

6 egg yolks
½ cup sugar

2 cups light cream
2 teaspoons vanilla

Whisk together yolks and sugar in a mixing bowl. In a nonstick medium saucepan, bring cream to a simmer, then promptly remove from heat. Stir hot cream into yolks, adding about ⅓ cup at a time. Pour mixture back into saucepan. Cook, stirring constantly, over medium-low heat without letting it boil for 7 minutes or until sauce thickens to the consistency of heavy cream. Watch sauce carefully as the change is subtle. Strain sauce through a fine mesh strainer into a small bowl. Stir in vanilla and cool sauce to room temperature. Cover and chill until cold. Sauce with keep up to 2 to 3 days. Whisk briefly just before drizzling over cake or apple crisp. Yield: About 2½ cups.

White Sauce

Thin White Sauce
1 tablespoon butter
1 tablespoon all-purpose flour
1 cup milk

¼ teaspoon salt
Dash of white pepper

Medium White Sauce
2 tablespoons butter
2 tablespoons all-purpose flour
1 cup milk

¼ teaspoon salt
Dash of white pepper

Thick White Sauce
3 tablespoons butter
3 tablespoons all-purpose flour
1 cup milk

¼ teaspoon salt
Dash of white pepper

Melt butter in a heavy saucepan over low heat. Stir in flour until smooth. Cook, stirring constantly, for 1 minute. Gradually add milk and cook, stirring constantly, over medium heat until thickened and bubbly. Stir in salt and pepper. Serve over poached eggs, poultry, seafood or vegetables. Add 1 cup shredded sharp American cheese for cheese sauce. Yield: 1 cup.

Whiskey Sauce

1	cup butter	½	cup heavy cream
1	cup sugar	½	cup whiskey or rum
1	egg, beaten		

Heat water in the bottom of a double boiler. When it boils, turn heat to medium. Cream butter and sugar together until light and fluffy in the top of the double boiler with an electric mixer. Add egg and cream and mix thoroughly. Stir in whiskey. Sauce will keep indefinitely in the refrigerator. To serve, reheat in double boiler. Serve over bread pudding, pecan pie or pound cake.

Bread Crumbs

If fresh bread crumbs are needed, remove crust from fresh bread and break the bread into chunks. Place in a food processor and process using an on/off pulsing action.

Bread crumbs may be made from stale bread by processing and putting in a zip lock bag. Store in freezer and take out as needed.

Make croutons by cutting stale bread into cubes and mixing with butter or olive oil, garlic and herbs. Bake at 250 to 300 degrees until crisp. These are much better than the ones you buy in the grocery store.

If you are in a hurry, you can brown the cubes in melted butter and herbs in a skillet.

Candied Violets and Pansies

It is best to gather flowers early in the morning while covered with dew. Wash the flowers and dry on paper towels. Separate one egg and slightly beat the white. Using a soft brush, paint the flowers with the beaten egg white; then sprinkle lightly with sugar and place in the sun to dry. When one side of the flowers dry, turn them over, paint and sugar the other side. Dry the flowers thoroughly. Store in an airtight plastic container with paper towels between until needed for decorations.

It is safe to eat nasturtiums, violets, pansies, carnation and marigolds. Nasturtiums, or pansies are a very attractive addition to a green garden salad in the springtime.

Chocolate Curls

Chocolate curls may be made from bittersweet chocolate or milk chocolate. Do not use unsweetened.

Chop chocolate and place in a double boiler over barely simmering water until melted. Stir until smooth. With a metal spatula, spread melted chocolate on a nonstick baking sheet as thinly and evenly as possible. Cool chocolate until firm to the touch but not hard. With a pastry scraper or metal spatula held at an angle, scrape chocolate slowly from sheet, letting it curl. Carefully transfer curls to a wax paper-lined plate. Chocolate curls may be made a day ahead and chilled, loosely covered. One ounce of chocolate yields enough chocolate curls to garnish 4 servings as decorations.

Chocolate Leaves

For chocolate leaves, select nonpoisonous leaves, such as mint or rose leaves. Wash leaves and pat dry with paper towels. Melt 1 or 2 ounces semisweet chocolate or chocolate-flavored candy coating over hot water in a double boiler. Let cool slightly. Using a small spatula, spread a ⅛-inch layer of chocolate on the back of each leaf, spreading to the edges. Place leaves on a wax paper-lined baking sheet, chocolate-side up. Freeze or refrigerate until chocolate is firm. Grasp leaf at stem end, and carefully peel leaf from chocolate. Chill chocolate leaves until ready to use. (Handle carefully since chocolate leaves are thin and will melt quickly from the heat of your hand.)

You can use melted chocolate to make a number of decorations. You can place it in a cake decorating bag with a writing tip to make hearts, musical notes, initials, lace or any number of decorations. Just pipe them onto wax paper and chill. In a pinch, I have placed melted chocolate in a zip-lock bag with a hole cut in the corner to make decorations.

Flowers for Garnish

Only use edible flowers or herbs for garnish. These include citrus blossoms, apple blossoms, scented geraniums, nasturtiums, roses, squash blossoms, pansies and violets.

Do not eat the following:
Amaryllis, belladonna, bird of paradise, buckeye, buttercup, caladium clematis, daffodil, gloriosa lily, hydrangea, iris, lantana, larkspur, lily of the valley, lupine, monkshood, narcissus, oleander, poinsettia, rhododendron, star of Bethlehem, sweet pea, tansy and wisteria.

Gum Drop Decorations

To flatten gum drops, place granulated sugar on a large cutting board. Flatten gumdrops on the sugar covered cutting board with a flat-sided meat pounder or slightly flatten with hand, coat with sugar and run through a pasta machine. The pasta machine does better if you are making rose petals or daisies. Use the color gum drop you want the flower to be; use green gum drops for leaves.

You may use orange gum drops to make carrots to be used on top of a carrot cake. Crush the gum drops by hand, using as many as you need for the size carrot you want to make. Roll the carrots in sugar. Press green gum drops out flat and cut with a sharp knife to form the leaves.

Yellow roses or yellow daisies are attractive on a lemon chiffon or coconut cake; also, at Christmas, it makes an attractive decoration for gifts of sweet bread.

Marzipan Decorations

Working with marzipan is like playing with play dough. It looks much more complicated than it is. Marzipan comes in cans and can be found in most grocery stores or in cake decorating shops. The texture is like pastry dough. The color is usually cream but you can use food colorings to make almost any color.

To color marzipan, cut off in tablespoon-sized chunks. Tint with a drop of coloring, working the color into paste with fingers. Experiment until you get the color you want. If marzipan becomes sticky while you shape it, dip shapes into powdered sugar.

Leaves: form leaf shapes by hand, or roll out marzipan into a thin sheet, sprinkle with powdered sugar and cut with a leaf-shaped cookie cutter. You may use a real leaf as a pattern and press the back of the leaf into the paste to make the veins. Roll the marzipan between your hands to make stems.

Flowers: Make a small cone by hand. Make little circles (by hand or with a cutter) for the petals. Press petals around the cone to make a bloom.

Bumblebee: Tint bits of marzipan with cocoa; press together with plain marzipan to make striped bee body. Press a sliced almond into each side of body for wings.

Pumpkin: Shape marzipan into a round the size of the pumpkin you want to make. Slightly flatten to resemble a pumpkin. Using the back of the angle tool used to make a zigzag pattern on a melon, create grooves around the pumpkin. Use a clove for the stem.

Small fruits and grapes can be made using your imagination to shape them with your hands.

Marshmallow Flowers

Cut large marshmallows horizontally into 5 pieces, using kitchen shears dipped in water. Attach these sticky pieces as petals to a miniature marshmallow, used as the center. Dust fingers with powdered sugar if pieces stick to fingers. Dip finished flower in colored sugar crystals.

Sugar Roses

Work 2½ to 3 cups sifted powdered sugar into 1 unbeaten egg white to form a workable dough. If you want different colors, separate and color as desired. Cover bowl or bowls with damp paper towels and a moisture proof cover. Store at room temperature several hours or overnight. Form balls (¼- to ½-inch in diameter) by rolling a small portion of dough between fingers; keep fingers dusted with powdered sugar. Flatten ball into a disk. Roll disk to form the center for the rose. Continue making disks, add to center to form a rose. You may also taper green disks to look like leaves, making a ridge in the center.

Vegetable Garnishes

Green Onions: Slice the roots off, leaving the bottom attached. Split the onion horizontally almost to the bottom and place in ice water. The splits will curl and make a flower. I use zip-lock bags filled with ice and water for these.

Onion Chrysanthemums: Using a sharp knife, split the onion from the top to the bottom several times, but not going all the way through. Place in ice water to spread.

Carrot Curls: Use a potato peeler to slice carrots into thin strips. Fasten with a toothpick and place in ice water until it stays in place.

Radish Roses: Slice sides of the radish almost through and place in ice water.

Squash ducks: Select yellow squash with enough stem left on for a beak. Cut slices from another squash to make wings. Cut slashes in the top of the wings and use toothpicks to stick the wings on the side of the duck squash. Use whole cloves for eyes.

Radish Mouse: Select a larger radish for the body, leaving the root on for the tail. Select a small radish for the head. Cut thin slices from another radish for the ears. Make a slot to put the ears on the side of the head. Use whole cloves for eyes. Use thin pasta for the whiskers.

Palm Trees: Cut the top off of a carrot so it will stand up. Trim the top off a large green bell pepper. Remove the seeds. Cut leaves around the bell pepper. Place on the carrot "trunk" with the bottom of the pepper on top and the "leaves" hanging down.

Tomato Roses: Select a nice large tomato and, beginning at the blossom end using a sharp knife, peel the whole tomato, trying not to break the peel. Place on your cutting board and using your fingers, curl the peel into a rose.

White and Dark Chocolate Ribbons

7 ounces white chocolate, broken into pieces	7 ounces semisweet dark chocolate, broken into pieces
¼ cup light corn syrup	¼ cup light corn syrup

Melt white chocolate in the top of a double boiler over gently simmering water; stir until smooth. Stir in syrup and pour onto a baking sheet. Refrigerate until firm. Transfer chocolate to a work surface and knead several minutes. Shape into a ball and wrap in plastic. Let stand at room temperature 1 hour. Repeat with semisweet dark chocolate.

Cut white chocolate into 4 pieces. Flatten 1 piece into a rectangle. Turn a pasta machine to the widest setting. Run chocolate through 3 times, folding in thirds before each run. Adjust machine to next narrower setting, run chocolate through without folding. If chocolate is more than ¹⁄₁₆-inch thick, run through next narrower setting. Lay piece on a rimless baking sheet. Repeat with remaining pieces. Repeat process with semisweet chocolate.

Cut four 8x1-inch strips from white chocolate and four 8x½-inch strips from semisweet dark chocolate. Center dark chocolate strips on white chocolate strips to form 4 ribbons. Run 1 ribbon from base of cake to be decorated to center. Arrange remaining 3 ribbons equal distance from each other in the same fashion, giving the appearance of ribbon-wrapped package.

Cut ten 5½x1-inch strips from white chocolate and ten 6½-x½-inch strips from dark chocolate. Center dark chocolate strips on white chocolate strips to form 10 ribbons. Cut ends of 2 ribbons on diagonal. Starting at center, drape ribbons over top and sides of cake to form "trailers". Fold remaining 8 ribbons in half, layered-side out. Cut ends into "V" shapes. Arrange ribbon halves with "V" shapes at center of cake to form a bow.

Cut one 3x1-inch strip of white chocolate and one 3x½-inch strip of semisweet chocolate. Center dark chocolate strip on white chocolate strip. Fold in ends and pinch to resemble knot. Place in center of bow.

This chocolate can also be used to make chocolate roses. After running the chocolate through the pasta machine, use a small circle cookie cutter to cut petals for the roses. Roll petals with fingers to make a rose. Using a real leaf or a leaf cookie cutter, cut leaves from the chocolate. I like to use a real leaf because you can press the leaf down and transfer the veins of the leaf onto the chocolate. Other flowers, e.g., calla lilies and daisies, can be made from this mixture.

You can also make small boats and sails out of this chocolate. Use the dark chocolate to form a small boat. Plate a skewer near the front of the boat and cut a sail out of the white chocolate; place on the skewer to look like a sail. This makes an attractive decoration for a birthday cake at the beach.

Menus & Recipes

A Ladies Luncheon

White Wine and White Grape Juice
Chicken Salad, page 53
Frozen Nut Fruit Salad, page 55
Cheese Straws, page 12
Helen's Tea Biscuits, page 39
Raspberry Tea
Lemon Chiffon Cake, page 181

The day before the party:

Prepare the fruit salad and put in attractive molds to freeze.

Prepare the cheese straws.

Prepare the chicken salad.

Prepare the lemon chiffon cake.

The day of the party:

Set the table. Place an attractive arrangement
of anything you have in your garden in the center.

Prepare the raspberry tea.

One hour before the party:

Prepare the tea biscuits but do not bake until guest arrive and are having wine or juice.

Remove the frozen salad from the molds and place on a plate in the freezer to be added to the plate about 5 minutes before serving. Place two leaves of lettuce shaped like cups on the plates. Place one scoop of chicken in one cup of lettuce. Place three cheese straws on the plate but not on the lettuce. Place the frozen salad mold on the other lettuce cup. Put ice in the glasses and pour tea.

Place the biscuits in a napkin lined bread server and pass to your guests.

After the luncheon is over and dishes have been removed, serve the cake and have ready a pot of coffee to offer guests.

Dinner for Six

Cocktails
Baked Crab, Brie and Artichoke Dip with Crackers, page 9
A Slice of Brie with Water Crackers
Watercress Soup, page 74
Roast Beef Tenderloin, page 127
Orange Walnut Salad, page 57
Potato and Pasta Gratin, page 89 ~ Asparagus, page 102
Yeast Rolls, page 45
Lemon Meringue Pie, page 232
Coffee

Early in the day:

Prepare the soup.

Wash your salad greens and dry. Store in a lettuce bag in crisper.

Section your oranges and place in a container in the refrigerator.

Prepare your rolls if you are serving homemade.

Prepare the lemon pie.

Marinate your beef tenderloin if desired.

Prepare the salad dressing.

Toast the walnuts for the salad and let cool.

Later in day:

Prepare the hot artichoke dip.

Prepare the potato and pasta gratin and place in the
microwave to keep warm. Pour water into your goblets.

Prepare the asparagus and cover with foil to keep warm.

Prepare your salad but leave off dressing until just before serving.

Place the soup on the lowest setting of your burner to heat.

Place the tenderloin in the oven to cook. This is going to take one hour.

Serve Cocktails & Appetizers

After the tenderloin is done remove from oven and loosely cover with foil; let rest while you bake the rolls, dress the salad, and place on the salad plates.

Put the soup in bowls on the table. Place the salad on the table. After the soup and salad; remove the dishes from the table; turn on coffee to brew while removing dishes. Serve the tenderloin with the potato and pasta gratin, asparagus and rolls. Clear the table of the entrée dishes and serve the lemon pie with coffee.

Bridal Shower For 50

Drop In From 3:00 p.m. to 5:00 p.m.

Cucumber Bites (3 dozen), page 240
Chicken Salad Filling (3 dozen), page 239
Shrimp Spread (3 dozen), page 242
Calla Lily Sandwiches (3 dozen), page 238
Spinach Balls (3 dozen), page 243
Shortbread Cookies (3 dozen), page 200
Petit Fours (3 dozen)
Meringue Mushrooms (3 dozen), page 198
Toasted Pecans (1 pound)
Heart Shaped Cheese Straws (3 dozen), page 12
Strawberries in Tuxedos (50), page 243
Cranberry Party Punch (2 gallons), page 22

Decide who will co-host the party with you. Three is a good number, but up to five is okay. Set up a meeting and decide the date of the party, where the party will be, what each hostess will prepare for the party, and what the duties will be during the party. The one who uses her house for the party usually greets the people at the door with the honoree. Another can keep the platters refilled, and another can collect the dishes as the guests leave and take them to the kitchen. If there are more than three hostesses, one can circulate with the guests, make sure the guests know where the bathroom is, and generally see that the party runs smoothly.

Count Down Week

Early in week order the flowers for the serving table, a floral ring to go around the bottom of the punch bowl, and a corsage for the honoree. Individual flowers may be ordered to decorate the food trays. Flowers or greenery at the outside entrance is a nice touch and gives the home a festive look.

Wash the punch bowl and cups and polish any silver you plan to use. Decide on what linens you will need and press them. I use the beds in the guest rooms to lay freshly ironed tablecloths on.

Read your recipes for the food you are going to prepare. Shop for the items you will need. Prepare any garnishes you are going to use to decorate the trays, i.e., gum drop roses, chocolate roses, spring onion flowers, radish roses, or tomato roses. The radish and onion decorations need to be put in a small container with ice water and placed in the refrigerator to be drained the morning of the party. The candy decorations can be placed in a plastic container with a tightly closed cover.

The day before the party, set the table or tables. I like to use a smaller table, (a card or game table) in the foyer for the punch and the dining room table to serve the food. There should be plenty of room around both serving tables so the guest can move easily from place to place. Place extra punch cups on a small table behind the punch table so you do not have to keep getting them from the kitchen. Put out the trays for food. Decide which food will go on each tray and write the name on a slip of paper and place on the tray. The other hostesses can quickly put the food on the trays suitable for serving.

Place napkins and serving plates on the end of the large table or on a sideboard.

The day before the party, make any sandwich fillings so that the flavors can blend overnight. Cut the bread for the sandwiches and store in an airtight container. Bake any cookies or savories you are preparing.

Day of Party

Make sandwiches from the spreads and bread you prepared the day before.

Place food and garnishes on the trays.

Spray the house with air freshener; put a pot of
lemon and orange slices in a kettle with cinnamon sticks, cloves, and allspice for
the fall or winter or use a light spring rain air freshener for spring and summer.

Set up the coffeepot for any guest who prefers coffee.
Do not turn on until you have a request for coffee.

Set up your music system for the music you want to play during the party.

Romantic background music is best for a bridal shower.
Turn music on before guests arrive.

Turn on all lamps in the party area.

Have an attractive pair of scissors handy for the honoree
to use in opening gifts. Have a pen handy for her to record her gifts.

Have fun!

Easter Dinner for 10

Baked Stuffed Ham, page 133
Potato Salad, page 59
Macaroni and Cheese, page 95
Asparagus, page 102
Stuffed Deviled Eggs, page 90
Yeast Rolls, page 45
Lemon Coconut Cake, page 182
Iced Tea

Thursday:

Make a copy of the recipes you will be using.
Prepare a grocery list from your menu and the recipes.

Saturday:

Set the table and prepare fresh flowers for a centerpiece. Get out the dishes and serving pieces you will need for your meal. I usually have help placing the food into the dishes so I place a small slip of paper in each serving dish indicating what is to be placed in the dish.

Ask a family member to prepare a blessing for the meal. When asking young people, it is good to give them time to prepare.

Bake the cake. You may add colored jelly beans or candy eggs to the top of the cake. Wash and trim your asparagus and drain on a tea towel. When drained, place in a zip lock bag and store in your vegetable bin.

Prepare the yeast rolls and place in the refrigerator overnight.

Sunday:

Put ham on to bake.

Roll out yeast rolls and cover to let rise.

Prepare the potato salad.

Prepare the macaroni and cheese.

Cook the asparagus.

Prepare the devilled eggs and refrigerate. Decorate each egg half with a tiny sprig of parsley.

Make tea.

Cook rolls just before seating of guests.

266

Christmas Dinner for 12

Crown Roast of Fresh Pork with
Wild Rice, Fennel and Sausage Stuffing, page 134
Candied Sweet Potatoes, page 105
Baked Stuffed Yellow Squash, page 103
Green Beans with Walnuts, page 109
Congealed Cranberry Salad, page 51
Yeast Rolls, page 45
Iced Tea
Caramel Pumpkin Pie, page 227
German Chocolate Roulage, page 178

Four days ahead, ask your butcher to prepare a crown roast with the number of chops that you are going to need for dinner. It takes at least 10 to make a nice round crown. A good number is 14.

The day before:

Pick up the roast. Prepare the wild rice dressing and place in
a zip-lock bag in the refrigerator. Prepare the yeast rolls and refrigerate. Wash
and prepare the green beans and place in a zip-lock bag in the crisper.
Prepare the German Chocolate Roulage.
Prepare the molded Cranberry Salad.
Set the table and place the serving dishes to be used on the table.

Early Christmas Day:

Prepare the pie and set aside.
Bake the sweet potatoes and prepare the recipe for candied sweet potatoes; set aside.
Place stuffing into crown roast and place in oven to cook. It takes 2 to 3 hours.
Roll out yeast rolls to rise.
Boil and prepare squash. Set aside
Prepare the tea.
Simmer a smoked ham hock about one hour for the green beans. After 1 hour,
remove the hock and cut any ham off and discard the bone and skin. Put the ham back
into the pot and add the beans. Salt to taste. Cook only until tender.
Remove the congealed salad from the mold and place on a serving plate.
Keep in the refrigerator until ready to serve.
Remove the crown roast from the oven and cover with foil. Let sit 30 minutes before carving.
Place the candied sweet potatoes in the oven. After the potatoes have been
in the oven for 15 minutes, place the stuffed squash in the oven.
Pour the tea.
Bake the rolls just before you sit down to the table.

Thanksgiving Dinner for 12

Baked Turkey ~ Sausage & Chestnut Dressing, page 269
Giblet Gravy ~ Pecan Rice, page 95
Seasoned Pole Beans, page 111 ~ Collard Greens, page 105
Sweet Potato Casserole ~ Cranberry Walnut Sauce, page 248
Rolls, page 270
Pecan Pie Dessert, page 234
Lemon Cheese Cake, page 180
Iced Tea

Monday – Prepare the cranberry sauce.

Tuesday – Shop for a 16 to 18 pound fresh turkey and other supplies from your shopping list.

Wednesday – Put turkey in brine to soak.

Make desserts.

Chop the vegetables for dressing and place in zip-lock bags in the crisper.

Wash and remove strings from the pole beans and place in a zip-lock bag in the crisper.

Make yeast rolls.

Get greens out of freezer and place in refrigerator to thaw.

If your chestnuts are frozen, get them out and place in the refrigerator.

Thursday ~ Early: Put the turkey in the oven by 7:00.

Boil the giblets.

Bake cornbread for dressing.

Rollout yeast rolls by 10:00 a.m. and set aside to rise.

Boil ham hock in a pot for the beans.

Prepare rice.

Prepare dressing.

Make gravy.

Bake rolls

Serve at 1:00 p.m.

The Turkey:

Remove the neck and the giblets and place in a zip lock bag in the refrigerator. Using a cooler or a very large pot, add 1 cup of kosher salt to enough water to completely cover the turkey. Put ice in the cooler or put the large pot in the refrigerator. Let soak overnight. The next morning, wash the turkey and dry with paper towels. Rub the insides of the turkey with salt. Place carrots, celery and onions, in the cavities. Grease the outside of the turkey with Crisco, tie his legs together and place on a rack in a roasting pan. Turn oven to 325 degrees. Place a thermometer in the thick short thigh of the turkey and cook until it registers 165 to 170 degrees. The thick part of the drumsticks should feel tender and move slightly when the turkey is done. Remove turkey from oven and place on a large platter; lightly cover with foil. Add a little water in the pan the turkey was cooked in to loosen all the brown bits left from the turkey. Strain into a fat separating cup to use in your giblet gravy. Carve just before serving.

NOTE: I prefer to cook my dressing in a casserole dish and not in the turkey. It works better for me. I can handle the leftovers better. After the meal is served, slice the rest of the turkey and place in bags. White meat in one, dark meat in another, and meat for a good soup in another.

The Gravy:

Place the giblets in a pot with onions, celery, and carrots, fresh sage, salt, pepper, and cover with water. Boil until tender (about 45 minutes to one hour). Remove giblets from pot and chop and set aside. Strain the broth into a container and set aside to use in your dressing. Discard the vegetables.
After turkey is done, skim off about ¼ cup of the fat from the pan juices. Place in an iron or copper bottom pot. Add ½ cup of flour and make a roux.
Brown slowly and do not let burn. When roux is ready add the rest of the pan juices from the baked turkey to make a thick, brown gravy. Add the giblets. If you do not have enough liquid from the turkey use a can of Campbell's chicken broth to the gravy.

The Dressing:
Sausage & Chestnut Dressing

Bake Cornbread

2	cups self rising cornmeal	2	eggs
1	cup self-rising flour	1½	cups milk
¼	cup Wesson oil		

Pour ¼ cup oil into iron skillet and put in a 425 degree oven. Meanwhile mix meal and flour and put eggs in center. Using a fork beat eggs slightly and pour in the milk mixing as little as possible. Last, pour hot oil in and mix slightly with a fork. Pour mixture into the hot skillet and bake in oven until very brown (about 30 to 35 minutes). Crumble into a very large bowl. Mix cornbread with one package Pepperidge Farm herbed bread dressing mix. Pour the chicken stock from your giblets over the bread. Brown 1 pound of pork sausage in an iron skillet. Pour into a colander to drain. In the same skillet melt ½ stick of butter. Cook 1 cup finely chopped celery, 1½ cups onion, ½ cup chopped bell pepper (any color) and cook until the vegetables are clear but not brown. Pour all into bread mixture. Chop 2 cups of fresh boiled chestnuts or one jar of chestnuts from Williams-Sonoma and add to mixture. (If fresh chestnuts are available, cut a slit in the

Thanksgiving Dinner For 12 continued

peeling of each chestnut and boil in water until tender about 15 minutes. Peel and remove the membrane over the nut. I am fortunate that I have a good friend who gives me chestnuts every year.) Add 1 can of cream of chicken soup, 6 beaten eggs and enough chicken broth to make the dressing almost like the consistency of the cornbread. Check taste to be sure it is salted just right and add coarse ground black pepper to taste. Put in a large baking dish and cook at 400 degrees until brown.

The Rolls

½	cup butter	1½	teaspoons salt
½	cup Crisco	2	tablespoons yeast
1	cup boiling water	2	eggs, beaten
¾	cup sugar	6	cups all-purpose or bread flour

Dissolve yeast in 1 cup of lukewarm water. (I always proof my yeast first by adding 1 teaspoon the sugar to the lukewarm mixture and letting it bubble. If it does not bubble up the yeast is dead.) Pour the cup of boiling water over butter, Crisco, remaining sugar, and salt. When cool, add yeast that has dissolved. Add beaten eggs. Add flour, knead a few times and place in a covered bowl and leave in refrigerator overnight.

About 3 hours before using, roll out dough on a floured board and cut with a biscuit cutter. Dip in butter and fold over on a baking sheet leaving enough room to allow for rising of the dough. Bake on a greased pan at 425 degrees until brown. Brush with butter after baking.

NOTE: As a special treat for my grandchildren, I began when they were small making special bear rolls for them at Christmas and bunnies at Easter. They are grown now but I still make their special rolls. Cut a larger round body, a smaller round head. Cut out small rounds for paws, feet and ears. Using egg white, attach the smaller rounds to the body and head and let rise and bake in the pan with the rolls. Cut a dark raisin in half for eyes and nose. At Easter, after the rolls are cooked, stick thin spaghetti whiskers on the bunny's face.

The Collards: Wash and prepare collards about one week before Thanksgiving. Freeze. Remove from freezer the night before serving. Place in refrigerator. Put in a pot and simmer about 30 minutes before serving.

How To Make Pesto

*Pesto sauce can have a variety of uses, such as for tossing
with hot pasta or stirring into soups. Double or triple the recipe and
freeze the extra in an ice cube tray for single serving portions.*

1. Strip the leaves from 2 large bunches of basil; discard the stems. Rinse the basil leaves and dry on paper towels.

2. Put the basil in a food processor with 6 garlic cloves, ¼ ounce (about 2 heaping tablespoons) of pine nuts, 1 cup grated Parmesan cheese, and 2 to 3 tablespoons olive oil. Puree until smooth, scraping down the sides of the processor with a rubber spatula as necessary.

3. With the blade turning, add ½ cup olive oil through the feed tube, pouring it in slowly so the sauce emulsifies and becomes thick.

4. When all the oil has been added, scrape the sides of the bowl and process again briefly. Season to taste with salt and pepper.

Makes about 2 cups

Vanilla Beans

The vanilla bean is the seedpod of an orchid. It grows in Mexico, Central America, and South America. To get from the original seedpod to the finished bean is quite a long tedious process. The beans are hand picked, spread out in the sun to dry, wrapped in blankets to perspire at night, and otherwise babied and pampered. This causes the high cost of vanilla. Vanilla beans are used more in Europe than in America. In this country, the flavor is extracted by alcohol and is sold as pure vanilla extract. This is probably easier to use, and that is why the bean is in so little demand.

The seeds in the long, thin bean seem to contain most of the flavor. They are edible, whereas the outer part of the bean must be discarded after use, as it is rather tough.

To flavor a hot liquid, one splits the bean and soaks a piece of it in the liquid. To flavor other items, such as cakes and cookies, one must split the bean, scrape out the seeds, and put these scrapings into the batter. Try using one quarter and one half of a bean at first for one batch of cookies.

The remaining "husk" of the bean, after the seeds are removed, may be used in baked custards, in rice puddings, etc. Sometimes it is placed in a canister of raw sugar, and it flavors the sugar. Even after the bean has been cooked with something, it may be washed and dried and placed in the canister of raw sugar.

To make your own vanilla flavoring, place two to three beans in one pint of Vodka or Brandy and let sit for two weeks; then measure and use the vanilla for flavoring cakes, etc. I like to use the Brandy for making my vanilla flavoring. You may add more brandy three times before adding more beans. When I add new beans, I do not remove the old ones.

Remembering

Life On The Farm

I grew up on a farm in North Florida in the thirties and forties. Daddy worked in town as a carpenter and Mama, with the help of a hired man, a wash woman, and my older siblings ran the farm.

I want my children and grandchildren to know how it was to grow up on a farm without electricity and modern conveniences. Most of the food we ate came from the fields, the barnyard, was caught in the rivers and streams or the Gulf of Mexico, or hunting.

A field of corn was used to provide fresh corn for the table, ground into grits and cornmeal, and food for the livestock. It was also made into corn liquor in the stills.

We grew cotton, which we seeded and sold. Many of our neighbors grew tobacco, which was a good money crop, but Mama refused to grow it because she thought smoking or chewing it was a terrible habit.

We had a thicket of pine trees on our farm, from which was harvested resin for turpentine. The bark from one side of the tree was removed in the shape of a chevron. A tin cup, and later a clay cup, was attached to the tree at the bottom of the chevron to collect the sap. This sap was collected by the turpentine men with buckets and loaded onto carts with large barrels to transport to the turpentine stills. The material was shipped to naval stores to be used for waterproofing ships. You could hear the black turpentine men chanting in the forest as they collected the sap. A turpentine still was an interesting place. The negroes used rhythm as they tapped out the hoops to hold the staves together for the barrels. There was always singing and chanting as the large barrels were loaded onto carts for hauling.

Mama was a good cook, and with the fresh eggs, butter, and fresh vegetables we always had plenty to eat. I grew up among women who loved to cook and men who loved to eat. I loved to hang around the kitchen and watch the preparation of food at an early age. As I grew older I liked to prepare food and decorate it to make it more appetizing and attractive. I think food should first of all taste good, and second, it should look beautiful.

I guess by today's standards we would be considered poor, but we didn't know we were poor because we had as much as the other people who lived near us; in many ways we were very blessed. We lived in a large rambling farmhouse painted white. It was the oldest and largest house in the area but we had a large family to live in it. We had a warm loving family, plenty to eat and a lot of freedom to roam the woods, swim in the rivers, ride horses, fish in the ponds and rivers, build tree houses, and dig caves. We always seemed to have a project in progress, so we were never bored. We did not have many bought toys, so we had to use our imaginations to make our own. A sugar tit was our swing. It was made with a crocus sack filled with moss. The top was closed with a large rope or cable and tied to a high limb in a tree. We climbed up to a high platform and jumped on the swing and soared back and forth until it died down. The sugar tit

was named for a smaller version made with soft cloth filled with sugar that was given to teething babies to suck on to soothe their gums. We also had a flying jenny, which was a long plank fastened on a slanted post and we whirled around with a person sitting on each end. We had no television, but we had a large radio that stood on the floor in the corner of our living room; on winter Saturday nights we listened to the Grand Ole Opry. Mama liked to hear Roy Acuff sing "The Great Speckled Bird". We listened to President Roosevelt during World War II, and I had trouble remembering if we were the allies or the axis. Ours was a slower life, but it had much to recommend it.

Chickens

Chickens arrived on the farm in two ways. When we were sent to gather eggs and a hen refused to get off the nest (and pecked at us if you tried to make her,) we knew we had a 'setting' hen. We would tell Mama, and she would mark with soot about 15 to 20 eggs and place under the hen. She marked the eggs that were to become biddies because the hen would leave the nest briefly for food and water; other hens would lay eggs in the nest.

The hen used her feet to turn the eggs daily and in 21 days she would have a little family of biddies. They were such cute little balls of fluff the smaller children like to try to pick them up. The hen would raise her feathers and attack anyone bothering her offspring. She would lead them around the barnyard, and if she heard a chicken hawk or other alarming sounds, she would spread her wings and cover the biddies until the danger was gone.

Mama also ordered baby chicks from Sears & Roebuck. We had a post office box in the small village about two miles from our farm, but if we had an order of biddies, the postman delivered them immediately. They arrived in boxes with four compartments and air holes punched in the top and sides so that they could get air. They arrived mostly in good shape, but there was usually one or two that had been stepped on or were just sickly. Mama removed these from the box, and would have killed them, but I always rescued the sickly ones and tried to nurse them back to health. For the most part they did not respond to my care and would die in a day or two. My sister and I would have funerals for them and put flowers on their small graves. This early in the spring there were not many flowers blooming in the woods so we usually picked the blooms off of the blueberry bushes for their graves.

My sister and I were walking in the woods one day after we were married with children, and we saw some blueberry bushes blooming; I asked her if she knew what they were and she answered 'Of course, those are dead biddie grave flowers'. The biddies that did survive became my pets and followed me around the farm.

The healthy chicks were put in a brooder house with kerosene heaters to keep them warm. When they got older, they were separated and most of the males were put in a coop for frying. The females were allowed to grow up to lay eggs.

Occasionally a rooster would take it in his head that he was the boss of the barnyard. He would run at anyone approaching and use his spurs to attack them on the legs. It only took a few attacks from him before he found himself in the cook pot surrounded by dumplings.

Chickens continued

We had several predators who liked to visit the chicken coops at night. Foxes, opossums, and weasels would sneak into the pen. The chickens would sense the danger and make a lot of noise and Daddy would grab his gun to do away with the offending creature. Sometimes, if he was not fast enough, we would lose a chicken.

On Saturday afternoons, Mama would wring about 6 or 7 fryers necks and toss them in a wash tub. She would scald them with hot water and we had to pluck the feathers off so they could be made ready for Sunday dinner. She would then singe the small pinfeathers off them, wash, and cut them up for preparing the next day.

All Day Sing at Deadman's Bay

Our family was Baptist. My Daddy had no middle ground. He was either living at the foot of the cross, reading the bible to the family gathered in the living room nightly, singing hymns, but never cussing, drinking, or using tobacco. He also did a lot of praying, and no one could out pray my daddy; he could put up a prayer that would make the angels weep. Sooner or later he would back slide. Then he would have terrible temper fits, have a nip or two or three, be cross with Mama, smoke, not read the bible and curse with more zeal and vigor than any sailor. If Daddy did anything with more proficiency than his praying, it was his cussing. He still attended church on Sunday with the family, but on the way home he complained about how ugly Mrs. Garey, a member of our church, was. He said you could grab enough ugly off her face to make a dozen screech owls. Mama always told him he should be ashamed because Mrs. Garey couldn't help the way she looked and his reply was always, "she could stay at home". He also complained about the preacher, and he hated to sing the hymn 'Holy, Holy, Holy'. If the preacher came to our house for dinner on Sunday, he always complained about how much fried chicken he ate. We always hoped that when Daddy died it would be during one of his good spells.

Once about every two or three months Daddy would load all eight children in the car for a trip to Dead Man's Bay (now Steinhatchee) for an all day sing with dinner on the ground. He had relatives living there, and they always sent word asking him to come. At that time there was no bridge across the Fenholloway River and we could only get to Dead Man's Bay by crossing the river on a ferry that was barely large enough for one car. It was a frightening experience on its own, but especially since we knew that the Coca-Cola truck had fallen off the ferry into the river. While we were crossing the river one of my brothers would always remind us of that Coca-Cola truck, as if we were not frightened enough already. We had plenty of religion when we arrived at the church because we had prayed all the way across the river.

The day would begin with singing of hymns with various quartets in the area performing. Then the preacher, who must not have participated in the singing or he couldn't have preached so long, would expound on sin and damnation until well past the noon hour. Finally, the highlight of the day arrived, and the ladies would spread their lunch on the wire fence nailed between the trees and covered with tablecloths. There was no end to the variety of wonderful food. There were so many different kinds of meat and vegetables from the garden and so many pies and cakes it was hard to choose. After the ladies put away the food, the people would return to the church for more singing and preaching. Daddy loved to sing, and he would become so engrossed in the singing and praying activities that he didn't notice when we children slipped away to visit the waterfront. The Greek sponge boats from Tarpon Springs were always tied up at the dock; my older sisters loved to flirt with the handsome Greek sponge divers, who were always lounging around the boats with no shirts on, showing off their bronzed bodies. The sponges would be hanging on ropes all over the boats to dry. My younger sister and

All Day Sing at Deadman's Bay continued

I had to keep going back to the church to make sure that the service was still in full swing and warn our sisters when it was time to return to the church and load up to return home.

Out of our parents hearing, we would dance around and chant:

All day sing; dinner on the ground,
Whiskey in the woods; and the devil all around.

Sometimes after the noon meal we would go to a special place on the river where the water was not so deep and have a 'baptizing'. Those who joined the Baptist church had to go through the ritual of total immersion to become a member of the church. The preacher and the people to be baptized would wade out into the stream, and the preacher would hold the persons nose and lower him backwards into the water and he would be pronounced 'saved'. The people would pray, sing a little, and then return to the church.

At the end of the day the dreaded trip back across the river didn't seem quite as bad as the trip over. Maybe we were just too tired from the day's activity to notice.

Cane Grinding & Making Syrup

A chore everyone on the farm hated was stripping the cane. Wooden boards were sharpened on both sides, and the cane stripper had to go between the tall rows of sugar cane, stripping the outer leaves from the stalks. The leaves were sharp and could cut your arms if you were not careful, and sometimes even if you were. The cane was then cut down and loaded onto sleds pulled by mules and taken to the sugar mill. After the cane was removed, the fields were burned and plowed to get ready for the next crop. Every farm did not have a sugar mill, so the ones who had the mill let the other farmers use it for a portion of the syrup yield.

A sugar mill consisted of a large contraption that looked like giant screws that turned when the mule walked around in circles pulling a long pole attached to the top of the screws. I always felt sorry for the poor mule that had to walk around in one boring circle all day. The cane was placed between large screws, which squeezed the juice from the stalks. The juice ran down a metal spout near the middle of the screws into a barrel.

A large vat was nearby enclosed in a brick foundation with a shelter. There was room for a fire underneath the vat. A small door in the foundation could be opened so that the fire could be fed and stoked.

The juice was strained through large burlap bags and then put into the kettle to boil. While the syrup boiled, the women used damp rags to clean the edges of the kettle. When the syrup was almost done, a sweet candy would form on the edges of the kettle. The children were given a piece of cane peel to use to scrape the candy off for eating. This treat was called "possum". The discarded peelings from the cane mill were carried out of the way and dumped into large piles called pummy piles. The children were allowed to play on these small hills. You had to fight off the bees because they would always come to the cane grindings for their share of the nectar. The men always set aside some of the cane juice to ferment into cane buck, a kind of home-made liquor.

After the juice was cooked into syrup it was poured into empty bottles and corked for keeping for table use or cooking until the next year. If you had a surplus of syrup, and cane grinding was approaching, you would have a party called a 'candy pulling'. The syrup was cooked in the outdoor wash pot until it was thick, and then every one buttered their hands and pulled the candy until it was a light caramel color and could be sliced or eaten in chunks.

The men celebrated the end of cane grinding by consuming the buck they had prepared. The women fussed at them, but I couldn't see that it changed anything because they did it again the next year.

Milking The Cows

Farming was really a seven day a week job. There was livestock to feed, chores to do, and twice every day, cows to be milked. Mama milked the cows but Daddy always went with her to the cow pen. He would shovel the cow paddies onto the fertilizer pile to be used later in the gardens. Mama milked the cows early in the morning before she prepared breakfast. She would bring the milk back to the house and put it on the milk shelf until after breakfast, then she would strain it and put it in large pitchers to place in the ice box for cooking and drinking. She then strained the remainder into large crockery bowls that were placed in a safe to sour into clabber with sour cream on top.

A safe was a tall wooden cabinet with shelves and two screen doors that closed with a wooden latch. After the milk soured, the sour cream was skimmed off the top and put into a churn with a little fresh milk to be churned into butter. The added fresh milk became buttermilk. Our churn was a five quart glass square container with the wheel and handle on top for churning.

One of our chores was to sit and churn the cream into butter. You could see little yellow flecks on the glass sides of the churn when it was nearly ready.

Milking The Cows continued on next page

Milking The Cows continued

You continued to churn until the butter made a ball and separated from the milk. The butter was then put into molds and placed in the icebox. The clabber was fed to the hogs and was especially liked by the small pigs.

We also ate clabber topped with sugar, honey, or syrup to sweeten as a snack when we came home from school.

After supper each evening, Mama and Daddy would return to the cow pen for the evening milking. They usually had their private discussions while doing this chore.

We were Baptist, and we were not allowed to dance. We would use the time Mama and Daddy were at the cow pen to turn the radio to the 'hit parade' and dance. We kept a sharp eye out for our parents so that by the time they arrived back from the cow pen, the radio was back on a religious station and we were not dancing.

The feed for the cows came in large one-hundred pound bags. These bags were made of sturdy, colorful cotton that was used to make clothes for the farm children. We did not like to wear these to school because the material was easily spotted as feed sack, and we were embarrassed. Mama would add a white collar and cuffs to the dresses to improve the appearance. Flour for baking also came in cloth bags. They were white and the women would wash them to use for dishtowels or to make undergarments for the children. The sacks sometimes would have "plain" for plain flour and "self-rising" for self-rising flour imprinted on the material. You can imagine the snickers if the seat of your panties bore these words.

The Ice Man

Before we had electricity on the farm, we had an icebox to keep the food cold. The iceman drove a big truck and with the back filled with ice, a tarp over it to keep it from melting too fast. The ice was scored into 100, 50, and 25 lb. blocks, and he would chip off the amount needed. Our icebox held a hundred pound block of ice if it was empty. The iceman came every other day, so we usually needed only fifty pounds each visit unless it was an unusually hot summer. We looked forward to the iceman coming because we would gather around while he chipped out our portion and catch the pieces of ice that flew while he chipped. He would always make sure there were enough chips to go around. The ice was placed in the top compartment of the icebox and the food was kept in the bottom compartment. There was a small drainpipe running down the back of the icebox where the water from the melting ice would run into a pan placed underneath the icebox. This pan had to be emptied daily, and we each had a day for that chore. My day was Tuesday, and sometimes I would forget to empty the pan and at supper I would see water oozing out from under the icebox. I would try to distract Daddy from looking that way until supper was over and I could quickly empty the pan before anyone noticed I had forgotten.

Hog Killing Day On The Farm

We had a lot of animals on the farm, and I liked most of them but somehow I just never did warm up to hogs. When they were very small they were cute with their little curly tails following after the sow, but they soon grew out of that stage and became nasty little creatures that refused to share and always seemed to be a nuisance rooting under the garden fence, into the chicken pens, or places they did not belong. Their pens smelled bad, and most farm activities with them were unpleasant experiences. The farmers let their pigs roam in the woods at that time and were not required to keep them in a pen or pasture. The farmers marked the ears with a special mark so they could tell their pigs from the other farmers' pigs in the area. The young pigs were held and an identifying mark was cut into their ear. It was covered with tar to try to keep the screw fly from laying eggs on it; they hatched out into screw worms that could kill the pig if it was not treated. The screw fly was finally eradicated in the late thirties. Pork was essential to the farmers food supply and crops were planted just for fattening pigs.

Before light on a cold day in autumn, I would awaken to the sound of gunshots and realize that today was hog killing day. The day before, I had watched Daddy and our neighbors dig the holes to place large barrels in slanted for easy access in which to scald the hogs, place the tables, and build the bar for hanging the freshly scalded hogs that had been fattening for weeks on chufas and peanuts. They gathered wood for the smokehouse and repaired or replaced the poles from which the meat would be hung for curing. They gathered the leaves from the palmetto bushes and cut strips to be used in hanging the hogs and for hanging the hams, sausage, and bacon in the smokehouse for curing. The leaves were green and very strong and did not burn when the meat was smoked.

The hogs were shot, and then the tendons at the back of their heels were slit and a foot- long stick was stuck through their heels so they could be hung from the bar. They were scalded in the large barrels, under which was built a fire, and hung on the bar so the hair could be scraped from their hides. Their throats were cut and the blood drained in the trench that had been dug under the rack. After the hair was scraped from the skin, they were washed down with fresh water and then split down the middle for the entrails to be emptied into the large tole dish pans and given to the women to clean the chitterlings, liver, lights and other usable parts; it seemed to me everything was used. My daddy used to say we used everything but the squeal. The chitterlings were emptied into a hole dug for that purpose and turned inside out for scraping. The smaller ones were plaited into short lengths for cooking. A lot of them were cleaned and put aside to be stuffed for sausage. The men then moved the hogs to the tables and cut the hams, shoulders, sides of bacon and even the feet were saved for pickling. The big black wash pot usually used for boiling clothes on wash day was heated up, and the fat was cubed and cooked in the pot for lard and cracklings. The lard was stored for use in cooking, and the cracklings were used for making crackling corn bread or just for eating. The smell of the fat boiling was very pleasant and overcame some of the other smells that

Hog Killing Day On The Farm continued

were not so pleasant. The hams and sides of bacon were set aside for curing. The meat for the sausage was cut in cubes to be ground and mixed with sage and other seasonings. The hams and bacon were salted and with the sausages were hung in the smokehouse for curing. A fire was built in the center of the smokehouse in a pit for that purpose. A lot of green hickory and other woods were used to create plenty of smoke and not much flame to slowly cure the meat so that it would not spoil.

While some of the women were helping with the hogs, the other women were in the kitchen preparing a large feast for the whole working crew. It was always a festive occasion; the neighbors visited around the dinner table, the children played, and the younger ones had to take a nap on quilts spread on the floors in the hallways or living room. The men usually retired behind the barn for a nip or two of home made liquor that always seemed to come from somewhere, and the women pretended not to notice.

The day after hog killing day, the heads of the hogs were boiled outside in the wash pot and the meat removed and made into what was called hog's headcheese. It was placed in a cheesecloth and drained, and then shaped into rounds or loaves of a jelly or aspic like dish that was sliced and served cold. No one in our family liked it except Mama.

Sitting On The Porch

In the evening, at twilight, when all the chores were done in the summer time, the family would sit on the front porch. We had rocking chairs and a swing.

Whoever was courting at the time would occupy the swing with their beau.

The smaller children would chase fireflies, and the older children and parents would rock and talk. We played all the old games: i.e., Blind Man's Bluff, Bum, Bum, Bum; May I; My Ship Goes Sailing, and Hellover.

We did not have grass in our yard. The house was surrounded by sand. The sand was swept clean with brush brooms. We made the brooms by going into the woods and cutting down gall berry bushes and whipping the branches against a tree to remove the leaves; then we would make a bundle of the branches and tie them together with rag strips for a broom that was used to sweep the yard. Outside the picket fence we had grass growing, and we would go out there if we were playing a game that involved falling down, i.e., Coach Whip, Statue or Leap Frog.

The yards were sand to prevent a fire from burning the house. We burned the fields every year in the autumn after all the crops were gathered. We also burned the pine thicket to burn out the underbrush and help the timber to grow. This allowed us to

gather pine straw for use in the hen's nests and in the stable and barns. We made a bin for keeping sweet potatoes by digging a cave in the ground, covering the potatoes with pine straw and then putting boards on top covered with more straw. I knew one family that survived a hurricane by getting into the sweet potato bin before their house was blown away.

When we sat on the porch, we would hear the stories handed down from generation to generation; some were funny; some were tragic; and some were just interesting or historic. News in Mama's day was often carried by song. She would sing The Knoxville Girl, who was murdered by her boy friend or about twins who drowned in a mill pond. Barbara Allen was a ballad. Mary Fagan was one of our favorites. It was about a young girl who was murdered in Atlanta when she went to the pencil factory to pick up her check.

We used kerosene lamps for light in the bedrooms, but we had no light on the porch; if the stories got a little scary, we would creep closer to Mama's rocking chair. Mama used this time to shell peas, butterbeans or remove the silks from the corn. It seemed she never sat with nothing to do. When it was time for everyone to go to bed, Mama always stayed on the porch to look at the sky to determine what the weather was going to do for the next few days and plan her farm chores accordingly. Irish potatoes were always planted on or near Valentine's day and all other plantings were done according to the sky and the Farmer's almanac.

Sitting By The Fire

During the winter, when it was too cold to sit on the porch, we sat by the fire in the living room. Daddy would often read from the Bible, or we would gather around the piano and sing.

Sometimes chores were done while sitting by the fire. We would shell out peanuts from this year's crop to save for seed to plant in the spring. We each had a pan of peanuts to shell. Mama would make a pot of syrup candy, and we would roast peanuts by the fire to put in it. The candy was poured out on a buttered board until it was cool enough to handle, and then we buttered our fingers and pulled the candy until it was a light caramel color. We added the roasted peanuts and shaped them into long bars for slicing. That was our reward for shelling the peanuts.

If we had no chores, we would play checkers or other board games to pass the time. We sat by the fire until bedtime, and then Mama would warm flat irons or bricks by the fire and wrap in old towels to put in our beds to warm our feet while we went to sleep. We had no heat in the bedrooms, and the beds were piled high with home made quilts.

Sitting By The Fire continued on next page

Sitting By The Fire continued

The quilts were made during the summer after the crops were planted and before harvest. Frames were hung from hooks in the ceiling of the living room and the neighborhood woman came; everyone worked on the same quilt until it was finished and then they would begin a new one. They sewed the tops on the old Singer pedal sewing machine; they put the filling in and attached the top, bottom and filling with intricate hand stitches over the entire quilt. It was quite an art, and some of the women were very proud of their skill with the needle and the neat small stitches they made.

We had a large clock on the mantel that my sister had won selling Rose Bud Salve, and the last thing Mama did before she went to bed was wind the clock. You did not need an alarm clock on the farm; the roosters would crow at daylight, waking everyone for a half mile.

Wash Day

Wash day on our farm was on Monday. Mariah, the wash woman, walked to our house early in the day. The fire was built under the wash pot, which was a large black iron cauldron. Homemade soap and bleach was put in the water, and we had to help hand pump the water into the large wash tubs for washing and rinsing the clothes. The sheets and other white clothes were washed first. The colored clothes were washed second and last the overalls and denims worn by the men while doing farm chores. They were put in a tub of soupy water, scrubbed up and down on the wash board made for that purpose, and then boiled in the wash pot. They were dipped from the boiling water with a long stick and placed into a tub of clear water for rinsing. They were wrung out by hand and placed in a final rinse tub of water before they were wrung out and placed in a basket to be hung on the clotheslines fastened with wooden pins for drying in the sun. The clothes that were to be starched were dipped in a starch that was cooked in a pan on the stove. If it was raining on Monday, the wash day was postponed until a fair day. After the clothes were dry, they were gathered into baskets and taken to the house for ironing. The skies were closely watched on wash day and at the first sign of rain everyone dashed out to gather to clothes before they got wet.

We had mulberry trees on our farm, and in the summer the smaller children were recruited to keep the birds scared away from the white sheets hanging on the line so the birds that had been eating mulberries did not sit on the clothes line and leave their droppings on the white sheets.

On Tuesday, a fire was built in the fireplace to heat the irons for ironing the clothes. It was a neat trick to iron the white shirts with a smutty iron heated by the fire and not get it dirty, but they somehow managed to do it. The starched clothes were sprinkled with water and rolled in towels to await ironing.

Canning & Preserving

During the summer, when the gardens were producing, we had plenty of fruits and vegetables; but during those times we had to think of the long winters when nothing grew and we still had a large family to feed.

We gathered vegetables from the garden. Tomatoes, corn, beans, peas, squash and butterbeans were cooked in large pots then processed and placed in jars for storing in the pantry for the winter.

We had peach trees, plum trees, grapevines, a black walnut tree, a pecan tree and a wild cherry tree on the farm.

We gathered wild May plums from the woods in May, wild hog plums in June, and dewberries, blackberries, huckleberries, and blueberries in early spring. Later in the summer we gathered wild fox grapes and purple grapes, from which we made jellies, jams, and preserves. We had a bittersweet orange tree on the farm, and Mama made an orange preserve from the thick-skinned oranges from this tree. Mariah, a black woman who helped Mama, came and helped with the canning and jelly making; she would take her share home with her in my brother's red Western Flyer wagon.

Going into the woods to pick the berries was a fun thing to do in the summer. Most of the berries grew near the Fenholloway River that was close to our farm. Mariah's house was also near the river, and we would always get Mariah to make some Kool Aid to drink when we were hot and tired from picking berries.

Index

Index

Index

O

##

Index

Index

Recipes and Remembering

Edith P. Middleton
1902 Tara Place • Dalton, Georgia 30720
Phone 706-226-6674
Email: jemidd@optilink.us

Please send _____ copies . . . . $25.00 each

Georgia residents add .07% state sales tax . . . . $_____

Postage & handling first copy . . . . $ 4.00

Postage & handling additional copies . . . . $ .50 each

Name_____

Address_____

City_____ State_____ Zip_____

Phone (_____) _____

Recipes and Remembering

Edith P. Middleton
1902 Tara Place • Dalton, Georgia 30720
Phone 706-226-6674
Email: jemidd@optilink.us

Please send _____ copies . . . . $25.00 each

Georgia residents add .07% state sales tax . . . . $_____

Postage & handling first copy . . . . $ 4.00

Postage & handling additional copies . . . . $ .50 each

Name_____

Address_____

City_____ State_____ Zip_____

Phone (_____) _____